A
DOCTOR'S
BORNEO

IN PEACE AND WAR

A DOCTOR'S BORNEO

by DERWENT KELL

Published by Boolarong Publications
Brisbane — Australia

First published in 1984
by Boolarong Publications.
Reprinted 1985.
Copyright© D. Kell

National Library of Australia
Cataloguing-in-Publication data
  Kell, Derwent
    A Doctor's Borneo.

  ISBN 0 908175 80 9.

  1. Physicians – Australia – Biography.
  2. World War, 1939–1945 – Borneo – Personal
narratives, Australian. 3. Borneo – History.
  4. World War, 1939–1945 – Hospitals.
  I. Title.
610′.92′4

BOOLARONG PUBLICATIONS,
24 Little Edward Street, Spring Hill, Brisbane, Qld. Australia.
Design, reproduction and photo-typesetting by
Press Etching Pty. Ltd., Brisbane.
Printed by James Ferguson Pty. Ltd., Brisbane.
Bound by Podlich Enterprises Pty. Ltd., Brisbane.

DEDICATION

To former patients in Sabah and Kuala Belait, and with thanks to the several Japanese doctors who treated me well in spite of the fact that our governments were at war.

Also to Lau Ham Chung of Kuala Belait whose help made three chapters of war-time reminiscences possible.

PREFACE

It is possible to read histories of countries in which there is no mention at all of doctors, ancillary medical staff or patients. Clearly they are of little or no historical importance. History is dominated by other and very different characters — kings, generals, politicians and the like. The world may have been a happier place if a sizeable percentage of these people had never been born. Records of their performances on this earth could, all too frequently, be more appropriately incorporated in works on psychiatry or criminology. Neither providence nor preventive medicine, nor indeed the law, has given us adequate protection against men of strong character with such characteristics as obsessive ambition and lack of real compassion for their fellow men.

The medical and other adventures of the Bill Smiths, Ah Fooks and Awangs of this world do not attract the attention of a Toynbee. During the few years I spent in the Far East I did not meet anyone of any particular importance or, if I did, I remained unaware of it. Admittedly I did meet a few Colonial gentlemen and some Japanese who, if the airs they gave themselves had been genuine, would have been veritable cyclones. Thus these memoirs cannot be regarded as making any contribution to significant history of the former British territories in North Borneo. But they do shed a little light, variously diffracted, on life as it was in a backward, lightly populated area of the Far East just before and during World War II. One thing is certain, if I had not taken the trouble to write about some of the people and some of the trivial things they said and did, and what many of them suffered, then they never would have appeared in print — surely a terrible fate!

Most personal names are correct, a few are not. My real name was pre-empted by a well-known professional writer and was therefore altered in this book.

M.C. CLARKE
COCOS–KEELING ISLANDS
1978

BORNEO 1938

Many places have since been renamed. Indonesian Borneo is now
known as Kalimantan and Celebes is now Sulawezi. British North
Borneo is now part of East Malaysia and is known as Sabah.
Jesselton, renamed Kota Kinabalu is the Capital city of Sabah.

Acknowledgements

The author gratefully acknowledges the assistance given by the officers of the Australian War Memorial in the selection of photographs relating to the Prisoners of War and scenes of Kuching, Sarawak.

CONTENTS

Chapter 1

KUDAT 1938–39

It is not very often that anything genuinely exciting appears in a medical magazine. An advertisement in the *Australian Medical Journal* provided a pleasant surprise. I read it, and immediately reached for pen and paper. Six weeks later I received advice that I had been appointed District Surgeon, Colony of North Borneo, with Kudat as my first station. My friends laughed when they heard about it, and, without exception, exclaimed "orang-a-tang-a-tang!" (Derived, of course, from "orang utan" — jungle man.) It was remarkable how uniform was this extraordinary response; it suggested a Pavlovian reflex, but in fact it came from a students' beer-drinking song, and it happened to express just about all we knew of this distant land.

I could claim that a spirit of adventure set me off to a remote outstation of Empire but this would not be true. Our family provider, a kindly country doctor, held to be one of the nation's best (and certainly one of its keenest deep-water fishermen) had not understood either money or rascals, and had died and left us in financial difficulties. The most that the skinflints of the day paid Resident Medical Officers was under two pounds a week plus food and lodging. The outlook at home seemed quite hopeless to me. I was 25 years of age and looked 18. I could not imagine enough sober citizens over 30 years of age paying ten bob to consult me on any serious medical problem.

And so in a few weeks I was off on a sea trip, on half pay, from Sydney through the Dutch East Indies, zigzagging from one interesting port to another. It was a short and useful introduction to a neighbouring but very different country and people. And the spectacular sunsets over the quiet seas separating the islands of the fabulous archipelago were something to be remembered.

In Singapore I stayed at the Adelphi. I still recall lying in bed listening to the sounds from the street below: the unusually cheeky and demanding car horns, the strange intonations of Chinese speech, and the clinking clip-clop of wooden clogs on the stone pavements.

An appointment had been made for me at a European emporium called Robinson's. There, a tailor measured me for a dress uniform which seemingly had been designed for tall, elegant African colleagues living in the tradition of nineteenth century imperialism. This regalia had a row of metal buttons running from pubis to Adam's apple. Being short and rather awkward, it made me distinctly uneasy, but I need not have worried — I never wore it again after the second fitting!

We crossed from Singapore to North Borneo on the S.S. *Kajang*. A lazy pleasant week. Drinks at noon and six o'clock, deck games, and sleeping — that was all there was to it. And, I reflected, all this time the half pay was rolling in to refill the near-empty family coffers. Some years earlier, an observant, pragmatic American had made this very same trip. Day after day, elbows on the deck rails, he took in everything that could be seen of Sarawak, Brunei, Labuan and then North Borneo; finally, when he reached Kudat, he asked, "Say, how long have you guys owned North Borneo?" The question had an inbuilt inaccuracy (the British did not actually *own* it) but there seemed to be a challenge in it. A government officer helped him continue: "Fifty years. Why?"

"Well", said the American, "Take my advice — give it back to the monkeys!"

The story entered local tradition immediately; indeed it became a sort of initiation ceremony. All future newcomers, including myself, going east from Singapore for the first time, had to listen to it at least a dozen times. What is more, the story had an unexpected sequel. A few years later, the American's energetic compatriots, aided by Australians, made sure we followed his advice almost exactly — they blasted every town in the Territory, indeed every village shopping centre, flat to the ground. Occasionally they hit a Jap, and everyone cheered them on. When the din was over, the monkeys came from the nearby jungle and settled amongst the ruins and resurgent jungle.

However, homo sapiens does not give in all that easily, and in due course the monkeys and apes were slowly driven back again by reconstruction.

But this is leaping too far ahead altogether.

The Kudat district is the most northerly part of the great island of Borneo, with Marudu Bay biting deeply into its northern coastline. In 1938 the Bay was a quiet, neglected spot which had, as yet, refused most invitations to enter the twentieth century. Mangrove forests, sullen estuaries and grey mudflats skirted a jungle ravaged annually by natives practising shifting cultivation. To the south, the district is rugged, its hills and mountains rising to a startling climax in Mt Kinabalu. So abruptly does the mountain rise over 4,000 metres that the winds are often sent swirling from its flanks to draw from the peaceful waters of Marudu Bay water-spouts reaching as high as the clouds.

There was an atmosphere of backwardness about the district which in its way was most refreshing. Piracy, rebellion, amuk, blackwater fever and delirium tremens featured convincingly in local legends.

Kudat — a small peaceful village nestling on the shore of Marudu Bay in the most northerly part of the great Island of Borneo.

In Kudat itself, the European community consisted of the Padre and his family, two Roman Catholic Fathers from Mill Hill, the District Officer and his wife, and finally myself. The District Officer and I had our houses on a low hill overlooking a Bajau village built in the sea. Further down, near the wharf, was a collection of two-storied shops: here, Chinese merchants sold everything necessary for a moderately civilised existence. Fresh meat and butter, and delicacies such as Chinese pheasant, Scottish haddock, and at odd times even Sydney oysters were obtainable from visiting ships. In the local markets there were plenty of prawns, crabs, fish, zebu cattle and water buffalo meat, and such vegetables as amaranth, Indian corn, bamboo and coconut shoots, and brinjals. The local dollar was worth a little less than two shillings Australian. A fowl cost 25 cents, and you could buy two tiny eggs for one cent. A bottle of Black Label scotch cost about five dollars.

Kudat was, in fact, something that tens of millions of Chinese would prize very much — a small peaceful village where they could sell and buy, chatter and drink coffee, and sleep, eat and breed.

The first day, I lunched with the District Officer, Riley Stackhall, and his handsome wife. There was no doubt they loved the life, and their enthusiasm was infectious. "Oh, it's fine, it's fine!" they said. We drank two gimlets, stirring them with swizzle sticks, and then had a Tennant's beer with the fried rice and prawns. Small, barefooted servants, dressed neatly in white drill, padded silently in and out. Two bull terriers used the couches like well-fed potentates: occasionally they got up and roamed about the room, beating the cane furniture with their tails. A kra monkey ran up and down a bamboo pole outside. Stackhall twiddled his moustache with satisfaction and looked into his wife's eyes with unrestrained intimacy and affection. They had never regretted "coming out".

I was clearly in another world. There was nothing like this in black-stump country. It was all very interesting.

The District Officer, Riley Stackhall, had a pet Kra monkey which roamed up and down a bamboo pole outside his residence.

By nightfall I had acquired a cook and a houseboy, both Chinese. Darkness set in before I had unpacked, and the rain pelted down, and the gekkos or chi-chaks chided me gently from the walls because the kerosene lamps, which attracted insects for their supper, wouldn't work. The phone rang several times, and from the receiver came sounds in an incomprehensible tongue as if a bibulous friend was attempting to be funny. A knock on the door and in came a short man with a small hurricane lamp which he put on the floor so that it illuminated only our shoes and lower legs . My visitor was the Padre from the S.P.G. Mission (Society for the Propagation of the Gospel) just beyond the coconut plantation up the road. We managed to shake hands in the darkness, each wondering, while so engaged, what the other looked like above the knees. The Padre offered all possible help, and as he left with his lamp he turned and asked, "Are you a practising Christian?" For some reason or other, the question amused me for days. After all, I was a G.P., but I must admit I hadn't had much practice.

After the Padre left I suddenly felt very sleepy and decided to call it a day. I had a bath in a Javanese jar, found and entered a mosquito-proof room, and flopped down on the bed. There was something there beside me. I cocked my leg over it and otherwise embraced a "Dutch wife" and quickly fell sound asleep.

The Civil Hospital, Kudat, had at one time been government offices and had been converted into a Rumah Sakit (House of Sickness) simply by the addition of outside toilets and a kitchen, putting bars in the windows of one of the back rooms, and a suitably inscribed notice on the front lawn. It was a two-storey building with wide verandahs and cement arches in front, so that it looked quite presentable in photographs, particularly so just after the bi-annual application of whitewash. Some sealing-wax palms and frangipani, a few rows of staked ground orchids, and a dozen colourful shrubs made the surrounds interesting and attractive.

The Civil Hospital at Kudat, previously used as Government offices, had been converted into a Rumah Sakit (house of sickness) and was set in attractive surroundings.

The hospital had accommodation for about 35–40 patients drawn with various degrees of difficulty from a district of nearly thirty thousand people. The male ward was downstairs, the female ward, dispensary and office-examination room were upstairs. There was no operating theatre for the "District Surgeon", nor any obstetric block. The beds were of wooden planks, and solid wooden blocks served as pillows.

The atmosphere in the wards was informal. Visitors wandered in and out almost at will, and sometimes occupied a spare bed at night if no-one was watching for this particular misdemeanor. No patient, however sick, was confined to bed, except during the morning rounds. When this main event was over, most of the patients went out to the verandah where it was cooler. They sat on the floor, backs to the wall, and discussed a limited number of subjects such as the next meal, probable causes of their illnesses (evil spirits, bad luck and wind in the joints), their medical treatment, and the chances of surviving their present ailments and resuming an active sex life. Incredibly old buses, amusingly dressed local identities on mediaeval bicycles, and buffalo and cattle-drawn carts passing along the nearby road kept them adequately entertained. When they felt better or had abandoned all hope of recovery they left hospital. This was often effected by amicable agreement with the staff, but alas, all too frequently their history cards were curtly marked "absconded". On these cards each patient's religion was also recorded — Catholic, Christian (Society for the Propagation of the Gospel or Basle), Mohammedan, Buddhist, Confucian, Taoist or Pagan.

Our medical records were brief: no words were wasted. Histories and clinical notes usually occupied less space than the list of diseases entered under "Final Diagnosis", for everyone had multiple complaints. A few of our patients were returned to Mother Earth, and always with dignity, for even paupers had free burial at government expense. Most of the patients were officially recorded as "relieved" or "cured" before returning to their homes. These were, with luck, in shops and houses, or on small peasant farms, or on coconut plantations; with less luck, on covered footpaths or perhaps even in gaol. Sea gypsies put to sea in sailing boats called kumpits, and the tough inland farmers (Rungus Dusuns) phlegmatically faced anything up to 160 kilometres journey on bare feet to reach their longhouses.

The Senior Dresser, Mr Thomas Boo Hian, was a big, chunky man: in this respect a little un-Chinese. He had an air of prosperity about him and many of inferior station addressed him as "Tuan". He weighed at least 95 kilograms, spoke with impressive force and speed in some eight languages, and even on the hardest day he laughed outright at least a dozen times: but in these brief intermissions there was no hint of any relaxation of his authority. Every day he dressed the same — white shirt, shorts and stockings, black belt and black shoes. Outside the hospital he wore a white helmet, and clenched a brown pipe between his strong white teeth. On entering the hospital office he hung the helmet on some antlers nailed to the wall and inserted the pipe inside the stocking on his left leg. He ran the hospital pretty well, albeit noisily at times, for he had a good pair of lungs and there was ample incitement to use them. While he bore the medical misfortunes of vagabonds with kindly equanimity, Thomas had a deep reverence for very sick people if they happened to be rich and Chinese. In the boudoirs of wealthy and influential people (i.e., in the local context), his countenance became solemn and he would study the mercury in a thermometer and apply a stethescope with profound gravity. In these matters he had me beaten, hands down.

And yet he had his moments of hesitation and uncertainty, just like the rest of us. Once, when I was travelling, he was called to see a very sick merchant and consoled the worried relatives by saying confidently, "I positively guarantee he will live two days!" Thomas knew exactly when I would be returning, hence the time at which the responsibility would be lifted from his shoulders. As it happened, his somewhat alarming prediction was accurate, but with not many hours to spare. It wasn't true that the merchant died of fright: I am sure a death certificate still survives to prove this.

The second Dresser at the Hospital was Mr. Shu On a hardworking and reliable assistant who accompanied the author on many visits to District clinics.

The second Dresser, Mr Shu On, was a different kettle of fish altogether: quiet, gentle, modest, he could have fallen into a lotus pond without frightening any of the carp. Any intelligent western scientist, for example Herr Schikelgruber, could have examined him and noted, without fear of contradiction, the complete absence of all Aryan stigmata. His body was long for his height, and his legs confirmingly short. His eyes were brown and narrow, and both epicanthic folds were sharp and genetically perfect. His hair was black, of course, and a lock hung down over his nose to cover an area between his dark eyebrows. When conversing, he frequently brushed back this lock with the back of his hand: and he always did the same thing after he had written down something in English. He spoke briefly and rather hesitantly in about five languages. In the hospital he often smiled, fleetingly but distinctly, but I noticed that when travelling in the jungle he never relaxed to this extent. Perhaps the wild animals and the weapons carried by the tough hard-drinking Dusuns reminded him that none of us is on this earth for ever. He was happiest at home amongst his family, with rice and pork and fish and vegetables spread on a table before him. At work, he was hardworking, reliable, and a very good Dresser.

The medical establishment was completed by one male and one female attendant, and a cook. And a part-time midwife should not be overlooked. This small Chinese woman nodded affably whenever she met me in the hospital and said something that sounded remarkably like ''Hai!''

Regarding endemic diseases — briefly, nearly everything we have at home was present in abundance. A primitive tropical country has primitive diseases — malaria, yaws, amoebic and bacillary dysentery and intestinal parasites (hookworm, roundworm, and a few others) were rife. Almost everyone had something on the skin that called for scratching. Oddities like cirrhosis and beri-beri were common. And we had our small share of leprosy. I had two patients with mossy foot and one with elephantiasis. Syphilis seemed to be absent and gonorrhoea was too common to mention.

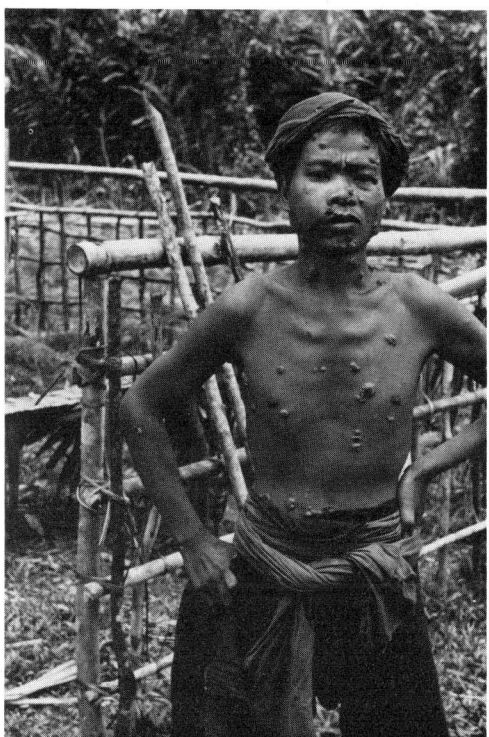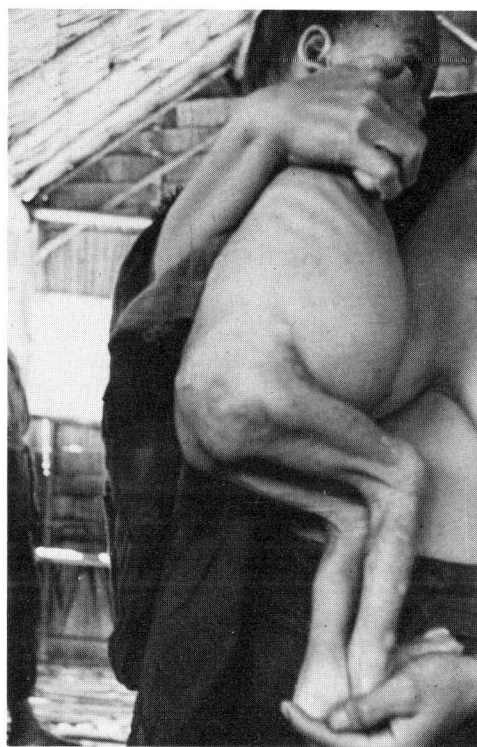

Among the endemic diseases Yaws (or 'puru') was most prevalent. It was often aggravated by malnutrition. European medicine worked 'like magic'.

Bad tempered honey bears and treacherous pet monkeys sent quite a few people limping to our hospital. Centipedes, scorpions, snakes and pit vipers, stingrays and even crocodiles made a contribution, sometimes quite amusingly. For instance, one of the River People (Orang Sungei) came with a nasty wound on his right hand. He had been filling a cooking pot with water when a spritely young crocodile seized his hand. "What happened then?" I asked. "I pulled the crocodile out of the river, Tuan!" Strangely enough, these exotic medical experiences were not entirely without profitable fall-out. Years later I was in practice in Tasmania. One day an agitated potato farmer limped into the surgery with several nasty holes in one calf, and exclaimed, "I was crossing the main street, doctor. You would never guess in a month of Sundays what happened to me!" I said, "You have been bitten by a Malayan Honey Bear!" It was quite straightforward — I knew there was a circus in town!

Clearly I hadn't been appointed to the staff of a great metropolitan hospital, but that did not worry me at all. In retrospect, I doubt whether I had chosen my vocation wisely: for me the great medical ant-heaps of civilised society were frankly and completely uninviting. So here I was in the small village of Kudat with no colleagues, no tutors, no medical students, no psychiatric or social workers, and not even a shapely physiotherapist: and, by the grace of God, no-one to crack a whip and tell me what to do. I could imagine a really ambitious doctor taking the next boat home. As it was, I gazed about me and said, "This looks good!".

One afternoon in July 1938 I made my first expedition into the Ulu, accompanied by the District Officer, Stackhall, and Mr Shu On. Our gear was packed in 20 bark containers known as boungins. These had shoulder straps, and kulis carried them on their backs for twelve cents a day. The government launch *Kimanis* took us toward the

Luggage and medical supplies being transported up the Bengkoka River.

head of the bay. We anchored opposite the mouth of the Matungong River and shortly afterwards a torrential downpour commenced and continued for six hours without a break.

At dawn the luggage was unloaded into canoes and a larger kumpit. We followed a channel through shallow mudflats and entered the river mouth. In mangrove forest lining the banks some proboscis monkeys were surprised in branches close to the water's edge. Stackhall joked, ''Look at the old man with a pot belly! Will I put a bullet into it?'' Punai or green wood pigeons were flighting, and we dropped enough for breakfast. Stackhall was a champion shot. When the paddlers showed signs of tiring, he raised enthusiasm by giving ''dozens'', like the cox of a racing eight. Progress up the stream became quite a boisterous affair. All the paddlers were stripped to the waist: they had golden brown skins. Several had neat moustaches. Their speech was direct and incisive. Their coloured headcloths gave an authentic impression of the legendary East. Eventually, the kumpit grounded. There was a short walk to a small bamboo rest house which was situated beside the market place. The area was normally deserted except on tamu (market) days when the Dusun farmers and sea-going Bajaus met to sell or exchange their produce.

About a hundred Rungus Dusuns had gathered for the Tamu and Clinic. As trading finished they collected under a shady tree. Some squatted on the ground, others wandered about carrying lumps of shark and stingray which they had obtained from the Bajau fishermen for coconut-shellfuls of native rice. The scene was colourful and I had the impression my patients-to-be had stepped straight from the pages of the *National Geographic* magazine. The men wore parangs — large knives with curved blades — in wooden sheaths on their left hips. Before the Clinic commenced the mata mata (policeman) shouted an order, and these weapons were piled ostentatiously in an untidy

The Rungus Dusuns gathered for the Tamu and Clinic. The women were small and shy. They wore highly coloured bajus and their lips were stained from chewing betelnut and sireh leaf. After the clinic they danced to music produced by drums and native xylophones.

The Rungus Dusun women adorned themselves with enormous spirals of brass around their legs, forearms and necks which clinked exotically as they moved about.

heap in front of the rest house. Apparently there had been bloodshed at earlier Clinics. How small the women were! How shy! Their clothes were of dark linen, but some had brightly coloured bajus. Their heads were covered with folded towelling and their feet were bare. A small plug of tobacco projected from lips stained red from chewing betelnut and sireh leaf. Their teeth were black and filed. There were enormous spirals of brass round their legs, forearms and necks. These clinked most exotically as they moved about.

When everything was ready, Shu On shouted "Chari botul obat! Get your medicine bottles!" There was a general rush for parangs. A nearby bamboo grove was attacked and stately limbs crashed down and were hacked into segments of suitable length to serve as bottles. A few minutes later the parangs were once again piled in a heap and the patients lined up ready to receive their treatment.

The Rungus Dusuns came forward one by one. Shu On interpreted. When asked their name, the majority turned their heads sharply to one side, seeking the assistance of friends. It was bad luck for them to speak their names: if they did so, the names might fall into the hands of evil spirits.

Nearly everyone wanted injections for "puru" or yaws. This disease was very prevalent amongst those living in the steamy lowlands. It is a particularly loathsome disease but, fortunately, European medicine worked like magic. Each patient came to me with outstretched arm, pointing to the vein in front of the elbow. "Minta susuk, Tuan." ("I want an injection.") They showed no fear of the needle. Shu On was very expert and gave 85 injections in about two hours. Every patient was given a vile-tasting mixture of carbon tetrachloride and chenopodium to expel the round and hookworm population which they harboured. How our patients performed after gulping it down! There was a tremendous amount of facetious retching. The little Dusun women almost turned themselves inside-out in efforts to be funny.

It was customary for government doctors to palpate all spleens. As my stubby fingers pressed under their ribs the women found it intolerably amusing. A humorous glint developed in their eyes, hands stole over their mouths, and finally their laughter was outright. It was impossible to remain serious.

"Kurrap" was the elegant name given to a fungus infection (Tinea Imbricata) which caused the skin to be shed in concentric whorls. A bowl of kurrap paint and two paint brushes were put out. The natives stripped naked and painted each other all over, delicately concealing themselves with one hand. The treatment was painful, and children stamped their feet in anguish.

The last patient was a middle-aged Chinese gardener. I asked, "What is your name?" The Chinese made a funny little sound twice. I did not catch it. "Shu On! Please ask this fellow his name."

The Dresser did as requested. "His name, Sir, is . . ." Shu On made what sounded like two intimate grunts of satisfaction.

"Write it down here", I said. Shu On wrote "Ng Ng."

"Does he really call himself that?" I asked.

"Yes, sir, though he may be called Ah Ng or Mr Ng instead of just Ng Ng."

"Indeed!"

The Clinic concluded with 73 tooth extractions without anaesthesia, all completed in about 15 minutes. The Dusuns knelt in a ragged line with their mouths open, indicated the offending "gigi" with their fingers and Shu On did the job with commendable expedition. About every fourth patient he dipped the forceps in hot water.

At the end of the Clinic Stackhall announced he wanted 25 kulis for the following morning. To solve this problem four Headmen gathered in a circle on the ground and each used his toes as an improvised abacus to calculate how many carriers his village should supply. It took them an hour.

It was a full day and the D.O. and I retired early. The split bamboo floor of the rest house was raised about a metre above the ground. Several dozen Dusuns crawled

'Kurrap' was the elegant name given to a fungus infection (Tinea Imbricata). Treatment called for an application of kurrap paint, for which the natives stripped and painted each other all over. The treatment was painful.

underneath. They chatted quietly in jungly vernacular for some hours, occasionally lapsing into brisk argument; others smoked native tobacco or chewed and spat betel nut. At 4 a.m. they decided that night was over. Three broke wind simultaneously, others followed suit sporadically; all began to clear their nostrils, light their native cigarettes and perform other active chores such as striking the dogs and making off into the scrub. The cook-boys brought tea, toast and eggs. We got up and changed.

At dawn, 25 carriers set off along the path leading to the village of Kuniong on the other side of the peninsula, each man carrying a load of 18 kilograms. An armed mata mata walked behind them. The line of Dusuns bearing the brown bongons formed a procession which looked like a strange segmented caterpillar as it wandered over the lalang hills. We walked in an amusing pecking order. Kulis first, then the policeman, after him the D.O.; then myself, a native chief, four headmen, some women, children and dogs, and a village pig. Several women opened waxed paper parasols and managed to look rather snooty.

After the clinic there was music and trading.

We passed through secondary forest. On all sides gibbons or wah-wahs were sending out their clear ringing calls. The D.O. and I made a detour to inspect a Dusun longhouse. A dozen little skinny pi dogs howled a welcome and a warning. The house was 40 metres in length, with the floor raised 150 centimetres above the ground. We entered by climbing a notched log. Along one side was a common thoroughfare, on the other a row of family cubicles. Women were de-husking padi in wooden mortars, the thumping poles shaking the entire house. We stopped to watch an elderly woman cutting up penang (betel nut) and sireh leaf, adding a little gumbir and lime and finally chewing the stimulating mixture as if the act passed away time which lay heavily on her hands. I bit a piece of nut, then spat it out. Stackhall asked the old lady "How is it, good?"

"Good enough, Tuan," she laughed.

As we left the village clearing, Stackhall said "Did you see that pig? I can make him follow me like a dog. Will you take me for five dollars?" I declined, but Stackhall walked towards the bushes, fumbling with his belt. The pig grunted with interest and then followed him. "There you are!" Mobile sanitation at its best! We went on, laughing.

At Kuniong another magnificent group of patients had collected to give us an equally interesting Clinic. There was one misfortune. One native, confusing his bamboo containers, drank some turpentine liniment. He performed as if his life was terminating in a particularly painful manner, but presently he recovered and said he felt better. The Clinic was followed by a tapai party. Under a mango tree Stackhall and I were surrounded by several score of grinning Dusuns. Now the advantage lay with them — they were administering the medicine! Native zylophones were playing, gongs were being beaten and some Bajaus thumped a smart rhythm on drums. The Dusuns poured native beer (tapai) into cups which they offered to us. "Drink, Tuan, drink! Do nothing but drink!" Tapai tastes something like rotten cider. I sipped and pulled a face, and everyone burst out laughing. After the D.O. and I had taken several drinks the party commenced in earnest. Headmen now joined in and then the rank and file of the villagers. After a while Stackhall said "They want to know if you feel drunk."

"Not yet!" The women refilled my cup.

"Minum, Tuan! — drink it down! Oop serabin mudja — like a young man!"

Dancing commenced. One of the Dusun men produced a red sash which he passed behind his neck and held with both arms outstretched like the wings of a wandering albatross. He then began to jog about turning this way and that, to the beating of gongs and gabangs. Four little Dusun women lowered their eyes modestly and entered the dance. Their bodies and arms stiffened perceptibly, their little hands dorsi-flexed most becomingly and they too jogged and revolved slowly, their naked toes nibbling at the ground. The tempo increased slightly, and suddenly the male came prancing towards them like a bird of prey. Hemmed in by the crowd, and agreeably terrified, the four defenceless women made their escape under his outstretched arms and resumed their quaint revolutions in the area just vacated by the predatory male.

The colourfully-dressed leading male dancer sets a high standard as he prepares to terrify four little women dancers.

The fun lasted until all the tapai was finished. Most of the natives were intoxicated. Worm mixture is an excellent foundation for a party! Two government officers were red in the face and grinning broadly.

We slept well that night. A mere dozen inebriates dozed fitfully under the rest house floor; the salute to dawn was dull by comparison.

The morning's walk lay back to Tegamon, a few kilometres south of Matungong.

After the Clinic there was a deer hunt. About 4 p.m. we set off, mounted on a dozen water buffaloes. I was handed the tail of my beast to hold, to stop me falling off. An hour out, someone spotted a herd of tembadau (wild oxen) in a clearing near the crest of a hill. We approached as closely as we dared on the buffaloes and then dismounted. Stackhall and I and the native Chief crept along a forrested gully to within range. There were three bulls in the herd. The cows looked curiously like domestic cattle. We sighted and at a signal from Stackhall, fired. One bull fell; another leapt ahead several paces and then sprang high on its hind legs, to be brought down spectacularly by the native Chief with his second shot. A third bull was wounded but followed the rest of the herd on three legs into the jungle. The natives arrived and cut up the game with their parangs. Every part of a tembadau was considered edible and only bloodstains remained on the ground when we left.

Darkness came quickly and on the way home we were caught in a thunderstorm. In the brilliant yellow glare of the lightning flashes the lalang plains looked extraordinarily beautiful. The Kerbau somehow made their way through jungle-covered gulleys. It was pitch black and I could see nothing except phosphorescent fungi and scattered colonies of fireflies.

The next morning the D.O and I separated, having first arranged a rendezvous. I set off on foot for Langkon Rubber Estate: a Dusun, carrying my toothbrush and paste and a pair of pyjamas, walked ahead.

The manager of the rubber estate and his wife were hospitable Scots. The estate contained the only shower bath in the district and it was certainly a treat to shower before dinner in the antipodean manner. That night, after whiskies and a five course meal, we listened rather sleepily to the nine o'clock news from London. It was almost absurdly grim.

At 3.45 next morning I left the manager's house and climbed into a sulky and sat beside the native syce. We set off along a dark road hedged in by rubber trees. Dismal enough by daylight, the trees were truly gloomy at this early hour. After a time we emerged from the rubber and passed through a village housing permanent estate labour. The upright tapioca stems and the broad banana leaves in the gardens had a quiet and sombre attraction about them. Stars were still visible and a few ghost birds fluttered awkwardly in front of the advancing pony. A steamy vapour hung over the young roadside growth and dew lay heavily on the leaves. The syce considered the day hadn't really commenced and his eyes closed and his head fell forward. The pony apparently agreed with him and came to a halt, eased off on two legs and joined the syce in a snooze. It was very quiet and for two minutes it seemed that the world had stopped. Finally I hit the pony on the rump with my hat and we got going again.

At the Pengkalan there was a canoe and four paddlers waiting. We pushed out from the muddy bank and started down the river. At first the banks were lined with nipah palms; lower down, we passed into purely mangrove forest. The tidal water was sluggish, almost greasy, and from the dark mudbanks came the clinking scuttle of crabs and an occasional loud "honk" apparently from the depths of mud skipper holes. Slender mangrove seeds plopped daintily into the water and bobbed up and down as they were carried away by the tide.

The Bajau paddlers went "easy" spontaneously as they slid past a patch of mangrove illuminated by twinkling cascades and streams of fireflies.

"Chantek, Tuan," murmured one of the Bajaus. Indeed, it was very beautiful. The early dawn cast a black shadow from the eastern bank. Some blunt-nosed mullet made smooth ripples on the water as they swam upstream.

It was full daylight by the time we reached the kuala (river mouth). Maruda Bay lay before us without a ripple on its face: the penchangs (piles) demarcating the channel through the offshore mudflats seemed to extend to the horizon itself. To the right was the Malay village of Tambun, mounted on stilts in the shallows, far from land, the very epitome of tropical beauty and charm.

The canoe continued on like a tiny insect crawling across a smooth silver plate. At the end of the penchangs it made its way to where the *Kimanis*, with the D.O. on board, was anchored.

The paddlers were given a chit for their wages. On the *Kimanis* a hand pump began to work, the Serang rang through to the engine room and the twin diesels sprang to life. The anchor weighed, the launch nosed round slowly to the north, and then surged ahead.

The D.O. and I sat forward on canvas chairs. A pot of tea appeared from below deck. On the way home Stackhall said, "Isn't the European news bloody? Any time now." He laughed, and added with conviction "It's getting close all right."

One day we received a shock. Advice came that His Excellency the Governor was on his way from Sandakan and would hold an inspection of the Civil Hospital in a few hours. Nothing to get excited about? Not half! Mr Thomas sprang into action — his voice swept through the wards, through the ceiling wax palms, and caused doors to open even as far down as the Baslc Mission. "The Tuan Besar (big boss) is coming! The Tuan Besar is coming! Get moving!" He galvanised the place in English, Malay, Hakka, Hokkien, Cantonese and Dusun.

It certainly was an event. Shu On seemed stunned for a moment, then cleared his forehead of hair and began gathering up files from the office table. Half-dead patients suddenly quickened and lent a hand in making our hospital spick and span. Dispensary bottles were arranged with every inscription facing foward. Wooden pillows were placed all on the same ends of the beds. Red blankets and mosquito nets were neatly arranged. Brooms swished to and fro. Less impressive relatives of patients were asked to remove their sleeping mats from the verandahs and retreat temporarily to the shelter and concealment of the coconut trees across the road. Two bamboo water pipes with their opium dross were hidden in the kitchen. The cook was instructed to have a bath and to wear something more presentable than underpants. Women put frangipani and hibiscus flowers in their hair. For a moment I considered wearing my Imperial African regalia but then asked the houseboy to put out a simple white suit. I was born too timid.

Everything settled down like an uneasy school of sardines after an attack by trevally. After dressing I went slowly round the wards and a curious feeling of contentment, even pride, came over me. The place was a veritable medical museum — malaria, three blackwater fevers; an array of very large spleens; two cirrhoses; a back room full of exuberant yaws; hookworm disease; a child with palpable lumps in her abdomen due to masses of roundworms; tuberculosis; a pit viper bite; even a mossy foot below a tropical ulcer. And, it must be admitted, a mistake — a Chinese who I thought had cancer of the bladder, was actually afflicted with schistosomiasis which he had brought down from China with him. Other people's misfortunes, often extreme, were indeed my luck — but "luck" really isn't the word to use. This was indeed a hospital, I felt.

As His Excellency was about to leave the Customs in a car, the hospital staff gathered formally on the front verandah.

Suddenly there was a wild cry from the male ward attendant. A patient with a fractured spine, finding the day unbearably hot, had decided to remove his plaster jacket. Two friends assisted him, and in no time there was a mess of plaster and strips of bandage scattered over the floor. The staff rushed in and tried to hide the broken back in the lavatory, but unfortunately the cubicle was occupied by someone with nervous diarrhoea. They then bravely decided to remove the rest of the plaster quickly and tidy up: ''Bring in the plaster shears!''

They set to work. The poor patient was dragged here and there as the plaster bandages were torn off. ''Hi-yah, Hi-yah!'' The shears bit their way erratically upwards from his thigh. In five minutes the ward looked like a bomb-shattered whitewash factory.

''A car is coming!''

''I say!''

Brooms swished more furiously than ever. Patients concealed lumps of plaster under the red blankets folded across their beds. Finally the staff rushed to the verandah again.

During the inspection the Governor looked slightly puzzled. Some forty Hakkas, Hailams, Dusuns and Bajaus saluted him as he passed and there was not a vacant bed. The hospital was obviously busy but he had not realised that everyone worked quite so hard — the entire staff was panting and sweating profusely.

Incidentally, this was the first and last full plaster cast I applied in the Far East.

Outstanding amongst the inventions of the Devil is the party telephone line. One of these contraptions stretched between Kudat and Pitas Estate, 160 kilometres distant around Marudu Bay. Far too commonly in the evening a lonely planter, feeling the need to commune with his medical adviser, would ring and ring and ring, finally successfully, and would then announce his diagnosis. ''Malaria again, Doctor!'' His voice would fade away as intermediate telephones were quietly raised and ''our friends'' (as they were called) listened in. To be fair, sometimes reception difficulties were due to local thunderstorms: but, to be accurate, ''our friends'' always copped the blame. It was no secret that there are three elements in Diseases of the White Man in the Far East: namely, (1) genuine fair dinkum parasites; (2) grog; (3) self pity. The contribution of each of the triad to any particular syndrome was anyone's guess. Always ''our friends'' analysed the clinical picture they overheard, confidently allocated the speculative proportions to (1), (2), and (3), and the final conclusion was always defamatory. Everyone knew it. Some laughed it off, some grew very irritable and described their symptoms with impressive heat in an attempt to carry conviction. At odd times language became distinctly vulgar.

One evening, three months before Christmas, Coleman rang from Pitas Estate: ''Is that you, Doctor?''

''Yes.''

''How are you?''

''I am very well.''

''Oh, how come? Is the Padre with you?''

I took this in my stride.

''Will you come over and join me for Christmas? Can you hear me? Can you hear me? Can you hear me?''

Every telephone along the party line was now applied to an ear and Coleman's voice almost faded away. Nevertheless, I had heard enough. Accordingly, I arranged a medical expedition up the Bengkoka River right on the festive season. And it was well worth it. For some reason I had always wanted to walk 50 kilometres in a day — just once! Medical supplies were sent across the Bay, and the *Kimanis* landed me and enough medicine for a Clinic just 50 kilometres from Pitas. Early next morning I set out alone along the bridle path. By 8 a.m. it was very hot and I was sweating profusely and thinking how foolish I was. The milestones seemed to be further apart as the day wore on. Twice I stopped at a Dusun house and had a drink of coconut milk. About morning-tea time I met a planter on a desolate stretch of beach and was invited for drinks to his home amongst dense secondary growth. He had only a small area of rubber and coconuts and was having a struggle to survive financially. His refrigerator was out of action but we had two scotches in warm, rather brackish water. He was eagerly awaiting the outbreak of hostilities in Europe. In his opinion war was preferable to functioning as a hard-up small planter on the remote shores of Marudu Bay. He preferred a tangible enemy, one of flesh and blood. After cheering him up with the news that World War II was inevitable, I pushed on and reached Oscar Belton's plantation in time for lunch. He had heard of my coming and welcomed me with cool beer, a fish curry, a tray of sambals, and sago and gula malacca. Visitors were rare and it was late afternoon before I could thank him and get away. Darkness came and I still had a few kilometres to go. The path became difficult to see and soon I began to think about cobras and banded kraits and pythons. Presently I was relieved to see a torch-light coming towards me. Coleman had despatched an escort. I was tired and sore on arrival: never have I enjoyed a rest in a Javanese jar more. I ladled warm water over my head with one hand and helped myself to cool Tiger beer with the other. Then a few stingahs, another great meal and blissfully to bed with several nightcaps aboard. Life wasn't too bad after all! I imagined this was how athletes must feel after a hard game of football and a few beers. Lucky fellows!

The village I had selected for a pre-Christmas present of chenopodium etc., was marked as ''Penapak''. It was a considerable distance up the Bengkoka River. I suppose it existed but in fact I never actually saw it. We left Pitas at mid-morning in five canoes. The river was in flood and the Orang Sungei paddlers had quite a slog against the current. Sometimes it took half an hour to pass a patch of sugar cane grass. The river was infested with crocodiles. Some hurried to the water on seeing us, others lay on the bank apparently sound asleep. We saw two lying on sandbanks with mouths wide open as if propped open with sticks. ''Are they dead?'' I asked.

On our way to Penapak up the flooded Bengkoka River which was infested with crocodiles. It took us half an hour to pass this patch of sugar cane grass.

"No, Tuan, they are waiting for monkeys to come down from the trees." I was told that the monkeys descended to the bank to chase crabs. The gleaming white teeth of the crocodiles apparently excited their curiosity to such an extent that finally the most foolish monkey in the crab-hunting group would practically seat himself in the reptile's mouth — snap, and it was all over!

River people and crocodiles usually live together in an uneasy truce. I was therefore surprised when they asked me to take up arms against the crocodiles. I shot three. The technique was to point the canoe towards a sleeping saurian, then the paddlers would sit very still while I aimed and fired. Immediately, with loud cries and shouts, we paddled furiously towards the bank to seize the tail of the wounded animal before it could re-enter the river. These exciting breaks relieved the monotony of the slow, tiring progress up the river.

We spent a night in a riverside rest house and on the second day reached a clearing where some bark and attap huts has been erected for our visit. Some 45 Rungus Dusuns and a few Orang Sungei (river people) had gathered for the Clinic from invisible villages. Several of the Dusuns had a curious nodding of the head and tremor and to and fro movement of the eyes which was apparently a familial complaint. We de-wormed everyone, injected most for yaws, and painted them all over for kurrap in routine fashion. After the Clinic I went for a long walk upstream, along a native path. Eventually I came to a tributary of the Bengkoka. There was a pool about 30 metres long with shallow rapids at each end. It was very hot so I stripped off and went in for a swim. The water was cool and pleasant and I spent two hours in pure enjoyment, occasionally diving, sometimes floating on my back watching the punai and imperial pigeons flying overhead. It was good and I was being paid for the pleasure. Reluctantly, I eventually got out and dressed, and went back to the rest house.

By 7.30 p.m. I had had two scotches, some tinned toheroa soup and fresh mudcrab. Two hungry River People decided I had had enough rest and so off we went hunting. Mata mata Gabuk, who had just distinguished himself by winning the annual police rifle shoot, came along to show us how it was done. Our luck was very much in. After a short walk, a small mouse deer showed up in the light of the hunting lamp and fell to a .22 shot. A little further on, we got a barking deer in similar fashion. We were lucky for it was "liar" (wild and agitated) and its eyes swung erratically in the light of the lamp. Pressing on, we crossed in the rapids below the pool in which I had spent such a pleasant two hours swimming. Another 15 minutes of walking, and then in tana payah (swamp) amongst some giant swamp lilies we came across two deer. The big payau raised their heads and their eyes "competed with the lamp", as the expression has it. It was a pretty sight. Slowly and gently I touched Gabuk on the side and indicated the animal on the right as his. The range was almost point blank. My Savage and Gabuk's shotgun exploded almost simultaneously. The male payau fell, its mate hesitated and then ran off before we could reload. The Orang Sungei were jubilant: being Mohammedans, they quickly — and just in time — cut the throat of the stone dead deer, as their religion demands. Poor Gabuk examined its body for traces of buckshot and then went amongst the lilies searching fruitlessly for traces of blood from the second deer. Alas, the champion had missed the unmissable at a few metres range and he was very ashamed. Obviously he had shot at one of those rare, but well-known, miraculous beasts immune to buckshot. Our prize was too heavy to carry home without assistance: we slung it 120 centimetres above the ground with rotan, beyond the reach of wild pig. Then we removed the leeches from our legs and set off home. We reached the rapids once more. On the far bank of my favourite swimming pool the hunting lamp showed a pair of baleful red eyes. "Buaya, Tuan. Besar sa-kali. A big one." As yet, I understood little Malay, but I knew that "buaya" meant "crocodile". The Orang Sungei added "It's always there. It feeds on pigs and deer." I was thankful its diet was so restricted. How crowded the small pool had been that afternoon!

A typical scene in the 'waiting room' at a clinic. Here the patients are resting after an injection for Yaws.

There was a small Clinic next morning, just a few stragglers and doubting Thomases, and we loafed about the camp until late afternoon. The paddlers spent quite a time trying to persuade me to shoot a great fat monkey watching us from a tree across the river. A young native then asked me to try my luck again in more legitimate shooting. We walked into the hills, upstream and behind the camp, for over a kilometre. Then we sat with our backs to a huge ara tree, and with a leaf began calling the kijang (barking deer). On the fifth call, a begging, plaintive, almost musical sound, a kijang answered. There was a hoarse roar and then a barking sound, seldom heard. I made ready. We could hear hooves thumping on the soft jungle floor, and a kijang came racing up and stopped in bewilderment a few paces from us. It was ours.

The sky had darkened. Chain lightning and thunder, and a rush of wind moving the jungle tops, were followed by very heavy rain.

We found reasonable shelter but were forced to get going when darkness came. Fortunately, I had brought along a small torch. We came to a deep gully, spanned by a thin branch which looked something like a reticulated python partly straightened out, and just about as thick. And wet and slippery. I shone the torch on it. Without hesitation, the young native, with the kijang on his back, walked straight across. So there we were, separated by a yawning gulch about 6 metres deep, with a metre of muddy water rushing noisily between some nasty boulders in its bed. A thin beam of torch-light pierced the inky darkness and showed me these dangers. My cheap Chinese boots were slippery with jungle mud. I had never been trained as a ballet dancer or tightrope walker for reasons undeniably sound, and so I made a most humiliating decision. I abandoned all attempts to maintain self-respect, and with the greatest difficulty went down the bank into the stream, waded across the waist deep torrent and, burdened by torch, rifle and a dozen leeches, I somehow crawled up the wet, near vertical, distant bank to join my nimble companion. He was frankly surprised at my performance. "Tuan, why didn't you use the bridge?" He didn't seem to realise I had just completed a most competent exercise in continued survival.

Next day we went downstream to Pitas, reaching the estate in a few hours, the floodwaters propelling us along at a very good pace. Hospitality in the East is open-handed, whatever the colour of the hands may be. In this case they happened to be pink, since my host, Coleman, was a red-headed Scot. There were no flaws in his hospitality that I could detect. Apart from one short walk through the rubber to view some smelly latex in the factory vats, we did not venture far from his overworked refrigerator. On Christmas evening we sat in cane chairs on the lawn, sipping beer, with Coleman taking occasional pot-shots at hornbills and mynah birds with his gun. He said, "How deep do you think that river is in the middle?" The muddy Bengkoka was swollen with floodwater and looked very deep. "Nine metres", I guessed.

Coleman smiled, "Quite wrong! Where the channel should be there's a great heap of empty beer bottles, reaching almost to the surface. Deceptive, isn't it?"

Next morning, as I left, I made the mistake of admiring an enormous ornamental carving of Chinese soapstone in his lounge. It weighed about a 100 kilograms and must have taken some poverty-stricken Chinese craftsman at least a decade to make.

"Do you really like it?"

"A fine bit of work."

After breakfast we went across the lawn to my kumpit. The craft sat deeply in the water: in it was the heavy soapstone monument, with all its dragons, snakes, parrot fish and curious little men eyeing me with amusement. What could I say? Coleman was grinning broadly, and wouldn't listen anyway. Short of jumping in the boat and hurling the thing into the river, there appeared no alternative to accepting it. As the kumpit moved off, Coleman shouted, "I've been wondering for years how I'd get rid of that!" He turned towards his house, very pleased with himself, grinning from ear to ear. I pushed on to some Dusun villages on the peninsula, and then, further on, to Suangduyong Laut on the east coast, where the *Kimanis* was waiting to take us home.

In Kudat I played chess once a week with an Austrian priest. We enjoyed the weekly tussle. One evening, Father Theurl made his move and walked across and stood looking at my recently acquired soapstone monument. In order to concentrate on the chess, I had to shade my eyes. The good Father returned to the table, remarking that the carving was an excellent example of oriental art.

"You really like it, Father?"

Father was concentrating on his next move. "Ja, ja, it is very goot", he muttered politely.

I went to the kitchen. A little later on, three servants were staggering to the Mission, heavily laden with oriental art.

Next day, the companion Father from the Mission greeted me. "Doctor, Father Theurl was overwhelmed. He says you are the most generous person he has ever met."

An interesting character at our hospital was the Male Attendant, a small, middle-aged man named Ah Kui. He swept the floors, washed sputum mugs, dispensed stock prescriptions, filled gelatine capsules with quinine, took temperatures, made entries on charts, and so on. He was a key man, and at any time of the day someone could be heard shouting "Ah Kui! A Kui-a!"

The Attendant's face was deeply lined, and he walked with a stoop as if deep in thought. Before long I noted that he often brought patients their medicines when both Dressers were occupied elsewhere. I asked Thomas, "Where did Ah Kui learn English?"

"He didn't, Sir."

"Then how does he know which medicine each patient should be getting?"

"Oh that! He can read the instructions all right. Without a doubt he taught himself."

Duty and curiosity combined to cause me to test Ah Kui's competence on several treatment charts.

"What is this prescription, Ah Kui?"

Ah Kui looked at the medical recipe indicated, then walked across and tapped the correct stock mixture with the back of his hand. I repeated the test seven times, and Ah Kui scored full marks. As he went away, the Attendant said something in Chinese to the Dressers. Their faces didn't change, but their eyes seemed to smile. Impressed, I watched this humble member of the Staff more closely. He was on duty 16 hours daily, seven days a week. He seemed to enjoy a working popularity amongst the patients. He was naturally well-mannered, but apparently very interested in hospital gossip, and when he heard anything amusingly derogatory about anyone, he often roared with laughter. Then his eyes almost closed, his sallow cheeks split into a number of deep vertical grooves, and his head bobbed up and down like a cork in the sea.

Many offences were committed by patients, such as throwing medicines away, abusing or even striking the cook, removing their own stitches, being seen at the house of ill-fame down-town without permission, or selling the hospital blankets. It was useless for a European or even an educated Chinese to argue with the hospital-blanket-selling class of Chinese. These rascals evaded, denied, threw the blame elsewhere, or suddenly lost all understanding of what was apparently their own dialect a moment ago. When things were going against the hospital in any such argument, Ah Kui would suddenly appear. He would shout the patient down, squashing all denials with angry hisses and blasts of air. Loyalty to the hospital? Perhaps so, but on the other hand he liked a lot of government property around, and possibly regarded hospital blankets as a personal reserve for the inevitable future emergency.

In his odd spare moments Ah Kui often sat chatting in the wards, instinctively rather than deliberately acquiring an intimate knowledge of everyone's private life and misdemeanours. Later, if necessary, he publicly hurled unsavoury abstracts in their faces. It did not pay to cross him. If any patient seriously annoyed him, then at the next meal his ration would be cut and a few pieces of worthless gristle substituted for the usual lumps of boiled water-buffalo meat; and his tin plate would be thrown down on the end of his bed with patent disgust.

A patient under mental observation had some clinically interesting yaws nodules on his head which I wished to photograph. Ah Kui was instructed to bring the patient to my house at afternoon-tea time. I saw the pair approaching. Ah Kui was leading the way, deep in thought as usual, and the patient followed, holding up his baggy hospital pants with both hands; but suddenly he let them fall, bent down and picked up a heavy lump of wood, and crept up behind the Attendant. I yelled, "Jaga, Ah Kui! Watch out!" Fortunately our patient was lacking in physical as well as mental skill, and by the time the wood descended and smacked the ground Ah Kui was facing his naked assailant from a safe distance. What a scolding he administered! Then he picked up the patient's pants and used this garment to drive him up the garden path to my front lawn. "That's enough, Ah Kui, give the man his pants."

The photographs were taken, including one of Ah Kui, and I then dismissed the pair.

"Thank you, Ah Kui."

"Sama sama, Tuan. The same to you."

The Attendant had recovered his sense of humour and went off laughing. No doubt he was preparing the menu for the patient's evening meal!

The number of in-patients gradually increased to over forty. This meant more work for everyone, including Ah Kui. All day long it was "Ah Kui, Ah Kui-a."

One day I returned from district work to find the female ward empty. A week later the male ward was similarly deserted. All in-patients had absconded. No-one was particularly concerned, but the event was quite interesting. I made a few inquiries and learnt that a young female patient had been awakened in the middle of the night by "something" in her mosquito net which attempted to smother her. She screamed, creating quite a scare. Later, she, and other patients too, could hear a wooden Chinese clock ticking loudly, although everyone knew there was no clock in the ward. Obviously the place was haunted, and at the first crack of dawn all female patients departed en masse for home and mother. In their turn, the male patients were disturbed by a figure dressed in white and groaning lugubriously, walking up and down in front of the latrines at midnight. Result — no patients at all!

Suspicion centred on Ah Kui, but nothing could be proved, and the matter blew over. Unofficially, crackers were exploded in the hospital, joss sticks were burnt, gongs were beaten, and the in-patients gradually returned from their vegetable gardens, coconut plantations, pig-rearing establishments, street corners and jungle longhouses.

From time to time normal hospital routine broke down. History sheets were found in the kitchen, buckets were not emptied, floors remained unswept, thermometers lay balanced on the verandah railing, and Ah Kui had to be shouted for twenty times before he finally appeared. Then, more often than not, he entered the ward dressed only in a pair of underpants and wooden clogs. He seemed stupid and worn, and his face was pale. He looked too long at people, his mouth hanging open. The first time I saw Ah Kui in this state I asked "What's the matter, Ah Kui, are you sick?"

"I've got a gut-ache, Tuan. Semua pechah — everything's broken inside!"

He had wind in the knees and his penis was being drawn into his abdomen — a grave disorder, and he hadn't even bothered to apply a clothes peg, mandatory in such circumstances. More questions, and I learnt Ah Kui was a registered chandu smoker, receiving a monthly allowance of opium from the government, which controlled opium smoking as a monopoly. As long as Ah Kui's supply lasted he was happy. But sometimes he smoked excessively and consumed all he had before the end of the month: and if he could not beg or borrow chandu, he felt and looked ghastly. No drowsy numbness seized and smoothed his ragged senses: his stomach played up, he complained of colic, forgot his manners, lost his grin, and his work just went to pieces.

Finally, I gave him a month's notice. For a time he improved. He kept on working sixteen hours a day and appeared with a cheerful grin whenever he was called. He appeared to be indispensable. Oft-times, he looked sad, and no-one knew what was going to happen to him. At the end of the month, nothing was said and Ah Kui went on working.

For a period he was as good as gold, as pleasant and as efficient five days before pay day as five days after. Then it was discovered that he was conducting an extensive private practice. His clientele was drawn from people of his own class (i.e. strata Z of Asiatic society) and from others who were too lazy to attend at Out-Patients themselves. Ah Kui raided the stock mixtures when the opportunity arose. Some patients were impressed by his skill, and it was only when they returned for "repeats" that the unusual Chinese characters scratched on the label by Ah Kui attracted attention and led to his incrimination. Accordingly, he was given a final month's notice.

One day, about this time, a demented Chinese girl bound for the asylum at Sandakan was landed at Kudat from a Straits steamship: the captain refused to carry her any further. She was confined to the Mad Persons' Room at the back of the hospital. She screamed day and night, smashed everything she could lay her hands on, and was dirty in her personal habits. At home, her husband had beaten her daily and poured pig food over her head. Finally, he had driven her from the house and installed a substitute.

By some mischance, this girl escaped from confinement one morning at dawn. She ran to the shore and made her way into the sea until only her head was above water. There, she turned and threatened to drown herself if anyone came near her. The problem was explained to some Bajau fishermen. They put to sea in a canoe, stole behind her and seized her before she could carry out her threat. Back at the hospital, the unhappy girl beat on the whitewashed wall of her room until, with great difficulty, she was given sedative injections. Gradually her grief and excitement abated, and she was left an occasionally tearful, habitually untidy, and thoroughly dispirited young girl.

One morning, Mr Thomas said, "Sir, Ah Kui has a very great favour he would ask of you."

"Yes, Thomas, what does he want? Call him."

Ah Kui came out of the Dispensary, saluted and said, "Tabe, Tuan Doktor."

"Tabe, Ah Kui."

Thomas continued, "Ah Kui says he has worked here for a very long time and now he finds that he has fallen in love with this mad girl. With your permission, he wants to marry her."

"What!" I was staggered. No-one was smiling. I turned to Ah Kui and asked quietly, "Is that correct?"

"Correct, Tuan Doktor" he replied.

"Why do you want to marry her?" There must surely be some reason.

"I love her", said Ah Kui.

I hesitated, then said, "O.K. Ah Kui, I'll weigh the matter. Let's finish rounds, Thomas."

I was puzzled. On the face of it, Ah Kui stood to gain nothing, not even a cook. What could have possessed the little man? How in the wide world would the idea of marrying this stricken girl ever occur to him? Did the request have anything to do with the fact that he was under notice? My thoughts wandered towards a possible explanation, but soon I gave up.

The matter wasn't really difficult to deal with. The girl already had a husband, and she had to go to Sandakan for further treatment. Ah Kui accepted this without argument. "That's my luck", he said. The girl was washed and smartly dressed, and sedated with such good effect that not a single person protested when she stepped aboard the steamer. Ah Kui was given yet another chance, but deprived of his private income, and thus of adequate chandu, he was hopeless. Some days he went round the wards looking sad, haggard, and utterly disreputable. Everyone who liked him said, "Stop eating chandu, Ah Kui, don't be a fool!" But Ah Kui could not stop being a fool, and even refused all offers to break him of the opium habit. "I like smoking chandu", he said; or just, "Never mind, never mind!"

On the final morning he was on the crest of one of such waves as were still available to him. Dressed in a white singlet, long white pants, a pair of brown canvas boots, and a freshly painted topee, at a quick glance the Attendent looked quite a respectable citizen. He shook hands with the two Dressers, with several out-patients, and finally with me.

"A safe stay, Tuan" he said, grinning politely.

"A safe journey, Ah Kui. What are you going to do now?" Ah Kui's eyes narrowed. No Chinese is ever beaten. He said, "I've got a friend who owns a charcoal stove, and I calculate to sell satehs. We have an arrangement with the butcher." Satehs are lumps of cooked meat and pork threaded on thin stems of coconut leaf and eaten after immersion in a special curry mixture — wonderful things with beer on a Sunday morning. An idea passed through my head. "I am very fond of satehs. We'll meet again, Ah Kui."

"I hope so, Tuan." Ah Kui appeared happy. He was now in business. He went down the steps and out into the road leading to the main bazaar.

Shu On said, "A pity. He was a nice fellow."

Indeed, Ah Kui was rather a pathetic sight, and everyone was relieved when a peasant in a buffalo cart offered him a lift and took him out of sight.

The medical party en route to the next clinic. Here they make progress through a field of belukar felled and burnt off for padi bukit (hill rice) planting.

Shu On inspects our rest house for the stay. It is located in a field of Indian Corn.

The magnificent Mount Kinabalu as seen from the Kota Belud District.

Two influential women of the Kudat hill-country towards Kinabalu.

Chapter 2

SANDAKAN 1939–40

After a year in Kudat I was transferred to the capital, Sandakan. The transfer was timely. It had been a bad year for health in the Kudat district. Malaria was rife. We had had ten in-patients with blackwater fever, incidentally, without loss. These malnourished people did well on a high egg-protein diet said to contain an anti-malaria factor. Recurrent dysentery and malaria had affected my health considerably. Neither natural immunity nor medical treatment seemed to afford any protection against further attacks. Stackhall preceded me to the capital as a result of an unusual near-fatal attack of malignant tertian fever associated with intestinal bleeding: at the time, he was far from home and had a barely-remembered trip back to Kudat by kumpit. He was sent to hospital in Singapore.

Sandakan was a big town of mixed population and I had a good hospital, a gaol, a police barracks, a paupers' institute, an asylum for the insane and a leper colony on the island of Berhala to look after. In addition, I was Port Health Officer and had to clear ships from overseas. For recreation, there was a golf club, tennis courts, a squash court beside an hotel, and the Sandakan and Recreation Clubs. Stackhall had discovered punai (pigeons) and golden plover on the golf course. All this was good, for there was no getting out of town except by boat. One road ran out from the capital for 18 kilometres, passing through Chinese gardens and rubber trees and it ended abruptly in the jungle. The last kilometre was used more by elephants, reticulated pythons, wild pig and mouse deer than by anything else. It wasn't even a lovers' lane for homo sapiens.

Hearsay had it that the senior government officers manning Sandakan had had more colourful lives when they first "came out". But now they formed a cosy, correct, but rather ethereal group, "very English" in their ways. Indeed, Mrs Agnes Keith was busily and brilliantly recording their stylistic performance for her book *Land Below the Wind*. A conservative outlook actually prevented us getting together a good tennis four for weekly games — the fourth player unfortunately being "in trade". At times the anaesthetic effect of this life style descended like an atmosphere of fifty per cent chloroform upon the jungle and sea-bound enclave; but here and there were little pockets of fresh air, and — so it seemed to me — every one of these was associated in some way with the Medical Department.

My boss, the Principal Medical Officer, was one of the most likeable men I have ever met. He was a big man, carrying a comfortable burden of weight, quiet, dignified and courtly. Good manners were his hallmark. I believe he was a Scot, but he had acquired an accent more commonly found well south of the Border. This was most noticeable when he first met you or was speaking to someone over the telephone. He was hard-working and ran his medical kingdom very well; in fact, with genius considering the small budget he was allowed under the Chartered Company. A more peaceful man could not be imagined, but he was a dedicated old-fashioned patriot and was actually delighted when war broke out with Nazi Germany. He loved North Borneo and after many years of medical work in this backward country, he had not lost his capacity for being surprised.

The waterfront at Sandakan.

Crocodile 'For Sale' at Sandakan market.

The Berhala Leper Station.

The armed constabulary at Sandakan.

After rounds one morning I was passing his office and he called me in. The police had asked him to examine a great vat of kampong medicine beside which a Malay woman had been found dead; so he filtered out leaves and nuts and berries from many litres of the medicine and then, scooping deeper into the vat, he was horrified to see a little wizened face appear above the surface on his wooden spoon. He was so astonished he gave an involuntary exclamation and stepped back a pace. The infant sank beneath the surface of the claret-coloured infusion. I watched with interest as he fished about the vat once again. And baby it turned out to be — one with a little tail! Its simian mother would have been very surprised to learn that her offspring had ended its days as a main ingredient in a Malay tonic! Dr Dingle washed his hands and, as it was near lunchtime, he invited me to his house for a gin sling. This was a far better recipe, and at least we weren't found dead beside it!

Another notable occasion was physically as opposed to pharmaceutically exciting. One morning a gentle little Chinese woman was admitted to the third-class female ward. I saw her and, when I was quite sure of the diagnosis, I completed the first of two forms legally essential for her detention in the Sim-Sim Mental Hospital. She had an excessive admiration for the opposite sex, and with it a disturbing lack of inhibition. She was dangerous and I had her locked up and then asked the P.M.O. to complete the second form.

On his first visit Dr Dingle was greeted with a courtesy equal to his own. For half an hour, patient and doctor conversed in Oxford and Chinese Malay. Both the woman's replies and the P.M.O.'s accent were flawless. Later, the P.M.O. said to me, "I'm sorry, but I couldn't find anything wrong with that woman. She seems as sensible as I am. I'll have to see her again." Which he did; they exchanged pleasantries, and the upshot was that the P.M.O. withheld his signature.

There is nothing more irritating (nor more salutary) for a young doctor than to have his clinical opinion disallowed by one of his colleagues. So I verified the stories repeated by Dressers and Nurses, sportingly entered the woman's cell myself, and then once again approached the P.M.O.

Meanwhile, and as luck would have it, our patient had fallen deeply in love with the P.M.O. But when he visited her again she said "Tabe, Tuan", without at once disclosing her feelings.

"Tabe, Ah Keng. And how are you now?"

"A little sad, Tuan, at being locked up all alone in this cell. Pannas — bah! It's hot!"

"Oh, don't worry. How is your appetite? Do you wish to eat rice?" Instead of answering, Ah Keng got down to tin-tacks. She sprang. In a flash she wrapped her limbs around the momentarily cataleptic European who gave a predictable shout of fear and astonishment. What revolting conduct! Nurse Alice leapt to his aid. Attendants, Nurses, Dressers, and even patients came running along, partly to help, partly to see the fun. And fun it was! The gardener entered the room and tore the hospital jacket off Ah Keng's back, leaving a skinny breast on each of the P.M.O.'s shoulders. The cook tried to unwind the human octopus from the head of the Medical Department. Cloth ripped, arms and legs and heads crashed against the whitewashed wall: shouts were made in several Asiatic languages, with occasionally a little muffled English breaking through.

"Let go! Apa macham! Eh! Hai-yah!"

It was an extraordinary way of spending a working morning. The squalid struggle went on and on and on. The gardener managed to straighten out one of the woman's legs, but when he tripped over an attendant the hind member went back into position with a thud. I laughed outright — I couldn't help it. In the end, numbers told, and finger by finger, limb by limb, the supple little Hakka woman was forced to relinquish her hold on the man she loved. As soon as he was free, the P.M.O. hurried up the hill towards his ice chest, tucking in his shirt as he went.

The same afternoon I received the second certificate, duly signed, in quite a firm hand at that. Ah Keng was swiftly transferred to the Mental Hospital at Sim-Sim. Days later the P.M.O.'s watch was found in her possession and returned to him. He put it on his wrist, checked the time, and resumed his humdrum administrative work.

The majority of my patients in Sandakan were Hakkas or Khehs, an agricultural people originally from Shantung and Shansi provinces in North China. They came to North Borneo under a scheme of government-assisted immigration. They were peasants rather than traders and did not maintain close connections with their homeland, a fact which made them desirable immigrants. Hakka (or Hak nyin) itself means stranger, guest or visitor, a name given to these folk as they gradually moved under the stress of famine and persecution from their homes near the Yellow River towards the southern provinces of Kwangtung, Kwangsi, Fukien, and others. In chaotic China, the peasants had found their main strength in family unity. However, in the safe and unrestricted atmosphere of their new country, their ways gradually changed. They had a passion for education and their children flocked to the Mission Schools. School finished, they sought positions in government service and in British-conducted companies. By 1940 the Hakkas were growing nearly all the vegetables, fruit and coffee in the state and comprised the bulk of the government subordinate staff: indeed, they were the soundest social element in the community.

Every dawn, I was awakened by Hakka women going to market. They walked along the asphalt road in front of my house like primitive ballet dancers, each bearing two baskets of produce on a carrying stick supported on one shoulder; this imparted a curious rhythmic motion to their gait. Distance was no bar to conversation between them. Without apparent effort, these lean, athletic women mustered the necessary power to hurl their monosyllables afar. Sometimes I followed the peasants to market which was conducted down near the wharves. An artist, probably French, must have been employed by the powers-that-be to plan the markets of South-East Asia, so colourful and attention-holding are the peasants and their produce and the fisher-folk and their catches. The strangest thing I ever saw for sale there was a crocodile about 3 metres long, its jaws tightly bound with rotan, its cunning eyes half-closed. It lay there awaiting an offer — Lord knows from whom!

The women gardeners had extraordinary taste in dress. Each wore a black hood called leong man (cool hat) with a curtain of cloth hanging down from the rim and almost hiding the face. A black coat (sam) and long black trousers (fu) were usually the only garments worn. Most had neither wooden clogs nor shoes. They gave an impression of suppleness and strength and, indeed, were often favoured for heavy labouring jobs.

I liked to know a little of what was going on about me. I therefore engaged a teacher from the S.P.G. Mission to teach me Hakka. This dialect has four tones, and to anyone with any musical sense is not a difficult tongue to master. I am nearly tone deaf, but by concentrating on hospital conversation I was soon able to understand common hospital questions and answers. In time, Dressers ceased to translate the more obvious of the patients' replies. In one of my earliest attempts, involving three tones, I asked a patient "Yu kaim mau? Have you a cough?" The patient's face remained blank. I tried again, and yet again — very carefully but without response. I turned to the Senior Dresser. "Thau Seng, ask him if he has a cough."

Thau Seng bent forward and said "Yu kaim mau?"

Without hesitation the patient replied "Yu kaim."

Slightly put out, I asked, "Didn't I say that correctly?"

"Very correctly indeed, Sir."

"Then why didn't he reply?"

"I have asked him. He says he is very sorry — unfortunately he did not realise you were speaking Chinese!"

The Hakka peasants regarded the heart (sim or sim kon) as the seat of emotions and thought. Anger was known as "kit sim" — congested heart; happiness as "ong sim" — tranquil heart. The liver (kon) controlled the temperature of the body. Mothers in the ward affectionately addressed their crying children as "sim kon! sim kon!" Surely not "my heart and my liver"?

"No, Sir" said a Dresser. "Sim means heart and kon means liver, but we combine them because it is better. All mothers say "my heart, my heart" because it is a very nice word for babies."

Many patients came to hospital with circular red marks on their foreheads as a result of cupping, and multiple bruised areas on their necks and chests. These latter were due to pinching, said to ease the nerves. A friend seized a fold of skin between the index and middle fingers and pulled sharply outwards. The process was repeated perhaps eight times in each spot. Another common practice, for the relief of abdominal pain, was to blister the skin of the upper abdomen by means of lighted wicks made of the pith of a certain swamp grass dipped in coconut oil. Permanent scarring resulted.

Mr Peter Lee, a Dresser, became my tutor in local Chinese medical customs. Peter's Chinese name was Lee Vun Chiang. Lee was the siang or family name. Vun means literature, and Chiang, green; clearly his parents hoped that Peter would distinguish himself in letters. Together, we undertook a "Cook's tour" through the fairyland of peasant Chinese medical belief and customs.

The Hakka gardeners considered the gall bladder an index of courage: the larger this little bile container, the braver the person possessing it.

Kidneys secrete urine and sexual energy. Excesses weaken the kidney. Great lovers had first-class kidneys.

Pregnant women were forbidden to hammer in nails, or to put together a jointed bed: such actions could lead to miscarriage. Eating goat during pregnancy caused epilepsy (yong thiau — goat fits) in the child, and eating monkey led to the birth of a marasmic child with heu chau (dry-as-a-monkey disease). It was a breach of etiquette for a pregnant woman to attend a wedding.

For thirty days after childbirth the mother was not allowed to eat green vegetables, fish, prawns, crab or fruit. Thus beri-beri was common after confinement.

Blue birthmarks on infants' backs and buttocks were known as "tee toi yiu" (re-enter pregnancy marks) made by the spirit entering the baby at the moment of birth. I also heard these marks described as "thumb-prints of the gods", a curiously attractive title.

A potent cause of disease was fung or wind: it entered the chest via sweat pores and caused pneumonia; the knee and gave arthritis; the bowels and led to diarrhoea.

In treatment, especially, I discovered the colourful slant of Chinese imagination. Everything strange and fantastic made an irresistible appeal to them. Thus, eye medicines made from sea-horses; diaphoretics and diuretics from the scales of the scaly ant-eater; aphrodisiacs from deer horns in velvet and tears of the slow loris, or the tendons of wild oxen and deer. Septic fingers were treated by insertion into the gall bladders of pigs. Bezoar stones (alimentary concretions) from "arrow pigs" (porcupines), monkeys and other animals were greatly valued as ingredients of medicine. The meat of domestic dogs was said to give more heat to the body. Cats were also eaten, and pythons or music snakes (kim sa). Rhinoceros horn (si nu kok, west cow horn) was used in the treatment of continuous high fever, by grinding it on a china plate containing a little water, which was subsequently drunk. To reduce the fever of tuberculosis a soup made of swallows nests and crystallised sugar was taken at midnight.

Most peasant bedrooms had a jar in one corner in which medicine was being made of cobras, monitor lizards, centipedes or scorpions — usually cobras, and this was the recipe. Capture a cobra. Place in earthenware jar without food for one week. Wash jar, wash cobra, replace latter. Fill jar brim-full of wine and close. Keep one to four years, then use as a linament for rheumatism or to relieve pains resulting from domestic strife.

Yellow wine (wong chiu) was made by nearly all gardeners. It was thought to be especially valuable in disorders following childbirth. The peasants often gave a dinner party for a sick person, with roast fowl and yellow wine.

In search of health, sick Chinese would try anything — their own system of medicine, that of Malay pawangs or of quack "professors" from far off Chinese cities, even that of their own qualified doctors. When all else failed they staggered to the Civil Hospital and sought help from water-carriers, attendants, cooks, drivers, nurses, dressers and myself — roughly in that order!

After a few weeks with Peter Lee and my sen-sang or teacher, I realised that in many respects both these young Chinese had abilities beyond my own. Both were quick, retentive, thoughtful, untiring in matters requiring a serious degree of cerebration. The objectivity of the pair surprised me. For instance, one evening Peter and I commenced an amusing discussion on possible defects in the Chinese character — gaps in their intelligence where jokes are concerned; the ant-heap instinct; servility and insincerity; gullibility; lack of a natural sense of sportsmanship at games; recklessness to an extraordinary degree in gambling; and so on. I asked Peter what he considered to be the weakest link in the Chinese character.

"Womanising" said the young Dresser, without hesitation.

"Not gambling? Talking too much? Or . . ."

"No, no, no other things. Most definitely, womanising is our chief fault."

"Have it your own way, Peter!"

Perhaps Peter was right. The chief fault of the Chinese lies in their prodigious numbers: teeming millions of whatever race gradually become a menace both to themselves and to their neighbours.

Be that as it may, all the Chinese ask for in this world is freedom to go about their business. Given this, the majority will prosper by their own efforts. British rule in the Far East, benign and adequately protective (so it seemed) was the best thing that ever happened to them.

Many people hold that the universe originated in a colossal "bang". Many more believe that God was responsible for all creation and on the sixth day he created Man. If this latter proposition is true, then it is certain He made the Chinese early in the day when He was still fresh and interested. He made a different people, alert and clever, lasting, trustworthy above all others, independent and self-reliant. The quality of his workmanship was good, but not uniformly so: for here and there is evidence of what amounts to pure devilment. A jaundiced American once recorded his views of the Chinese in a book, *Ways that are Dark*, but we can console ourselves with the fact that he was not writing about the King's Chinese. A wiser man than this author was Archdeacon Mercer of Sandakan who lived and worked amongst them and spoke Hakka fluently. I remember him saying, "Doctor, they are the best people and the most interesting study on earth." The simplicity of this sentence gives no indication of the depth of feeling with which he said it. His eyes half-closed, and smoke from his pipe passed in front of his inscrutable face. I could see the Archdeacon was busy entering the Chinese mind; and so I sat quietly and watched him with great interest.

The Archdeacon looked for all the world like a particularly eminent Confucian. He had come East to reform the heathen Chinese. Yet who was influencing whom? Where did the balance lie?

It is said that Chinese babies cry at birth because they are born into a very sad world. Nevertheless, the less fortunate Chinese often show a remarkably tenacious hold on a life that scarcely seems worth preserving. One of my patients was an old kuli who had been blind for five years. Most nights he slept on a pavement in the main bazaar and he took pot luck at the tables of charitable people. In both his eyes there were dense cataracts. There was, of course, no specialist help available in Borneo, and as there were many more in town similarly afflicted I obtained the necessary instruments, read how the operation was done, and in due course sent the old man to the theatre. After I had removed one cataract, and before he could be prevented, the old chap sat up on the operating table and pointing to several of the staff in turn, he asked "Are you the doctor?" He said the first person he wanted to see was the doctor who had given him back his sight again. A little later, and without permission, he removed his eye coverings and stood in the door of his ward and enumerated the things he could see — the jungle on the far side of the harbour, an island, a ship perhaps? This was very surprising, as well as gratifying. One night he took French leave and went down to the coffee shops to tell everyone about the miraculous restoration of his sight.

Unhappily the day came when he did not greet me as usual during the morning rounds. Something had gone wrong and he had lost his sight again and also had become deaf in one ear. The days passed and he could not persuade me to operate on the other eye. I was inhibited by a first failure in specialist work. One morning Thau Seng translated, "He says he is very grateful to us for letting him see his friends again, if only for a few days. Now he does not care if he dies."

But he did not die, and after a time he was sent to the Paupers Institute. Twice a week another pauper and he walked several kilometres into town, had coffee with friends, and then returned to the Institute. On other days he worked with a companion on a vegetable plot. This man had spastic paralysis and his legs were crossed like the blades of a scissors, but he had eyes for the two of them and a very good heart. They were a remarkable pair, and, being industrious, they lived in fair prosperity. They often expressed gratitude to government: they knew that when they died each would be buried in a wooden box and the dogs would not be able to disturb their bones. This was a great comfort to them.

One morning, when I was seeing out-patients, a sergeant rang from the Police Station. "Tabe, Tuan! We can't find the C.P.O. (Chief Police Officer). Can you come down immediately? A person's had his heart cut out."

This sounded like an emergency so I drove down to the Police Station immediately. Half a dozen mata mata saluted as I entered.

"Tabe, Tuan. That's him."

Standing against the wall was a slightly built Chinese in late middle-age. On his left arm was a cane shopping basket. "Tuan can see what I've got here." He removed some strips of banana leaf and exposed a human liver.

"Where did you get this?" I asked, quietly.

The Chinese replied, "Forgive my Malay, Tuan, I'm not very capable. A guest in my house had a very bad heart so I cut it out."

He looked at me searchingly, hoping I could follow the logic behind his action.

Later in the day, I accompanied the Chief Police Officer to a bamboo shack on the outskirts of Sandakan. The door, walls and floor were spattered with blood. Lying in front of the cooking place was the body of the guest, with wounds on his head, neck and back; the cervical spinal cord was divided and his liver had been removed, evidently with some skill. It was a spectacle of violence and rather difficult to reconcile with the physique of the fragile old man.

The story behind the crime was this. A stranger, down on his luck, was offered shelter for the night. As the days passed he showed no signs of leaving. Moreover, he complained about the food and told lies about his host to the local shopkeepers, who thereupon denied further credit to the host. Feeling gradually developed. The ultimate quarrel came when the guest kicked his benefactor's dog away from the fire. There was an immediate protest. "Why do you kick my dog? You know it's not a human being. So why kick it?" The guest then struck the dog with a piece of mangrove firewood. This was intolerable. The kindly Chinese lost control. He hurled himself at his guest, shouting reproaches at him, but was pushed back against the wall and then thrown to the floor. Desperate now, he seized a chopper and slashed out: his persecutor fell with blood spurting from his scalp. The old man kept on striking until his anger had disappeared. Then he placed the chopper on a shelf and sat down.

After a time, he got up and rolled the body of his enemy over, made an incision with a smaller knife and removed the organ responsible for all the trouble. Then he put it in his shopping basket, washed his hands and covered the basket with leaves, and made his way to the main bazaar. Here, he chatted to several friends, bought some salt and a tin of condensed milk, and then went to the Police Station to report his morning's work.

Subsequently, I visited him in prison and was present when he was hanged. Quiet, affable, polite, and somewhat stunned by his experience, he looked and behaved like anything else but a murderer. He was a decent old fellow who had been tried beyond the limits of his endurance.

A different personality altogether lived in the Leper Colony on Berhala Island at the entrance to Sandakan harbour. Most of the houses in this rather sad settlement were within 40 metres of a fine sandy beach. Just behind the houses, towering over the attap roofs and dozens of tall swaying palms, was a massive cliff of red sandstone which formed a landmark for incoming ships. A well-to-do merchant would have paid a high price for the island if it had been vacant. As it was, a small, complex, greatly-feared bacterial enemy of mankind had assuredly discounted its natural beauty. To live there was compulsory for the afflicted: and treatment with chaulmoogra oil gave such a poor chance of clinical cure and freedom that it was given on a purely voluntary basis.

The subject of this story was a stocky fellow in his early thirties named Abdul Majit. Here was a man who, by his own efforts, could cause anyone getting hysterical about the virtues of the Chinese race to have second thoughts. No-one knew for certain why he had emigrated from China to North Borneo, but every guess tended to his discredit. Another leper had, on one occasion, cast reflections on his ancestors by advising "Don't look behind you, Abdul!" Abdul had become so angry at this that it was apparent he had been hit on the raw: clearly, his forebears were not worth tuppence. After coming to North Borneo he was impressed by the songkok, sarong and baju worn by sea-going folk, and so he entered Islam (without permission or any formality) and assumed a Malay name that tickled his fancy.

By nature, Abdul Majit was irked by restrictions of any sort and, contrary to regulations, he and several others began visiting the mainland at night in canoes. They went to coffee shops and generally joined in the night life of the capital. Abdul had singularly low tastes and was as happy as Larry in the company of prostitutes. Before long, indignant townsfolk reported his nocturnal adventures: they were evidently selective in their worries about infection. As a result, the lepers were ordered to destroy all their canoes and not to visit town again.

Some time later, Abdul described to me how, when out fishing on the harbour two nights previously he had driven his canoe through an area of sea illuminated by untold millions of soft phosphorescent lights. This was a common phenomenon on the harbour along lines of current. Clearly, canoes were still being used, and to impress the prohibition upon the lepers, the Principal Medical Officer himself visited the Colony. Standing on a mound on the beach he addressed them and warned that anyone found leaving the island would be punished. In the sand beneath his feet, Abdul's canoe was buried. For days after, Abdul could scarcely contain himself as he described the incident. Needless to say, he continued to visit Sandakan.

It came about that he and an associate named Wong Yu quarrelled with a third leper; a few nights later, they met this man in mid-channel, ran their canoe beside his, killed him with parangs and dumped his body into the sea. Next morning, they foolishly boasted about their deed, wishing to impress the other lepers.

Three days later the victim's body was washed up under the Malay village at Sim-sim. The inquest was not a resounding success, for when it was held, a leper had not yet been reported missing from Berhala. Abdul Majit and Wong Yu were eventually arrested, but they escaped conviction on the matter of identification of the body. The other lepers, having less legal knowledge, but decidedly more worldly wisdom than the magistrate, petitioned the government not to send the two murderers back to Berhala. As a result, this bloodthirsty pair were quartered in a hut at the Sandakan Civil Hospital while arrangements were made to send them to Singapore. I saw Abdul Majit daily and soon understood him perfectly: he was a cold-blooded habitual killer, albeit with some sense of humour. One day, seeing him kill a mosquito which had landed on his knee, I said, "You like killing things, don't you, Majit?"

It was a simple joke, but one Majit could appreciate. He laughed heartily. Indeed, his reserve was so broken by this incident, that he admitted killing two persons before coming to North Borneo! Killers command a certain respect, and Abdul became quite a character at the hospital.

One night there was a car accident in town and an emergency operation was necessary. Some wild bees had settled above the theatre verandah: in the middle of the operation, attracted by lights, they found a hole in a gauze window and streamed into the theatre in force. Mr Kong, the anaesthetist, was the first of several to be stung. Attendants were summoned, and the hole in the wire was covered with a long mop and the invading insects were assailed with fly swatters. I removed one from the wound and covered up with a wet sponge until the battle was over. I had resumed the operation when Abdul Majit's name was mentioned. I looked up to see the killer gazing at the open wound with the utmost interest. I said sharply, "Get out, Majit!"

Abdul hesitated. The Dresser spoke to him in Chinese and he turned slowly and reluctantly towards the door.

On rounds next morning Dresser Thau Seng said to me, "Majit says you are a very clever doctor. He wants to become an Attendant and help in the theatre. He says he is very interested in potong orang (cutting people) and hopes he will give good service. He says it does not matter much about pay."

Everyone present was smiling. After all, what an amusing request it was! However, I decided to refuse it for, after all, a professional association with a murderous leper like Abdul Majit might have been unethical, even in Borneo!

One day, learning that the two lepers were now employed grass-cutting in the hospital compound, I asked "What are you cutting the grass with, Majit?"

"A slasher, Tuan."

"Where is it? Go and fetch it."

It was wise to have some knowledge of the implements Majit was handling. Abdul looked beneath his hut; incredulous he looked again — someone had stolen his slasher! The Dressers laughed — the killer outwitted! Majit was livid with rage.

His "face" went down a little in the hospital. Other patients teased him, asking "Have you lost your slasher, Majit?" This was rather a silly thing to do and not entirely devoid of risk.

The two lepers decided to recover prestige by perpetrating a patriotic assassination. China was at war, of course — this time with a neighbour, Japan. It followed that local Japanese were suitable subjects for liquidation. The patriots decided to commence with

Mr Fukui, a quiet, portly commercial agent living just below the hospital hill: a good golfer, and not at all a bad citizen. I often gave him a lift to incoming Japanese ships when the Chinese refused to take him. The two lepers set about planning their attack, but presently Wong Yu got cold feet: and so he backed down, giving reasonable excuses. At this, the vicious Abdul Majit could not control his anger. Wong Yu was opposing him!

It was Nurse Alice who saw Majit coming down the steps of his hut carrying a bloodstained knife in his left hand, and she raised the alarm. Later, in the operation theatre, four wounds in Wong Yu's stomach were sutured, but subsequently he died.

And Abdul Majit? He was caught, he was tried, and he was sentenced to death. As usual, the Adjutant and I attended the hanging. Abdul's head was covered with a black hood. Some 95 seconds after the "drop" his heart stopped beating. Without a doubt, his spirit went straight to the lowest of the thirty-six layers of hell, the place of unending torture.

Because Majit was a leper, the rope was changed before the next hanging.

One morning the Adjutant rang me. He was extremely concerned about an outbreak of venereal disease amongst the mata mata in the Police Barracks. He told me he had arranged a "short arm" inspection for the next morning. And so at 7.30 a.m. on the morrow I found myself involved in this peculiarly British procedure. The police force stood in ranks at attention, fully dressed except for the absence of trousers and underpants. The Adjutant and I slowly passed along the ranks. Tall recruits from the Punjab stood proud and confident, a suggestion of a smile at the corners of their mouths. The much smaller natives were unhappy and humiliated because the inspection strongly conflicted with their customs. Afterwards, over a cup of tea, the Adjutant said, "Doctor, it's serious and we are worried. I want you to frighten hell out of them."

I had never frightened a policeman in my life, and future prospects in this respect were not encouraging. And so, with a certain zest, I set about complying with the Adjutant's request. Clearly, it was for the good of the force. From the Paupers' Institute, the Asylum and the Leper Colony I gathered a magnificent group of halt, lame and blind, and one morning we transported them to the Barracks in a P.W.D. (Public Works Department) truck. If any of them had venereal disease it was purely coincidental.

The police listened to my lecture in stunned silence. The climax came when I opened a book on tropical medicine to reveal a picture of a case of massive scrotal elephantiasis. I didn't say so, but the mata mata must have inferred that this condition could be an unwanted bonus of promiscuity if their luck was out. "I say!" one of the police exclaimed quietly.

The Adjutant was very pleased with the lecture-demonstration. He turned on tea and cakes for the visiting patients who quite enjoyed their morning out.

The armed constabulary was recruited partly from the Punjab, but mainly from the up-country Dusuns and Muruts. One could not but admire the way in which the Constabulary officers could take even the most primitive natives and turn them into smart mata mata in a matter of months. A policeman on point duty could stop the Governor of the State by simply raising his hand: and only two years previously the same mata mata could have been living in a jungle longhouse with long black hair to his shoulders, and dressed only in a bark loincloth. Recruits were taken, dressed and drilled, sent to school to learn to speak Malay and write it in Romanised fashion, and any necessary medical treatment was given. The transformation was startling: the British are very skilled at this sort of thing. The police were introduced to soccer and they took to it like fish to water. I was invited to several boxing tournaments held at night under lights out in the open, and they were dignified and sophisticated events.

Yet there were often reminders that the transformation was merely superficial. In one dreadful episode which occurred only a kilometre or two from the Sandakan hospital a mata mata's wife got into trouble at childbirth. The placenta did not come away: so the umbilical cord was tied to a stick and a native midwife pulled on it, obviously very hard. When the anterior lip of the cervix became visible it was seized and evulsed. Then, to cap it all, a great mass of mushy grass and herbs was applied to the bleeding area and all over the perineum between her thighs. She arrived at the hospital shocked and almost exsanguinated and I could not save her.

Government officers in Sandakan had a "conservative" attitude to other Europeans working outside government — that is, they kept them at arms length, but of course, with impeccable good manners. For this reason we saw little of the business people or even doctors in private practice in the town. However, an instrument called "Board of Examiners" brought me into contact with Dr Stookes, a World War I pilot who practised in Sandakan and was the visiting doctor to a number of commercial estates in the East Coast Residency. He flew a light seaplane from his property on the banks of the Kinabatangan River and was an independent and adventurous man.

Dressers were classified into three grades, and they rose from one grade to the next by attaining a certain seniority and then passing an oral and written examination. Stookes and I conducted the examinations for the East Coast. It chanced we had a similar problem.

Mine was Dresser Richard who was in charge of the Mental Asylum at Sim-Sim. It was a tough assignment and Richard was the best man we had for the job. He was a Grade II Dresser and had remained so for many years. He knew three "nervous" drugs very well and had a good knowledge of several others, and was a competent manager in the rough environment at Sim-Sim. This was good enough for us: but when it came to examinations he was asked about very advanced modern things like M&B 693 and anti-sera for lobar pneumonia. Instead of pricking up his ears intelligently, he was honest and just looked blank. He neither wrote nor spoke English particularly well, and he had a stammer and a blink which came on when he was either nervous or thinking hard, and this did not help him during oral examinations. His family grew, as did his expenses, but his salary stayed put at Grade II level. Justice was not even appearing to be done. I had always regarded exams as one of the outstanding evils of civilisation, a disease attacking adolescents like acne and warts. And so with the zeal of a Crusader I set about the difficult task of coaching Richard to pass the examinations.

To my delight, on the day of the test Dr Stookes quite frankly admitted he had a problem: namely, an excellent Dresser working in an isolated timber camp up in the Kinabatangan jungle; a resolute fellow who tackled any medical or surgical problem with confident determination, but as regards academic study he had a head like bilian, which is one of the best of the jungle hardwoods.

When Stookes' candidate came up for the Oral I had his written paper on the desk in front of me, with "Pass, 51%" prominently displayed in red ink. I asked him, "What would you do for a man who has been bitten by a crocodile?"

"Stitch up the holes, Sir," he replied.

It was a sensible answer and I knew that this was what he would do, and quite competently. "Very good. No further questions."

Dr Stookes sat back happily. Instinctively he knew we must not be too hasty, so he recounted an amusing story of a big Dutchman named van Veyn who was wading across a sandy lagoon beside the Kinabatangan when he was suddenly attacked by about three dozen crocodiles. He survived because the crocodiles had only just emerged from their eggs in a nest nearby. We laughed and sent Stookes' man on his way.

Then Richard came in and sat down looking like an unhappy cat that was just about to miss out for the tenth time on a bowl of milk. Stookes smiled benignly, and I nodded reassuringly. I looked at Stookes, and he said to Richard, "A man is constipated. Name one purgative you could give him for relief."

"Garam Belanda" said Richard.

"Correct", said Dr Stookes; for garam belanda (Dutch salt) was a local name for Epsom salts, and it was the only one Richard knew. Stookes took up his pen and chivalrously wrote "Pass 52%".

To my surprise, Stookes asked a second question, possibly for his own edification. "What would you do if one of your insane patients became violent?"

"I'd lock him up in a cell."

Good, but scarcely enough. I drew Richard on because I knew I was on firm ground. "How would you quieten him?"

Richard blinked several times, but he knew he was in the hands of a friend, and controlled his stutter very well. "I would hold him down and inject paraldehyde into his pantat (behind)."

"Excellent!" exclaimed Dr Stookes. I think he was impressed by the chance I took.

And so two good Dressers accomplished the seemingly impossible feat of passing the examination for promotion to Grade 1, with its increments of salary annually, right up to the maximum. For me, it was a very good investment. Two mornings a week I visited Sim-Sim. My approach was always under observation through nail holes in the great galvanised iron gates. These swung open uncannily, with no visible operators, and in I walked to be greeted and conducted around the Asylum by a grateful Richard as if I was the world's most distinguished psychiatrist.

One of the most influential in-patients at Sim-Sim Mental Hospital was a Javanese called Awang. Awang spoke an obscure Indonesian dialect at a very rapid rate. He had a huge grin and great square teeth, and eyes which protruded and gleamed when he grew excited, and this was his normal response to the most trifling stimulus. His history card recorded details of two dramatic escapes from Sim-Sim in the course of which he demonstrated he could be quite a muscle-man.

On learning that Awang had artistic inclinations I gave him some coloured crayons. On the walls of his private cell he drew pictures in the Javanese style of the Prince of Heaven, the Prince of Earth and other celebrities, all with very sharp features and looking extremely demoniacal. One day I photographed two of the murals and from then on I was "Number One". Many successful artists carefully ration the amount of divine excitement permitted to illuminate their countenances, but our Javanese was quite uninhibited in this respect; indeed, but for this carelessness he might have regained his freedom quite legally, but those blazing eyes and spiritual frenzy made such a concession imprudent. Unofficially, Awang was given the position of Mandor or Foreman of the Mad House. With Richard, he always met me at the gate and showed me round the wards and cells. He was keenly interested in every patient and gave his opinions freely. Only one patient had him completely baffled. This young man lay naked every day on a cement verandah, his hands behind his head: he never spoke a single word to anyone. He had amputated his own penis when his girlfriend refused to submit to his advances. "Why didn't he ask another woman before he chopped it off?" asked Awang. This sensible question almost earned Awang his freedom. Sometimes neither Richard nor I could understand Awang, but there was always someone who reckoned he had grasped the gist of what the Javanese was saying, so we didn't miss out on much he said. But one

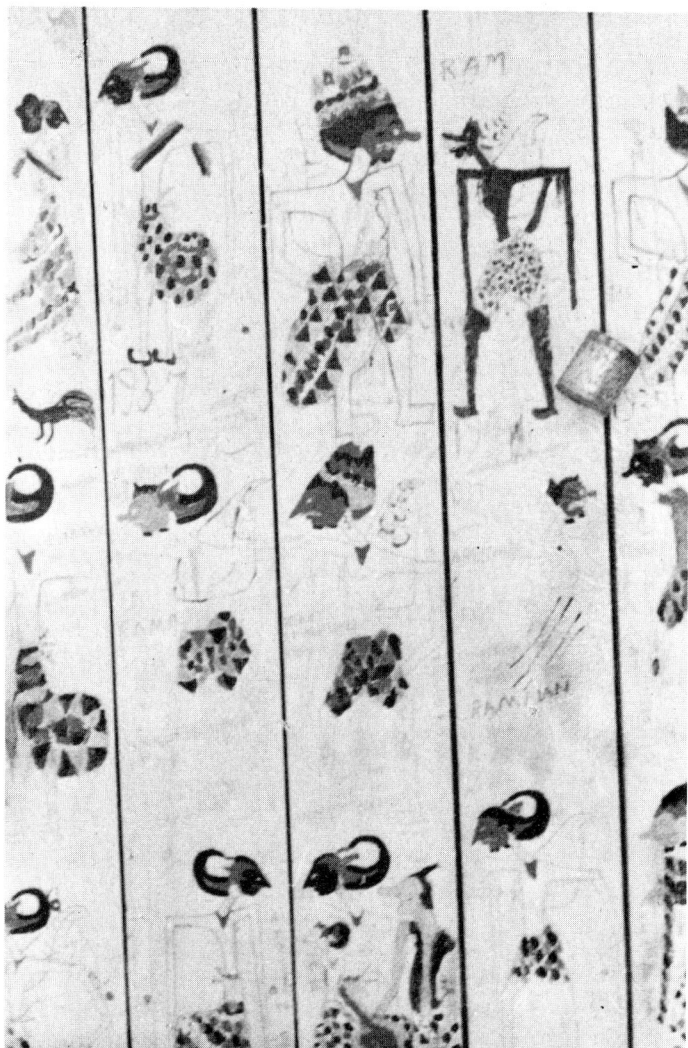

Wall of Awang's cell at the Sim-Sim Mental Hospital.

day I thought Awang said, "Tuan, there's a cat inside the wall of my room." This was interesting and I stopped. Awang repeated his story very, very fast. Finally everyone was quite sure they understood what he meant — there was a cat inside the wall of his room. "I've been talking to it for three days", he shouted.

This sounded bad.

"Why didn't you tell someone? The cat will starve to death."

"No! No!" shouted Awang. "I've been pouring in milk through a crack in the wall. Look at the puddle!"

The mental patients collected outside Awang's cell and when amused disbelief showed on several faces his eyes and teeth overwhelmed every other feature of his face. He went inside the cell and knocked against the wall and mewed like a cat. He listened for an answer, but none came.

I was about to go when Richard drew my attention to two new planks in the cell wall. The wall was a double one, and presently we learnt that Awang had persuaded some carpenters renovating the kitchen to do some repairs for him. Had a cat got into the narrow space between the two sections of the wall during the repairs?

The matter was important. I said "Richard, send someone to call the carpenters."

Few of the patients would be able to tolerate a dumb animal in such confinement and it seemed important to have rescue operations in sensible hands. The Mad People now gathered in force. When one expressed the opinion that Awang was imagining things, Awang became extremely excited. His sanity was being called into question!

The carpenters appeared, and to their surprise the mental patients greeted them enthusiastically. A little frightened, they set to work and quickly removed the two planks. Amidst dead silence everyone looked at the dark space. Nothing happened.

Awang now took a stick and beat against the wall. Next he mewed, and then squatted down and inserted the stick between the walls and prodded right to the end. He looked perplexed and worried.

"That cat was a ghost," said a Chinese. "And how can ghosts drink milk?" Everyone laughed. It was sad, but I had seen enough.

"Oh, Richard! Make sure the carpenters take all their tools with them."

I was moving away when there was a tremendous shout. From inside the double wall had come a mew! Awang was transformed.

As we packed around, a small grey kitten with white feet walked out of the wall into the cell. It was quite dazed and seemed not to notice the very great enthusiasm and even cheers which greeted its appearance. Awang picked it up and pressed it to his chest. His friends thumped him on the back as if he had won the Singapore sweepstake. The kitten had meant a great deal to him, and he hurried off to find the hungry little animal something to eat.

Map of the Colony of British North Borneo showing the major towns and villages visited by the Resident District Surgeon.

Chapter 3

KENINGAU 1940–41

Finally, I got the appointment I wanted — as District Surgeon, Beaufort and Interior. I was delighted.

Keningau was the administrative centre of the Interior District. Here, early in 1940, I made my headquarters. This, my third district, stretched from Mount Kinabalu in the north, southwards to the Dutch border, and from the headwaters of the Kinabatangan River to the shores of Brunei Bay. Population numbered some 60–80,000: Chinese in the small trading settlements; Dusuns, Muruts, and Kwijaus amongst the inland hills; Dusuns, Besayas, Kedayans and Brunei Malays in the swampy country of the Padas delta.

In front of my house at Keningau was a polo field. I had barely arrived when word came that the District Officer, Robertson, had a pony saddled for me to play polo. Everyone knows that Australians are expert horsemen. In fact, I hadn't sat on one of the animals since childhood, and I had never seen a game of polo in my life: nor, indeed, had I ever wanted to. Nevertheless, I changed into khaki trousers and scrambled on to what appeared to be a Timor or Mongolian pony.

The opposing teams were lined up in the centre of the field. I reached them at a walk, wondering which side of the stick to use. The D.O. said "Good show!" At this moment my pony swung round and set off at full speed towards an irrigation ditch on the edge of the field. Dropping my polo stick, I tugged on the reins, without achieving anything. Immediately in front of the beast and I appeared a section of ditch 150 centimetres deep, with vertical sides: no horse on earth could possibly have cleared it. I suspected my life was about to end. Fortunately, the same idea must have occurred to the horse; it couldn't stop, so it fell on its knees and shot me over its head like a bullet. I landed on my back and went over and over for some metres. Finally, I found myself standing on my feet beside the ditch none the worse, physically at least, for the adventure.

There were jungle-style rest houses every 16 kilometres or so along the bridle paths of the Interior. These served as Clinic centres, the natives attending from villages amongst the local hills. Ponies were essential for district work. Before long Dresser William Chin said, "Sir, we've found a pony for you. Mr Chin Tin On, the Dresser at Tambunan, has one. He wants $40 for it." This was just over four Australian pounds. I said, "If he'll take $35, tell him to send it down."

Chin Tin On accepted my offer with alacrity. When the pony arrived, I took an instant liking to it, but I asked: "Why is it so thin? You can see every bone in its body!"

"Mr Chin Tin On has been keeping it thin under orders, Sir. It's his wife's pony. She is nervous on horseback. If it's weak it can't bolt with her."

Within a month I had a stable of three ponies and two Murut syces to look after them. I learnt not to fall off a horse too frequently and presently was rearing to go. There was no hospital to hold me, and government never questioned the expense of medical expeditions. And so I quickly set about arranging a series of trips which took me to most parts of this very big district over the next two years. Early, I made trips to Ranau in the north and Pensiangan in the south; to Sipitang and Mempakul on Brunei Bay, and to Sandakan on the east coast along the length of the Kinabatangan River. Most of our expeditions took about a month and we covered about 320 kilometres on each trip. The easiest travelling was along the bridle paths of the Interior on horseback. The hardest, up and down the steep foothills of Kinabalu and in the jungle-covered mountains south and west of Pensiangan. Canoeing down the Kinabatangan through one of the most valuable stands of primaeval forest in the world was an easy passage, for it was in flood. Poling up the rapids in the Ulu Tagul was extremely laborious, and rather a trial. Most jungle walks of 8 to 24 kilometres were pleasant outings: but climbing steep jungle mountains of 920 to 1,500 metres, carrying a complement of leeches, while the rain pelted down and the kulis screamed and yelled to relieve the oppression in their chests, was sometimes hard, slogging, uninspiring work. But all in all, these two years were probably the best and most interesting of my life. Occasionally, I got restless and handed in my resignation. The war in Europe had started while I was still in Sandakan: and all the young government officers wanted to be in it, but had no success, except a few who were on leave in England at the outbreak. It was government policy not to denude the colonies of personnel and, of course, there was no-one to replace us. So I just had to go on having a very good time.

The summit of Mount Kinabalu.

View from the summit of Kinabalu.

Before long the temptation to climb the two highest mountains in the Interior proved irresistible.

The rest house at the Dusun village of Rendagong was situated on a high ridge between two broad valleys. One evening, I accepted an invitation to visit native Chief Kabindong's village nearby. From behind the village was a fine view of Mount Kinabalu. Standing with me on a grass covered slope, Kabindong said, "In a few days Tuan will be standing on the summit. I've looked at the mountain for over 50 years but I've never climbed it."

How close the great mountain seemed! And what a glorious spectacle in the cool evening light! If anything can produce tranquillity of mind it is majestic scenery.

We were standing near a large, round stone lying on the grass. According to legend, one day, a long time ago, a hunter went to the hill on the opposite side of the valley in front of us, where he met and speared a jungle pig. To his consternation it immediately turned into stone and he ran home as fast as his legs would carry him. Years later, the stone was carried to the village. A thin, rusty, white line was all that remained to show that the pig's hair was white. A little knob represented its snout and two holes showed where it had been pierced by the spear. Kabindong's son said that, in headhunting days, any head taken was placed on this stone which was then lifted up chest high by the celebrating villagers, each person using only one fingertip.

I doubted this was possible and said so. The stone was a massive piece of granite, very heavy. The Dusuns laughed me down and insisted on a demonstration. Kinabalu was forgotten. Ten villagers and I squatted round the stone and each inserted an index finger beneath it. At a given signal we all pressed upwards, and very slowly the stone rose from

A Dusun plantation of sweet potatoes on a typical steep slope at Bundu Tuhan.

the ground. As we tried to maintain it at chest level the group of laughing people moved slowly along the hillside. Brown-eyed children followed us, leaping up and down, clapping their hands.

"There you are, Tuan! It's even heavier with a head or two on top!"

At Bundu Tuhan, living on a steep mountain slope with their backs turned on Kinabalu, was the largest aggregation of Dusuns in the Interior. The rest house was 1,050 metres above sea-level. A messenger was sent to the village of Kiau, some 8 kilometres away, to obtain the services of the traditional guide to the summit of Kinabalu. Three Bundu Tuhan headmen (Gunting, Gilau and Guntau) announced their intention of accompanying me. They were queerly assorted friends. Gilau, an ex-policeman, was a genuine bon viveur who was never happier than when he had a stomach full of rice wine. Gunting or "Scissors" was tough and adventurous; twice in his life he had apprehended homicidal maniacs and his ambition was to join the select group of legendary men who are immune to rifle bullets. Just how he would join the club was not clear. Guntau was a fine little fellow, quiet and pleasant and something of a scientist. By tremendous exertions, he had proved that, where there is impenetrable rock just below the surface soil, pit-latrines simply cannot be constructed with native tools, in spite of government wishes. The discovery profoundly influenced departmental ideas on sanitation in the Interior. Government was converted to Dusun opinion, held for centuries, that pigs are better than pit-latrines, at least in some areas.

Our party left Bundu Tuhan early one morning. The village was enveloped in cold swirling mist. Above Tenompak, at 1,500 metres, we entered the jungle. We climbed along a rising escarpment leading to the mountain. The first stop was at Lumununu: here, the native priest offered a fowl, some rice, an egg and a betel nut to the spirit of the mountain. About mid-day we arrived at a camping place named Kambaroonga which is also the name of a magic charm.

The second day's walk lay to Pakka, a small cave at 3,000 metres. As we ascended, the trees became stunted and their branches were covered with mosses and orchids. Some steep ascents had to be made, sometimes up short ladders. A large stag crossed in front of Gunting, actually brushing against his chest as it did so. I lost 150 metres following it in hopes of a shot.

It was quite a slog along the ridge leading to Pakka. Often we trod only on roots from amongst which most of the earth had long since slipped away.

After a cold night at Pakka we set out early for the summit. The climb was now steep; in time, we passed beyond vegetation level and made our way slowly up over the granite pavement to the crest. The final gradient was not steep but every 20 paces it was necessary to pause to regain breath. The panting natives sought relief from the restriction in their chests by shouting loudly.

The straggling climbers passed slowly by several of the ten peaks in the crest on their way to the highest point attainable. There, it was several minutes before everyone was fit to enjoy the view. Sundang, the Chief Health Inspector, had vertigo and lay flat on the granite like a body in a mortuary.

The climb was worth it. Kinabalu rises abruptly from the parent mountain. On the coastal side, just in front of where we stood, was a deep chasm, and beyond it a scene of rugged grandeur. To the north-east, the sun was behind a battlement of jagged crags, throwing black shadows into the hollow in front of us. The two limbs of Maruda Bay looked almost quaintly small; it was easy to understand how the great mountain twisted the prevailing winds to produce water spouts so frequently on its waters. Below us, towards the sea, was the stretch of lalang-covered hills in Kota Belud. South from Kinabalu and between Mount Terusmadi and the Crocker Range, the Tambunan plain was clearly visible; and further down, the Keningau plain could just be seen. Underneath, the Ranau plain showed in a gap of rising cloud, looking no bigger than the palm of one's hand. Brunei Bay, and the hills behind Jesselton, and even Sandakan, could be seen. Incredibly, below us, on the Ranau plain, within a few years was to be enacted one of the ugliest pages in Japanese and Australian history.

At the top of the mountain there was a small pool. The pawang or Mononolob with us sacrificed two fowls, one pure white, to the Mian Kinabalu and the blood was sprinkled over its surface. Gunting, Gilau and Guntau and other Dusuns present washed themselves in it and filled small bottles to take home. Pieces of granite were smeared with the blood of the sacrificial fowls. Later, they would be hung over house doors to prevent evil spirits from entering. Water in which these stones were immersed was considered a useful medicine for treating disease.

On a small peak near the pool was a bottle in which all climbers left a record of their visit; for Kinabalu was an amateur's mountain, free of danger, and many climbed it. Only those failed who were not willing to pay tribute to the spirit of the mountain or threw stones down the slopes or laughed too loudly. The Dusuns even described to me how they had assisted a very fat Governor to the summit with ropes. I couldn't see him about, so presumably they had carried him home again.

By request, I fired shots in the direction of several villages to bring good luck their way.

At 9 a.m. clouds rose from ravines at the foot of the mountain. The white vapour came rushing towards us over the crazy pavement mountain top. In a few seconds we were enveloped in cloud. We descended to Pakka, gathered our luggage together and returned to Bundu Tuhan before evening.

After climbing Kinabalu the party and guides, Gunting, Gilau and Guntau, rest on the return journey.

Dresser Micky Robert holding Rafflesia found growing on the jungle floor near Mount Terusmadi.

Well, that was Kinabalu, but Terusmadi, a lesser but more difficult mountain, remained. So, not long afterwards, during a tour amongst the goitre-bearing foothills of Mount Terusmadi, the medical party tackled this 2,550 metre peak and, sad to say, did not particularly enjoy it. True, the Monsok Kwijaus were an interesting people and the jungle was alive with game and strewn with dangerous spring-traps; indeed, the spear from one flashed through a leaping Health Inspector's legs! Our carriers enticed ground pheasants towards the party by imitating their calls. We came upon young trees fractured and marked with the teeth of mountain-living rhinoceros. I photographed kukuanga (Rafflesia), a brown, horribly-smelling flower 100 centimetres across and reported it to Keith, the Director of Forestry in Sandakan, causing him great excitement: my photographs ended up in Kew.

Nevertheless, when Angkai, Headman of Kengaran, led us in a single day to the bottom of a narrow, chilly ravine called Pampang; and on the next, while it rained heavily, up through fantastic moss forests to the cloud-enveloped summit, no-one was particularly elated. We were wet and very cold. In turn, we dashed from cover and stood on the highest point for a few bitter seconds; then crouched together in protection, hoping the weather would clear to permit a view. Dresser Robert, teeth chattering, said "The Headman says we are the first outsiders to reach the top. Two others have been up Tolot, nearby. He guided them there because it's easier to climb, and anyway they didn't know the difference!"

Angkai grunted, then almost laughed. Presently, he said, "If we don't get out of here we'll die."

And so we returned to Pampang. The following day we trudged through heavy jungle-covered hills to the bottom of a gloomy ravine called Kipau; and then went on to Ponontomon and other Dusun villages for Clinics. One evening, we were pitching camp on a rough jungle path closely fenced in by thick secondary jungle, but at the last moment I found a small clearing a short distance away which was more suitable. In the early hours of the morning we were abruptly wakened by a great herd of stampeding water-buffaloes. The heavy beasts pounded over the area which we had first chosen as a camp-site with a din suggesting a combination of tornado and earthquake. They passed by in a matter of seconds, and presently all was quiet again.

Angkai's parting remark was, "This is the last time I'm taking anyone anywhere on this mountain."

Dresser Micky Robert answered for everyone — "It's certainly the last time you're taking me!"

Late one evening we descended to the Tambunan plain. Everyone was ready for an early night but we had been seen and I was summoned urgently to a village behind Timbau. Robert and I went on foot. In a small bamboo house we found a Sister from the Roman Catholic Mission at Teboh attending a complicated childbirth. As soon as I entered she said "You must be very tired, Doctor. Will you have some tapai first?"

"A little later, Sister", I said. Elderly native midwives were present. When I turned for an instrument, one reached to show me a manipulation which she thought was appropriate. I thanked her and sent her to boil some water.

When it was all over, we sat for a while in the small bamboo house and had a cup of tapai: and then the Sister and I set off home across the terraced rice fields. The moon was out: clusters of native houses could be seen about the plain. The Sister looked attractive in the white robes of her Order. She was the first European girl I had seen for months and I looked forward to her company for the walk across the rice fields. But after half a dozen paces across each terrace, we had to step up on to a mud mound and then jump down to the next terrace. I was tired and frequently jarred my frame by landing on my heels; and thus we went down the moonlit slopes with our eyes chiefly on the ground, walking a few paces, stepping up and jumping down; walking, stepping up and jumping down.

The Tambunan plain is a narrow 19 kilometre strip of undulating land lying snugly between hills which fall away from Terusmadi to the east and the Crocker Range to the west. Golden-skinned Dusuns lived on the plain — Tambunan, Bundu and Liwan Dusuns. Basically the language was the same, but it differed in its "lagu" (tune or accent) considerably, so that people from one village often had some difficulty in following speech used in another village a short distance away. Clusters of family houses formed the various villages. Most of these swarmed with children, a fifth of whom had no sharp epicanthic fold above their eyes, such as most Chinese have; but in almost double this number it was well marked and in the rest it was present to some degree. Centuries before the Europeans came, North Borneo had been a Chinese colony.

Living in the village of Pomotobon was a respected native practitioner named Goiyoi. She was aged about 50, barefooted and conspicuously bandy. She wore a piece of towelling wrapped on her head and a dress and blouse of blue-black linen. Most days, she did not bother about brooches or bangles, but sometimes she had a coil of black rotan around her half-concealed waist, with little brass ornaments threaded on it. Goiyoi enjoyed a reputation for her skill in treating disease. I decided to consult a colleague and find out something of their methods.

Goiyoi was delighted. There were no secrets in the profession. She was pleased to have a frank discussion with me. I could cure yaws and de-worm children, and she was impressed with my treatment for guk (goitre). This complaint had puzzled her for a long time. The hill people had it. She had tried scratching the skin over the swelling in the throat and applying pounded tatapis leaves, but with indifferent success. I advised her to give dried sea fish to persons affected. "Tuan, you may be right. The people on the plains don't get goitre and they eat dried fish bought from the Chinese, but the hill people can't afford it and most of them have guk."

The profession had no reason to be ashamed of Goiyoi. She showed me her armamentarium. There were two main instruments, ganding and susukuon.

The ganding consisted of eleven crudely-shaped triangular brass pieces, each 25 to 50 millimetres long, tied to a small iron ring by an untidy mass of knotted string. Threaded on one string were three pieces of kambaroonga root. The susukuon was a small magic parang (chopper) about 30 centimetres long. Near the end of its broad flat blade was stuck a piece of beeswax, called sapilot, from which hung eight strands of string: on these were pieces of kambaroonga root, two lengths of red beads and a dried fruit called buah lubah. By means of the susukuon, Goiyoi was able to communicate with members of the spirit world.

I said, "Goiyoi, tell me exactly what you do when called to see someone who is ill."

Goiyoi removed the ball of tobacco projecting from between her lips and sat on the floor. She took her European colleague back hundreds of years in the history of medicine. She told of medical ceremonies such as renait, mengalubuk and manimbubu; of magical recitations called bacha-bacha in a strange language only understood by spirits; of blood sacrifice of fowls and pigs; of herbal remedies; and of various taboos which their patients were asked to observe.

I listened intently, but occasionally my imagination took hold of my attention as I thought of man's age-long struggle for knowledge and health. Finally, when Goiyoi paused for a moment, I came down to earth. I asked, "Goiyoi, what about your fee? How much do you sting them?"

Goiyoi's eyes sparkled. 'If the patient is very ill, I ask for one dollar, four gantangs (gallons) of padi, a fowl, a plate and two yards of black cloth. If only slightly ill and I can fix them by putting the point of a vegetable knife on their chests and sprinkling on water, well, ten cents and a cigarette tin full of rice is all I can get.''

''You do pretty well, Goiyoi.''

''Oh, not so bad, Tuan. But I've only told you a little of what I know. I could go on talking for a week. Why, I know one bacha-bacha which lasts three days!''

Goiyoi had me laughing now; she was boasting! I said, ''Goiyoi, if I could take you home to practise your art, you'd be a success overnight.''

Joking apart, if the RSPCA (Royal Society for Prevention of Cruelty to Animals) could be pacified, Goiyoi, her ganding and susukuon, could easily be the principals in a very lucrative practice in George Street West. She would do just as well as we could do with some patients, not as well with others, but a damn sight better with many a hypochondriac!

A short time before I came to Keningau, a keen Cornish doctor had gallantly set about training native Health Inspectors to teach hygiene and sanitation to the inland natives — people who still sprinkled their sick children with fowls' blood, paid great attention to calls of omen birds, and hunted the bearded pigs with poisoned darts.

I inherited this major headache. The few tonnes of excreta put down daily over thousands of square kilometres of jungle and mountain caused more disease and administrative trouble than a hundred tonnes produced daily in a civilised city. When the Health Inspectors were first released from the school, they were regarded as peregrine falcons on the warpath. At first, the natives understood that a government ''hukum'' (order) had been issued. Accordingly, hundreds of pits were dug all over the Interior. In wet rice areas and in the mountains water or solid rock, respectively, were often met a few centimetres below the surface. Scores of shallow pits were used for a few days as a gesture of goodwill and were then abandoned. Outhouses were built, and presently they were put to more practical use for storing wood. Fences were erected around houses and villages to keep pigs at a distance, as the government wished; then ramps were added or holes were left in odd corners to admit them: someone rolled a stone over these holes whenever a Health Inspector appeared.

One Headman objected to pit latrines, quoting the native belief that digging deep holes in the ground would be followed by a death in the village; it was too like digging graves and was asking for trouble. However, he agreed to give it a go. Shortly after work started, a death occurred in his kampong and everyone downed tools immediately. On his next visit, the Health Inspector pointed out that the death was obviously due to senility. Most reluctantly, the Headman decided to try again. Immediately, as luck would have it, three other villagers turned up their toes! That decided the matter: the Health Inspector himself was shaken!

The outside pig-latrine represented a brilliant attempt to compromise with native custom in the pig-rearing districts. The latrines were shifted from under the bedrooms to over a pigsty or back fence a few metres away. Even this type led to some opposition. At a remote village an old Headman explained to me how such a latrine might be dangerous. ''If we use it at night an enemy will seize the chance to shove a spear into our buttocks!''

I couldn't argue with him. His objection was based on precedent: he showed us the scar!

Some resolute natives countered the health work by refusing to allow Health Inspectors into their villages, by threatening to take their heads, or simply by lodging complaints at the local District Office. Some of the complaints were quite clever.

''We have been instructed to cut down all our fruit trees to improve the appearance of our gardens.''

A Headman reporting from the Bokan area was asked by the District Officer, ''What news?''

"No news, Tuan. There's absolutely nothing to report."

"Nothing? Is everything fine?"

"Yes, fine, Tuan. Except that we'll all starve to death this year."

"Why?" asked the surprised D.O.

"We haven't got time to plant rice."

"How is that?"

"We're too busy arranging our houses in straight lines. The Health Inspector ordered it."

I went down the line to Beaufort once or twice monthly. This small township, which technically qualified as a railway junction, had a club, two tennis courts and a nine-hole golf course which were patronised by as friendly and convivial a group of planters as you could muster anywhere — Wren, Morris, Lingard, Tuxford and Lutter. Baxter of Sapong and the Lacks of Melalap and other visitors dropped in from time to time to help the small Club pay its way. At weekends there were often as many as fifteen relaxing sportsmen in the Club. We all drank too much and had what we assessed later (not necessarily next morning) as a helluva good time.

I had a large, gloomy, sparsely furnished house the other side of the town, just beyond the hospital, beside the muddy Padas River. A family of enormous monitor lizards lived beside the kitchen, and I suspect they drank out of the same Javanese jar placed to catch rainwater as did my cook and I. Bats flew around inside the house as soon as evening came and from the windows facing the river I was able to shoot two crocodiles on the opposite bank the first time I was in residence: subsequently, I acted more sensibly and left the reptiles alone.

The current District Officer was John Savage, young, chunky, weighing over 95 kilograms. He had been to Cambridge but I suspect he had not acquired any academic degrees before he accepted a position in the service of the Chartered Company: honorary ones are hard to come by.

Our first two meetings were rather memorable.

I had just assumed duty when he rang to say he would like to conduct the annual administrative inspection of the hospital. The usefulness of this hospital, and indeed the annual inspection, had been sadly reduced when the local rubber estates had opened their own medical establishments. About a dozen in-patients, mostly paupers, was the usual tally. On some high ground behind the office and O.P.D. (Out-Patients Department) Block was a large infectious disease ward which was almost never used. When we entered to inspect it, an uncommon and startling sight met our eyes. Hanging from the rafters, with a rope around his neck, was one of our patients, as dead as a doornail. I glanced at the Hospital Assistant, Mr Liew, and the dressers for enlightenment, but they were just as flabbergasted as I was. After a long silence, Savage said, "Doctor, you really should report this sort of thing at the District Office." From this I deduced that Savage was an exponent of the art of understatement: no doubt his Cambridge training.

The second incident was decidedly more lively. Once again an equine adventure was involved. The villain of the piece was Pretty Polly, an elegant, Australian bred mare, standing, I should imagine, several hands higher than Phar Lap. I finished rounds at 10.30 one morning, and there in front of the hospital was Pretty Polly all saddled up and in charge of Sangkai, Savage's Murut house-boy. It was an invitation to what Savage called "luncheon". There was no way to get out of it. Sangkai gave me a leg up. Pretty Polly swung round, knocking Sangkai over, and jumped a drain to reach the road. She then set off towards town and home at full speed. She had demonstrated at many race meetings that she was the fastest racehorse on the West Coast. One minute I was doing a quiet round in the hospital, the next my structural integrity was once again at stake.

Beaufort town consisted of two short rows of wooden shops, facing each other. At morning-tea time the bazaar was always crowded. On this particular day every member of the community seemed to be chatting quietly in the middle of the road or was crossing it peacefully from one shop to another. The prospect of avoiding disaster seemed hopeless, but the townsfolk were alerted by Pretty Polly's thundering hooves. "Hai-yah! Yi-sang loi! (Good Heavens! The Doctor comes!)" It was a miracle but a thin lane appeared between the shoppers and in a second we were through without killing anybody. Then Pretty Polly sprinted along one edge of the golf course. Near the office was a right angled turn. I gripped hard, and managed to stay aboard. On we went. The police guard on duty at the office sprang to attention and saluted as we galloped past. At the bottom of the hill supporting Savage's house was another sharp turn. I crouched low to avoid a tree branch and without further ado I left the saddle. It had rained very heavily some hours before and the water had collected in pools on the path. I was dressed in white shirt, white trousers, white socks and white shoes.

The whole episode, from start to finish, was completed in two minutes flat — except laundering, of course!

Savage's day began at 6 a.m. with coffee, followed by eighteen holes of golf. While bathing and breakfasting he used the telephone half a dozen times: this seemed to be for the purpose of activating the administrative mechanism. About 9 a.m. he went to the office and with his Chief Clerk he dealt with all outstanding correspondence expeditiously. Then, if there was nothing urgent, or any Court work, he went to the golf course again. One hole was near the Club and its telephone, another close to the railway station and its telephone, a third was beside the District Office. The windows of Savage's office on the second floor were always open, so that the Chief Clerk could transmit intelligence, receive instructions and throw out golf balls. The dignified Sikh Sergeant Major walked up and down in front of the office, watching the golf and suspecting skullduggery somewhere in the district. From time to time, he confided the more disturbing of his suspicions to Savage.

After "luncheon", the energetic and seemingly tireless District Officer was partial to a short rest. Then he liked three sets of tennis and/or a round of golf, with a game of billiards and several stingah whisky sodas in the Club before dinner at 10 p.m. He had the capacity of a city reservoir and kept a remarkably good table. Often, after dinner, if he had someone willing to listen, he would read selected pages of Somerset Maugham to them.

Savage had his finger on the pulse of every department except the medical which was out of sight, down the river. He corrected this by having me to stay with him during my monthly visit. This suited me. Living with Savage eliminated hourly walks to the phone to reply to the stock inquiry: "Derwent! What's doing? Anything?"

The star member of Savage's household was Betsy, a bull terrier bitch who qualified for local fame by having more energy and go even than her master. When roused, her activity was positively cyclonic. I was not particularly fond of the breed. They dominated government officers' houses: lay about in armchairs, sprawled across beds, attracted nine-tenths of all conversation, and killed too many pi-dogs for my liking. However, there was something about Betsy that made me almost suspend judgment. She was exuberant and fearless and interested in everything. On occasions, I even reached a state of wary friendliness with her. After lunch she usually lay on her back in the upstairs lounge looking at the young District Officer through pink, half-closed, diabolically humorous eyes. Now and again she thumped her tail on the floor to attract his attention. She understood Savage perfectly and liked to keep in touch with him. "What's doing, John? Anything?" If any interesting noise came from below Betsy sprang to life. Her legs began to work like pistons even before she had rolled over. Once on her feet, she set out to investigate with a total disregard for the consequences of her speed. The polished floor was slippery and in these wild rushes she frequently fell flat on her face.

A friend going on leave gave Savage a monkey to mind. It was kept on a long chain in a tree in front of Savage's house. It could reach the top of the tree and descend to the ground when it felt so inclined. This monkey became a major factor in Betsy's life. Often she would be dozing on the upstairs verandah when a metallic clink and a light thump would announce the descent of the monkey to the ground. Immediately Betsy swept across the lounge and tumbled down the stairs and was out of the house in a flash: but the monkey wasn't deaf and was always safely amongst the branches by the time Betsy arrived. At first Betsy tried to climb the tree after it, but more recently she just bounded from the house, took a quick half-concealed look to convince herself that the esteemed monkey was not within range, and then continued on to the edge of the hill; there, with ears pricked up, she looked across the golf course to see what it was that had attracted her attention. She paid no attention to the jeering laughter issuing from the tree top.

Things went on this way for weeks. Then one day Betsy did a very clever thing. From the verandah she heard the clink and light thump which meant so much to her. She got up carefully, trod lightly across the lounge, and slipped quietly down the stairs. Savage, busy reading *Macintosh*, put down his book in astonishment. Then suddenly he realised the import of this behaviour and rose from his chair with a shout.

Too late! It was all over before the monkey knew what had hit it.

Savage was aware of my opinion that no-one in the country knew how to train bull terriers; or if they did, they did not have the necessary strength of character to put their knowledge into effect. Here lay an interesting chink in his armour. Betsy, in her occasional episodes of excitement approaching mania, tested his overlordship to the limit. She was just impossible. One thing that frequently acted as a trigger was the sight of Savage mounting Pretty Polly on the padang. On two occasions, with my own eyes, I saw Betsy actually leap up, seize Pretty Polly by the backside, and hang on. The mare had spun round like a top, with Savage in an uproar on her back.

One day Savage invited me to attend a party being thrown by some progressive Dusuns to celebrate the opening of a new dam for irrigating their rice fields. I said, "I'd love to, John, but not if you're taking Betsy."

Savage flushed. "Look here, Derwent, don't be ridiculous. Betsy's changed. She hasn't killed a pi-dog for weeks. Honestly, I give you my word."

"Nothing doing, John! You know she'd ruin the whole afternoon."

However, after a crab luncheon and several pink gins, I raised no further objection. We set off up the line in a trolley. Betsy sat on the seat between Savage and I, ears pricked up, intent on every living thing we passed. Occasionally a long red tongue shot out of her mouth and swept over half her very long nose. She certainly was a comic! I began to play with her, pushing her head away and saying, "Get away with you, Betsy!" Betsy enjoyed this. She stroked my arm with one paw and pretended to bite. Savage looked on approvingly. Nevertheless, he was on the alert, and when we came to a sago island, with several monkeys on the fronds, he held Betsy by the collar and covered her eyes with his hands.

Finally, the trolley stopped. To reach the new dam we had to cross several hundred metres of rice fields. The fields had just been flooded and the paddy had not yet been planted out from the nurseries. We walked along the mud mounds which divided the rice-growing area into rectangular plots. Suddenly Betsy spotted a pig wallowing luxuriously in the mud. She set off at full speed along the mound, negotiated two right-angled turns and hurled herself into the quagmire. The pig was a domestic one and consequently fairly tame, and before it showed the slightest trace of alarm, Betsy had it by the scruff of the neck. My forebodings were fully borne out and I could not help laughing, but Savage was very very angry. The same old business! He ran along the mound, stooping to pick up a stick which someone had dropped. Betsy was shaking the domestic pig vigorously and its squeals could be heard a kilometre away. As Savage approached, the bull terrier saw him, so she made off, struggling with the pig amongst the mud and slush. Savage followed on the nearest mound, shouting and throwing lumps of clay at her. Finally, coming very close to Betsy, he stepped off the mound and went in after her — through the mud!

It was a brilliant opening to the afternoon's amusement. The fun came to an end, of course. Some Dusuns ran around to cut Betsy off. She flung the pig to one side and made her way to a mound. After shaking herself vigorously, she ran off towards the hill. By now, Savage was neither immaculate nor self-possessed, but he joined me and we went across to the dam and had some tapai. It wasn't long before he recovered his habitual good humour. He chuckled, ''It wasn't a pi-dog, anyway! You must admit that!''

A dog's life is short. Some go to the full span, some do not. Poor old Betsy! One day, some months after this incident, she went into the jungle to chase squirrels and pig, and a damnable python seized her. A great battle developed and the courageous Betsy gave as good as she got. When found, both bull terrier and python were dead.

Chapter 4

MURUT COUNTRY 1940-41

A most interesting part of my practice lay amongst the Muruts, a jungle folk living south of Keningau.

Native tradition has it that when, centuries ago, their forebears penetrated into this jungle-clad wilderness they followed or displaced no other people: they were the first to come. There were still a few tigers living on the slopes of their highest mountain. Murut villages were now scattered throughout this inland equatorial forest, situated some 8 to 24 kilometres apart. Though seemingly one people, the Muruts could be separated roughly into a number of loosely-bound groups. Some had plain district names like Dalit or Keningau. But others had thoroughly primitive names like Sumabu, Minakok and Tagal O'Kolod. In the headwaters of the Kinabatangan River I came across people calling themselves Romanoffs: unfortunately it wasn't a headline-catching discovery — they were Muruts, not Russians. Some of the coastal riverine people known as Besayas were Islamised Muruts. Between these groups there were differences in language, in native law and social customs such as tattooing and effecting improvements to natural ears and teeth, but the distinctions were largely geographical and slowly breaking down. And in the disintegration of village life and custom the rubber estates on the edge of their territory were the most important influence.

Perhaps half-a-dozen times a year a European doctor, District Officer, or Cadet made brief expeditions into Murut country. But if our government had suddenly been withdrawn completely, within a year or two no signs beyond a few baubles and metal weapons would have persisted to give an inkling that these natives had been governed by a civilised power for several Murut generations. The one great mechanical innovation, a rickety telephone line connecting Pensiangan to Keningau, would have been swallowed by the jungle in a matter of months.

Each Murut village consisted of a small communal house with 30 to 60 golden or dark brown pagan animists in residence. There were private cubicles for families, lofts in the rafters for adolescent girls, and bamboo beds in a common room for bachelors. Village sites were chosen in accordance with the dreams of babalians (priestesses and healers). Since headhunting had been suppressed, the babalians seemed to dream more often of comfortable, convenient sites beside the rivers, rather than of high escarpments only approached with great difficulty. In the remote mountains of the Ulu Tagal near the Dutch border there were children who had never walked along 50 metres of level ground in their lives.

Many Murut men still wore their hair long with a bun pierced by a long brass or deer-bone pin. They plucked hair from their faces and armpits, perforated and dilated their ear-lobes so that in extreme cases they reached their shoulders, and about puberty their front teeth were levelled by filing with riverbed stones. Lower incisor teeth were often sharpened to points. If necessary, anxious teenagers were sedated with alcohol and

Murut men.

forcibly held down for these painful procedures. Teeth were also blackened with landioh woodash or tapal stone powder and special leaves, a process taking about three days. Normal attire consisted of shorts and shirts, but many still had bark or linen loincloths. They carried parangs (choppers) on their left hips, and a spear, or spear and blowpipe combined, in the right hand when travelling.

The Malay dress of sarong and blouse was accepted by all women. They wore rotan bangles and necklaces and precious carnelian or cheaper multi-coloured Chinese beads. Like the men, they tattooed their brown skins in simple designs such as lines and stars and scorpions. Babies were carried in shawls slung over the shoulder. Nearly all the Muruts practised shifting cultivation, moving from one area of hillside to another year by year. Secondary jungle was felled with parangs and burnt after it had dried out. Crops included hill rice, tapioca, sweet potatoes, Indian corn and keludi. Vegetables such as fern tips, bamboo shoots and various tubers were gathered from the jungle. River fish were obtained by using cane traps or poisoning streams with derris root. In the jungle the Muruts were very clever. Remarkable ingenuity was shown in devising spring and noose traps to capture jungle animals and birds. Using a suitable leaf, skilful hunters were able to imitate the barking deer's call so closely as to entice them within shotgun or blowpipe range. Similarly, the larger deer (payau) could be called by the use of a segment of split bamboo. Occasionally, an inquisitive clouded leopard would answer such a call! Small hunting dogs were used in bringing the larger deer and wild pig to bay. It was considered an excellent indication of future hunting ability in a puppy if a pair of nipples and the navel were in line.

Making a blowpipe from jungle hardwood was a highly skilled and tedious procedure. Poison for the dart tip was prepared from maloh and bina. When hit, small animals died quickly. For large beasts, a tiny cup filled with additional poison was often fitted on the dart. When a monkey was struck, the hunter followed leisurely, listening for the sound of vomiting which occurred prior to the animal crashing to earth. Monitor lizards took to the river, to crawl out on the bank just before dying. We were told that human beings could often last an hour or two after being struck by a dart, which surprised me. A nick was put in the dart so that the tip would break off if extraction was attempted.

Suburban type newspapers flourished in the jungle. Signs called "tatandu" were set up typically near the intersection of native paths. These tatandu consisted of small branches marked appropriately and stuck in the ground. A few bones tied together and hung on the tatandu clearly indicated the nature of the last meal eaten by the Murut travellers. If a hunter had killed a deer he hung a forked branch resembling deer horns on the tatandu; if a python, a coil of rotan; if a pig, a broken stick bent acutely and with the bark sliced off each end, this representing a pig's lower jaw. Direction of travel was indicated by the inclination of the tatandu, a return journey by breaking the top of the tatandu over backwards. Often we stopped at the intersection of jungle paths and had someone read to us the latest jungle news as recorded in the tatandu. It was all food, weddings and deaths, but chiefly food.

The jungle was still the main Murut medicine chest. As we travelled along the narrow jungle highways, it was surprising how often Dressers and kulis fell into discussing the merits of various path-side plants as herbal remedies. A sense of well-being and sexual potency were the yardsticks used to assess the efficiency of any jungle medicine. Our sophisticated standards may be marginally more accurate, but the Muruts had the edge in bedroom laboratory testing. The native doctors (babalians) were all women and they practised both curative and preventive medicine.

When a serious epidemic broke out in a kampong, visitors could be discouraged or actually forbidden to enter a village by appropriate signs erected beside and across paths leading to and from the village. During certain berubat (medicine) ceremonies, there was an absolute prohibition to the entry of strangers. A bamboo rail was erected across all paths leading to the village, and flowers were hung from the cross-piece. On one upright there was attached a piece of knotted rotan (tembuku) indicating the number of days the ceremony would last. Before British times the death penalty could be inflicted on anyone ignoring this sign.

In the face of serious chronic disease the Muruts put forth their greatest medical efforts in a prolonged medical ceremony called "kalatong". This consisted of a series of feasts and ceremonies extending, with intervals, over a period of weeks or even months. For the climax of the ceremony every respected babalian in the neighbourhood, and her pupils, gathered at the sick person's house. Any babalian called and not attending had to pay compensation. After two full nights of mengaji (praying), early in the morning the babalians went to a pig pen. A pig was dragged out and, with all the babalians and pupil babalians chanting and reciting and showing signs of emotion, the animal was bound and carried to the river. Seven times the chief babalian forced the pig under the water. It was then taken to the bank and held firmly by several men. The chief babalian now took hold of a special dagger handed down from generation to generation. It was about 16 centimetres long and grooved and used for no other purpose. The dagger was driven deep into the chest through the axilla, and left in place. Blood issued from the pig's heart and was caught in a cup. The men bore the carcase back to the village. There, some pure rice tapai was mixed with the blood from the pig's heart. Seven different types of leaves were tied together and dipped in the blood and tapai. The patient's coat or shirt was now removed and the whole of his chest, front and back, was painted with the mixture. Sometimes a dab was applied to the forehead. All this was done to the accompaniment of singing.

Hair was then removed from the pig with hot water. The heart was taken out and divided into two. One half was now cooked. The cooked and uncooked portions were placed on separate saucers, which were laid in the centre of a circle of babalians who forthwith proceeded to pantun (sing). After the pantun the sick person ate as much of the cooked portion of the heart as he could. What remained, plus the uncooked portion of the heart, was then thrown from the window, to the delight of the village dogs. It was hoped that the sickness which afflicted the patient would accompany the discarded heart out of the window.

The rest of the pig was cooked. The husband of the chief babalian divided a portion of the pig into small pieces. Everyone present at the kalatong had to partake and were called upon to do so. A pupil babalian held up a saucer containing pieces of pork and shouted "Who hasn't eaten? Who hasn't eaten? The disease will go to anyone who hasn't eaten!" Even babies in arms had to take a little.

Throughout this last night the babalians continued mengaji. They and their pupils were allowed to drink a little, but to become intoxicated was frowned upon. As for everyone else, they were duty bound to finish all the remaining tapai, whatever the consequences. The rest of the pig was eaten with rice and vegetables.

After a long, rather tipsy night, the sun came up and terminated the kalatong. Everyone staggered off home. The babalians ordered the patient to take no rice for one week, nor tapai made from rice for one month. But potatoes and tapioca, and tapai made from the latter, could be consumed in any quantity.

If his luck was in the patient overcame his illness and survived. If not, it was beyond any doubt that his family, his friends and his neighbours had done their very best to help him. Ultimately, as the poor fellow breathed his last, they forced food into his mouth and down his throat so that he would enter the next world with a full stomach, a sign that he had not been neglected. His spirit survived on a nearby mountain for as long as living memory, about a decade, seldom more, then faded into nothingness. If he lived in the heart of the Murut country his physical remains were forced into a large earthenware jar. A small saucer was placed across the mouth of the jar and sealed in place with clay. The jar would then be placed against a wall on the closed verandah and in about three months time, when the sounds of decomposition within the jar had ceased, it would be carried out to the burial house and the dried bones emptied out into a heap on the floor.

The Murut burial house was something of a jungle masterpiece. The floor was raised above the ground beyond the reach of pigs, flags fluttered gaily from all corners, and the outside walls were decorated with designs in coloured pigments. Quite a pleasant, cheerful place to settle for the final rest.

In the latter half of 1941 I undertook my longest and most enjoyable tour through Murut country. Dresser Micky Robert and two Health Inspectors accompanied me. We walked south for 130 kilometres through the Dalit and Pohun Batu to the river Seliu. Daily walks of 8 to 19 kilometres were followed by Clinics, blowpipe and tug-of-war competitions, hunting expeditions for fresh meat and, in the evening, by drinking and dancing.

On the fifth day out, after a Clinic, a snooze and a bucket bath, I noted it was a pleasant evening and not yet 6 o'clock, so I set out on a stroll, carrying my .22 rifle, just in case. Presently I was walking through a fire-burnt area, with the lalang grass razed to the ground, when to my surprise I spotted a big boar about 30 metres away, coming slowly towards me, sniffing the ashes and deep in porcine thought. Solitary boars are evil-tempered beasts and this one had large finely honed tusks. The immediate problem was straightforward: would a .22 slug stop him in his tracks? For surely, if not, there was going to be some unexpected, even desperate, activity in the next few seconds. Never once had I out-distanced man or beast in a sprint. I extracted a second bullet from my pocket, then aimed and pulled the trigger and immediately reloaded. Allah be praised! The fabled moment of truth! The great boar slumped forward, transformed from pig to pork before it realised my bullet had produced cardiac arrest.

Nothing puts a village in better spirits than a hunter with large amounts of fresh meat, and that evening I was made very welcome on the drinking platform.

The object of Murut hospitality is to make all visitors happily intoxicated. Native beer or tapai is brewed and stored in great earthenware jars. When broached the tapai is sucked from the depths along bamboo tubes serving as straws. The neck of each jar is converted into a bowl by means of a leaf diaphragm between the neck and the body of the jar and this bowl is filled with water. As the tapai is aspirated the water percolates downwards through fermented tapioca or rice, replacing what is drunk, and at the same time acquiring its alcoholic kick. A notched stick in the bowl shows the exact amount consumed by each person. We were urged to drink to the limit. An element of blackmail was introduced with the phrase "Nanti kapunan" which implied that a visitor would bring bad luck both to himself and the village if he persisted in showing even reasonable restraint. "Drink like a young man, Tuan!"

The dancing floor (papan or lansaran) gives visitors an excuse for escaping from the drinking platform. It consists of a platform about 3 metres square, sunk below floor level and mounted on very long bowed saplings under the house. These act as springs on which the platform can be bounced up and down rhythmically, in a remarkably efficient way. In a typical dance the centre of the floor is occupied by naked children, smiling with excitement; round them a circle of women, hands linked; and outside these again, a circle of men; in all, some 15–30 persons. They make their way step by step round the platform, in rhythm with the bouncing movement of the floor. The dancing is accompanied by singing. The men often chant together, with women joining in the choruses, or individuals sing a verse, with everyone joining in as they finish. In the singing during our visits, the medical party was always thanked for bringing medicines to the village.

Tapai is usually laced with chillies and other corrosives so that the first mouthful burns your mouth beyond any argument. Having spat it out, it is polite to say "This is very strong", because it pleases the Headman and causes everyone to laugh.

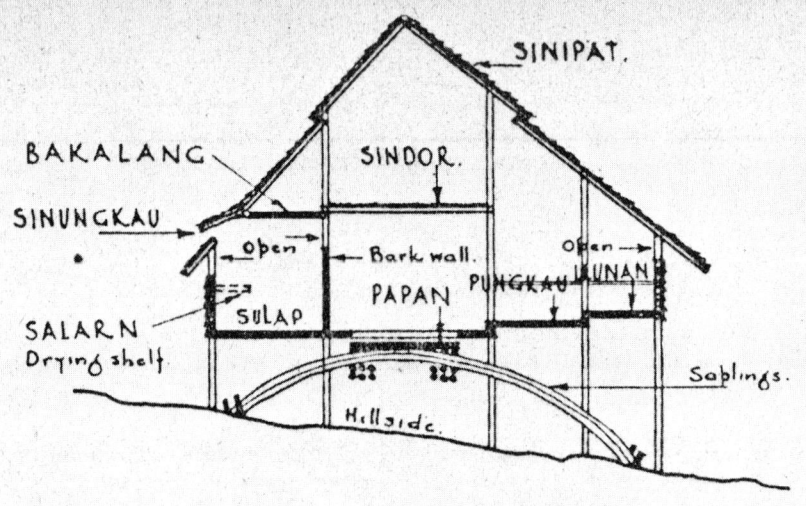

SINIPAT.

BAKALANG

SINDOR.

SINUNGKAU

Open — Bark wall. Open

PUNGKAU ULUNAN

PAPAN

SALARN
Drying shelf.

SULAP

Saplings.

Hillside.

MURUT HOUSE - CROSS SECTION.

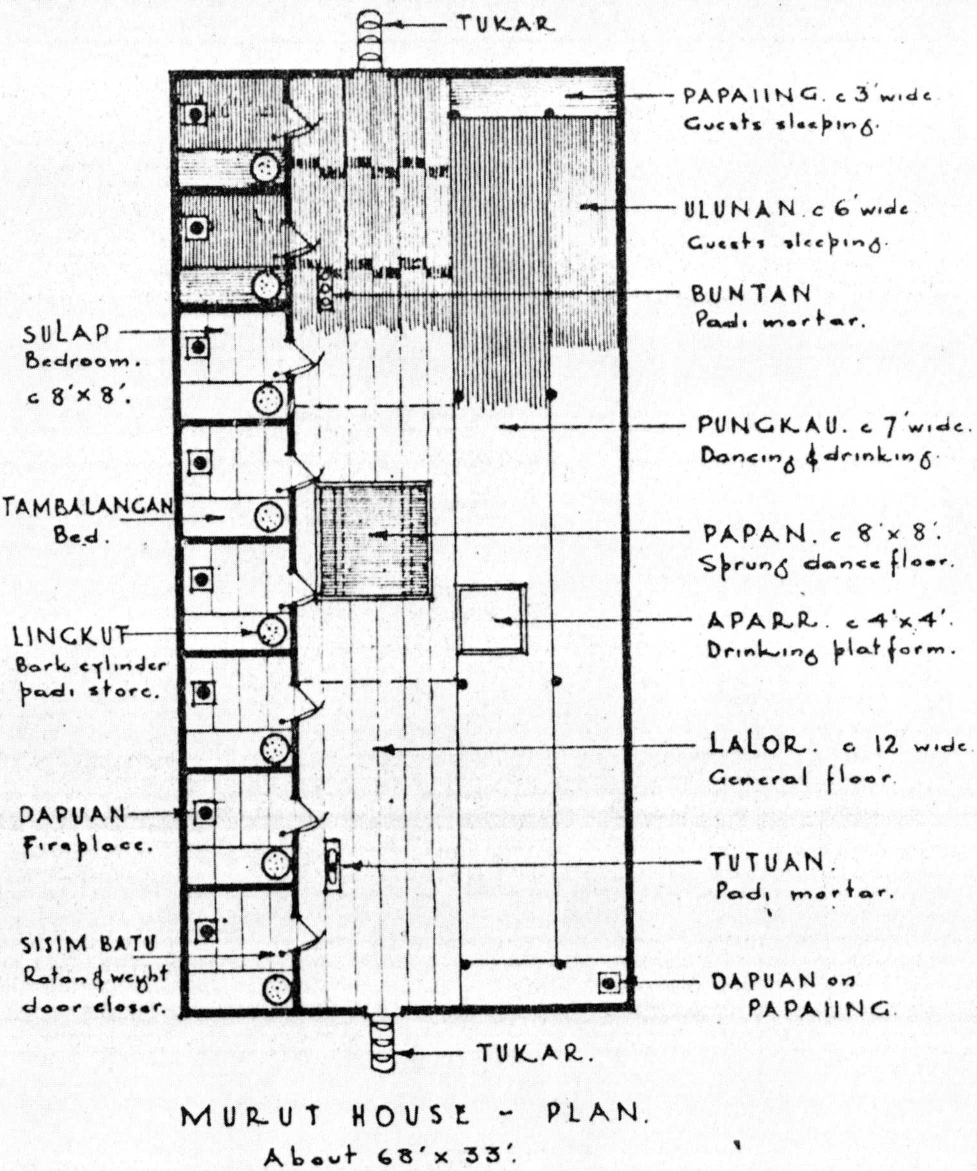

TUKAR

PAPAIING. c 3' wide.
Guests sleeping.

ULUNAN. c 6' wide
Guests sleeping.

BUNTAN
Padi mortar.

SULAP
Bedroom.
c 8' x 8'.

PUNGKAU. c 7' wide.
Dancing & drinking.

TAMBALANGAN
Bed.

PAPAN. c 8' x 8'.
Sprung dance floor.

APARR. c 4' x 4'.
Drinking platform.

LINGKUT
Bark cylinder
padi store.

LALOR. c 12' wide
General floor.

DAPUAN
Fireplace.

TUTUAN.
Padi mortar.

SISIM BATU
Ratan & weight
door closer.

DAPUAN on
PAPAIING.

TUKAR.

MURUT HOUSE - PLAN.
About 68' x 33'.

KAMPONG MESAPOH.

R.G.S.

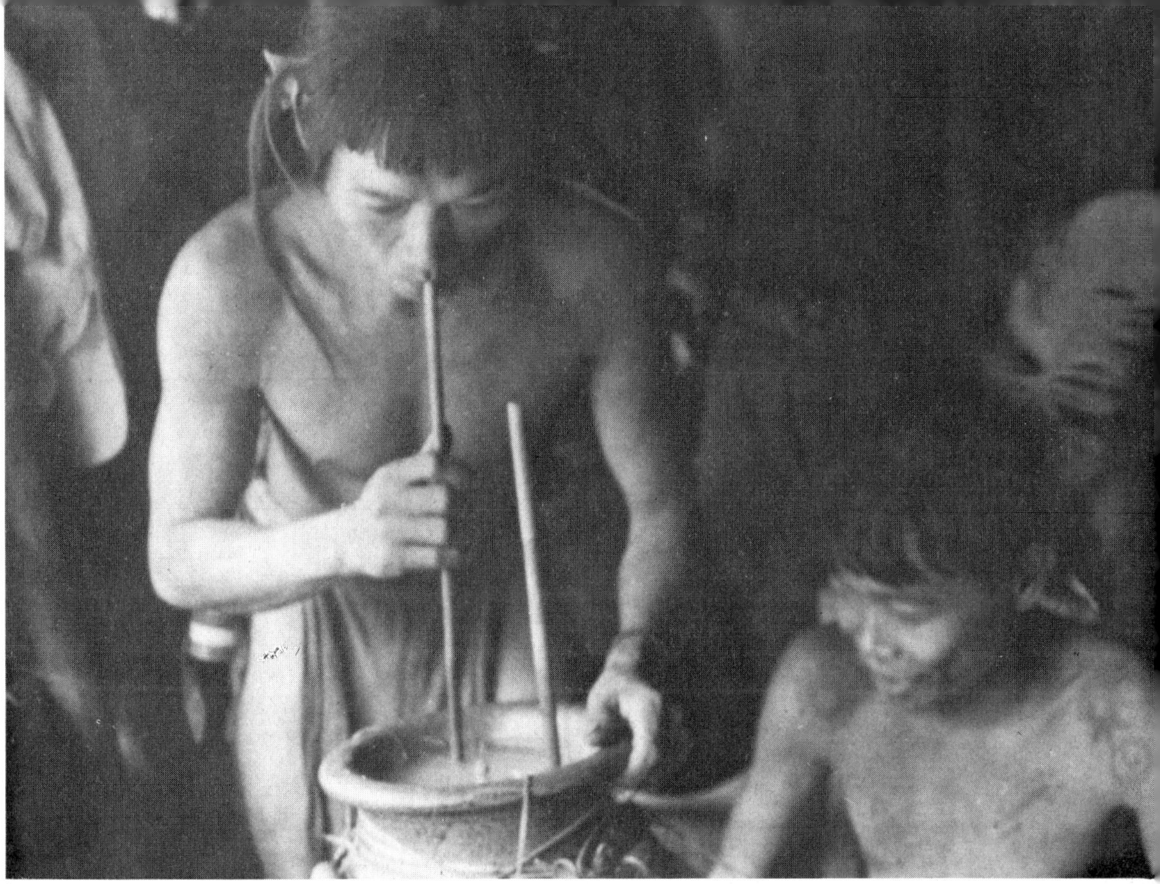

Murut native sucking tapai through a bamboo tube from a typical great earthenware jar in which it was brewed.

The dancing floor built for Muruts attending Annual Tamu at Sipitang in 1941. The floor is inside the hut mounted on saplings. On the ground are loads of damar, which are carried by up-country natives to the market.

On the night immediately following the shooting of the great boar, the last thing I remember saying was, "This is not very strong." It was a reasonable statement, for some fool had forgotten to add the chillies. Next morning, I woke at 5.30 a.m. feeling awful and was horrified to see a vast concourse of natives sitting on the hillside patiently waiting to be assaulted with de-worming and other medicines.

Every one has at least one moment of grit in their lives which they can recall with self-satisfaction. This was mine. I rose, dressed, climbed down to the ground, and examined every single patient meticulously; then crawled over two great mountains to the next village.

Unhappily, in these years, the Muruts were facing extinction as a result of disease and malnutrition. Doctor Copeland had travelled amongst them and had recorded his pessimistic impressions in the *Lancet*. Around Pensiangan and in the Bokan area particularly, they were decreasing at the rate of an average sized village (45 persons) every year. There was a curious tradition in certain areas that appointment as Headman carried with it the probability of an early death. One evening, when we were still in the Dalit, a young Headman asked me to take his photograph. "When I am dead the village will have something to remember me by."

He sounded so glum that I asked, "What makes you think you are going to die? You are still young!"

The Headman ticked off on his fingers an impressive list of persons who had died within a short time of receiving their letter of appointment. "Now the government has made me Orang Tua. I didn't want to become one, but I had to. I suppose I'll die. But what can be done about it?"

Murut carriers taking luggage packed in boungins across a flooded stream.

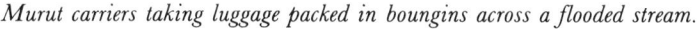

He had a short dry cough which frequently interrupted his nervous, hesitating speech. It was curiously pathetic to hear him reveal such a depressing tradition. We went into the kampong and drank some tapai. Dancing had barely commenced when a gong rang out sharply from another house half a kilometre away. Yet another Murut had died. Following custom, dancing ceased and I returned to my sulap (hut).

During the night there was a violent thunderstorm. The flashes of lightning and claps of thunder were nearly simultaneous. With each reverberation came cries from the Muruts. Men, women and children were standing out in the rain hacking at trees with parangs as the lightning flashed, apparently in an effort to appease the angry spirits.

In this very same village I had a delightful medical experience. A young native came to me and said, "Tuan, I've got sugar in my water."

"How do you know that?"

"Tuan, whenever I pass water I notice the ants come to it but they don't come to other people's water. So I tasted my urine and it was sweet, and I knew there was sugar in it."

To me, this seemed a remarkable observation. Medical history would indeed be interesting, in fact transformed, if an omniscient being had recorded the significant discoveries of the primitives and presented the manuscript to our libraries.

We reached the river Seliu to find it heavily in flood. There were twelve canoes waiting for us. We piled in the luggage and set off. Some people have the knack of attracting attention to themselves by multiple misfortunes and we had one of them with us — a long, lanky, aging, nervous, Hailam immigrant extracted at short notice from a comfortable coffee shop in Api-Api and appointed without ceremony to act as cook for thirty miserable dollars a month. As we raced down some rapids he distinguished himself by falling overboard. Fortunately he was rescued before life was completely extinct. To him this incident seemed the last straw. Already he had been attacked and bitten by ground wasps, and an evil, yellow-striped leech had climbed high up his lower limbs and had proceeded to feast in a forbidden area. Yet again, he had jumped on to a tree lying across our path and had sunk up to his crutch in the rotten wood, completely trapped! We pretended to walk on, leaving him to his fate — pigs or pythons? "Hai-yah! Hai-yah!" he wailed. If there is anything in this world more miserable than a water-logged, traumatised, Chinese cook staggering about in the Borneo jungle, going God knows where, surrounded by doubtfully reformed headhunters armed with parangs, spears and blowpipes, then I do not know what it is. However, Kuki smiled fleetingly after we treated him with a double dose of a well-known Scottish distillate.

At Pensiangan there was a Dispensary and Dresser-in-charge. We paused for two days to see about a hundred patients from the nearby jungle and to give old Kuki a rest. Then we pressed on by canoe and on foot into the Ulu Tagal and Ulu Salilir near the Dutch border.

Along these isolated rivers lived the healthiest of the Tagal Muruts. They ate beautiful red rice three times daily and boasted of it. They poled us up the rapids laboriously, each canoe going up slowly like a daddy-long-legs climbing up a tree with rough bark. Success in reaching level water was celebrated by everyone holding their poles and paddles upright and giving a long crooning cry of triumph. We were welcomed at all villages by the beating of brass gongs and the wolf-like howling of pi-dogs. At the village of Apa, Headman Andal entertained us with cockfights. Further on, at Kalagunon, I photographed the Muruts on their dancing floor by flash-light. It was a beautiful scene, with everyone in festive dress; comely young maidens, naked to the waist, stood beside the tapai jars watching the dancing. At times the tempo of bouncing of the dancing floor suddenly increased to a climax at which a centrally placed dancer was flung upwards perhaps 5 metres towards a prize dangling from the rafters. What an imaginative and poetic people they were! Improvised verses in song and apt descriptions and stories flowed from them effortlessly. For example, in the shadows of their vast, dimly lit hunting grounds lived the nightjar or tok-tadau, its flight awkward and jerky like a dead leaf swirling irregularly in a current of air. If a child could not sleep, the Muruts said its spirit was darting to and fro like the tok-tadau - surely an excellent simile! To banish sleep at night, hunters often ate one or more of the night-jar's eggs.

From the Ulu Selalir we had some stiff climbing up and down high ridges to the village of Alak-Alak in the Ulu Telikosan. The large house was about 1,300 metres above sea level: at night, it was bitterly cold. The next three days were spent in uninhabited, largely primary jungle.

I had two dozen kulis to feed and fortunately the shooting was incredibly good. Everywhere were the intriguing "tub-oh-h! tub-oh-h!" of Argus pheasants and the shrill screams of pakiak (Bulwer's pheasant). In the gloom of the thick jungle the dazzling white tails of the pakiak attracted my aim from their dark bodies. Every morning we shot several pigs; one, a great bearded pig, weighed over a hundred kilograms. Curiosity proved its downfall. The gun boy had lagged behind and while we waited for him the big fat pig faced us from fifty metres, wagging its short tail and studying us with interest. Twenty minutes later, every scrap of its carcase had been divided amongst the carriers, and only bloodstains on the ground remained to record the incident, and very briefly at that. At the next river, portions of meat were sunk in pools, weighted down with heavy stones. The Muruts would call for them days later when returning to their villages from the Pa Matang.

At night it rained very heavily. The jungle was sodden and leeches were active. Late one evening, after a hard day's walk, we slithered and slipped down some dismal dripping slopes to the upper Padas River. The water was muddy and running fast and had risen to invade the lower edge of the jungle. Everyone was tired and some were very irritable. I looked across some fifty metres of racing water and wondered how we were going to cross it in the morning. Three kulis set to work making a small hut for me and the rest simply disappeared. I must have been too exhausted to give the matter a thought. Kuki had boiled some drinking water very early in the morning and put it, still hot, into a thermos flask, so that we had to wait an hour or more before the usual evening noggin which seemed the only hope of brightening the immediate prospect.

While thus wasting time and sharing a load of self-pity with a cook trying to light a fire with wet wood, I missed an interesting feat performed by the carriers. One hundred metres above where I was camped they slung a long cable of coiled rotan between two great trees, one on either bank, built quite a large raft of bamboo poles lashed together by rotan and connected it by several loops to the cable arching across the flood waters. Further rotan ropes fixed to the raft and to the sling enabled the raft to be drawn backwards and forwards across the river.

It was an impressive feat. Only a very brave swimmer would have tackled the flooded river, dragging across the first rotan cord. The dog-paddle and sidestroke were the only swimming strokes known to the Muruts. In the event, about 9 o'clock next morning we collected on the bank and sent some luggage and the cook across on a trial run. After several crossings, with water splashing almost to our knees on the laden raft, all luggage and personnel were safely across to the other side. Not far below our point of crossing there were rapids and a broken cable could easily have precipitated a tragedy — as my terrified cook pointed out! Presently, we were struggling up the far slope and on our way again.

It was an interesting experience travelling through quiet, misty moss-forests to the summit of Mount Ilui, which seemed to be about 2,500 metres high. From there we looked down on the valley of the Pa Matang and the Padas River and across at a table-top range within the borders of Sarawak.

We descended into the valley and spent two days with the Lundaya Muruts at the villages of Kuala Miau and Pa Sia. These were a fine people, in physique amongst the best in the state. About 1939, a native Christian had come over from Dutch territory and had converted the Lundayas to Christianity. As a result, they gave up smoking, drinking, dancing and the practice of bachelors sleeping with the unmarried girls, formerly sanctioned by custom, provided they entered the girls' sleeping places with a burning brazier in their hands so that everyone knew who was sleeping regularly with whom up to the inevitable time of pregnancy, and hence marriage. At Pa Sia the Lundayas had built their own church of roughly-hewn timber. I attended a service. The men sat on benches on one side of the church, the women on the other. The service was quite emotional, with much clapping of hands and singing. The Headman produced a long tin containing colourful illustrations of various miracles recorded in the Bible. He explained the pictures to me, showing he knew the stories well. As he finished describing each miracle, he looked very intently at me and asked, "Is that correct?" I answered responsibly. The Headman noticed me having a stingah whisky-water before dinner and asked me if I was a Christian. "Yes, indeed" I said, wondering about a second drink.

I was met at Kuala Miau by Mr Chin Tin On, now Dresser at Sipitang on the coast, and native Chief Labau, quite a famous person from Kampong Iburu. They brought food and medical supplies with them, and a story of some excitement they had had on the way up from the coast. Chin Tin On was not a particularly outstanding athlete; yet, when charged by a ferocious wild ox (tembadau) he had climbed a tree without any branches under 16 metres, like a goanna, as if he had been doing this all his life!

Strangely enough, Labau's turn for excitement came on the return journey. He was young and proud of the fact that he owned the only shotgun in his district. Having shot numbers of pigs at something beyond blowpipe range, I emerged from the mountains with quite a reputation. As the combined party travelled back to the coast, I had all the luck, Labau had none. Every evening there was fresh meat — payau, pig or barking deer — but Labau supplied not a morsel of it. One day we made camp under a steep hill, with low grass-covered hills on the other side. In the afternoon I invited Labau to accompany me shooting. Labau had a red, tense, painful boil in his crutch which he was too afraid to let me open. In spite of this, he was still determined to demonstrate his skill. Politely, he said he would be pleased to go, but would Tuan Doktor mind if we went out separately? This would increase the chances of success, he said. I agreed and quickly chose the low hills. I was making towards a deer when suddenly a shot sounded on the hill above the camp, and it was followed by others. Of course, every deer in the district went to cover, and I had no luck.

That evening, the story of Labau's expedition was told. With two friends he had set off up the slope behind the camp. Presently, they spied a deer near the top of the hill and made towards it. They were climbing in the lalang when suddenly a tembadau emerged from the nearby jungle, saw them and immediately charged. His two friends ran but Labau stood and fired, and then ran towards a solitary tree standing in the centre of the open grass. He inserted a fresh cartridge into the breech as he ran. In the tall grass the bull tembadau was faster than Labau. Just in time, the Murut Chief swerved to one side and fired a second shot; blood gushed from the tembadau's wounded side. Labau ran on, threw himself down behind a tree and reloaded. Again the wild ox came on and when it was quite close Labau shot it in the face. It rose sharply on its hind legs and threw its head about. Then, to Labau's intense relief, the animal turned and limped off into the jungle.

Back in camp, Labau lay flat on his back, emotionally exhausted. An inquisitive Robert asked, "Labau, what about your boil? How did you manage to run so fast?"

Labau replied, "Half way to the tree it exploded!"

"What a way to open a boil!" exclaimed Robert. "Why didn't you let the doctor do it?"

Even Labau joined in the general laughter.

Next day we travelled about 16 kilometres. It was easy walking, mostly downhill. We were joined by several Muruts carrying heavy loads of resin (dammar) which they would sell for a few dollars at Sipitang. In the afternoon I picked up my Savage rifle and went out hunting again. We had enough meat, but there was always tomorrow and the appetites of the carriers seemed insatiable. A kilometre from camp I entered fairly thick jungle along the banks of a swiftly flowing stream, some thirty metres wide. Presently I saw a fully-grown payau enter the water only fifty metres away and make towards the opposite bank. I sat down and took aim and soon had its mid-thorax just above the silver-tipped sight. The bottom of the stream was very rocky and the big deer was making heavy weather of the crossing, like a fussy woman in high-heeled shoes. It had a pair of very big antlers and often stretched out its neck and peered myopically at the water in front of it.

Si-Langkap, a Tagul Murut from Bole was an expert hunter. He proudly carries the Kijang or Barking Deer which he shot after coaxing it from cover by calling on a leaf whistle.

What the devil! We had enough meat, though I knew thirty voracious kulis would not agree with me. I lowered my rifle and sat watching the beast. It reached the other side, raised its head and looked about it. Then, to my delight, it shook the water from its flanks in the same way as does a wet dog, and then trotted off amongst the trees.

Si-Langkap was a young man, about 19 years of age, married, with one or two children, an accomplished hunter who a year or so ago had helped supply a medical expedition with fresh meat.

By chance, our carriers found him lying very sick in a crude bark shelter, some distance from our path. With him was a very short, thick-set companion with a goitre.

I remembered Si-Langkap well. Once he had paid me a compliment which I rather treasured. That was on a day when we were in the jungle our backs against two jungle giants, trying to coax a kijang or two from amongst the trees. Si-Langkap had had no luck with his calls, so I folded a leaf over my index fingers, put the edges between my lips and sent several calls up and down the slopes. No answer. I handed Si-Langkap the leaf and at that very moment a kijang roared about fifty metres away. Si-Langkap gave me back the leaf, and, delighted, I called again, gently and plaintively. There came a thudding of hooves and in a second the kijang came to an abrupt halt barely three metres from us, bewildered beyond immediate flight. Si-Langkap shot it. To this day I have a photograph of him with the deer slung across his shoulders.

Now we were shocked at his changed appearance. His skin and eyes were yellow and he told me he had had shivering and high fever for some days and he had been unable to walk and his friend had built the shelter over him as he lay. It looked as if he had blackwater fever, but I had never seen this in a native, only in Chinese.

We offered to carry him to the coast, but he said he couldn't stand the long journey and all he wanted to do was to get well enough to get home to see his wife and children before he died. His village was many kilometres away.

I gave him aspirin, which could do little harm, and a little quinine and sulpha-pyridine which could do a lot of harm. However, I thought that blunderbuss therapy gave him the best chance, and Micky Robert and Chin Tin On spent half an hour explaining to the thick-set companion how and when to give the "Obat". Pieces of broken stick were set out beside the pills to help him remember. We gave them condensed milk and other food, and after lingering for half an hour we turned away and left them to it.

Half a kilometre away old Kuki said, "A curse on this jungle! If we don't get out of it we'll die too!"

I never heard of Si-Langkap or his companion again.

After two months in the jungle we finally reached a hilltop from which we could see the sea. Most of the carriers had never seen it before and quite spontaneously they all emitted a curious harmonious call which expressed their wonderment appropriately. I rested a few days at the charming village of Sipitang on Brunei Bay. The sight and sound of the sea is the tonic par excellence. Miasin, the native Chief's son, worked in the local Dispensary with Chin Tin On, and he supplied us with fish, crab and prawns. Chin Tin On invited us to a dinner, and Labau came to it in native ceremonial dress, including a necklace made of monkey's teeth. His buttocks were covered by a great colourful tabil or sitting-down-mat with clouded leopard skin on it, and he was prouder of this than his shotgun. There was no doubt he was spectacular and he knew it. Had Minnie-Ha-Ha been present, she would have called for smelling salts at the sight of this noble savage. Chin Tin On had a refrigerator and a bottle of scotch which, with all due allowances, is a more sophisticated and acceptable poison than tapai.

The village of Sipitang.

Our rest house in the jungle on the way to Bole Valley.

We gave the carriers from up-country their wages and presents of salt and tinned fish. Labau was intrigued by the ice cubes in Chin Tin On's refrigerator. He asked for and was given half a dozen. He wrapped them carefully in banana leaf and said he was taking them back to Iburu (days away) to show them to his children.

When we reached Beaufort my cook invented a critically ill relative and handed in his resignation and went back to his job in the coffee shop at Api-Api.

After returning to Keningau, I decided to take things easily for several weeks, confining my travelling to short trips to Beaufort. Savage had been transferred to Kudat and consequently there was no difficulty in escaping back up the line to the peace and quietness of Keningau. I had had a number of attacks of malaria and dysentery, and a rest from long jungle tours seemed indicated.

It was pleasant enough in Keningau. In the evenings, after polo, volleyball or badminton, the District Officer and I sat in cane chairs in front of one or other of our houses. At intervals, a house-boy dispensed stingah whisky-ayers and, a little before darkness, appeared with a plate of salted groundnuts or other small eats. The syces brushed and fed the ponies, the water-carriers prepared hot baths and the dogs lay on the grass growing more and more excited as their mealtime drew near.

In front of my house, just across an irrigation ditch, was the padang with its herd of cross-bred zebu cattle. Beyond this, near the Liawan River, were the villages of Tuarid Tuad, Tuarid and Dangulad. For months on end from these villages came the sound of gongs being beaten in houses where tapai was being drunk. "Come and have a drink" said the gongs. "Come and have a drink!" And near harvest time, vying with this sound, were the sharp clatter of tangkabak and the shouts of old men in imbus on the edge of the rice fields, scaring away the birds.

In the distance, the slender dimpled peak of Mount Terusmadi rose from a purple waste of foothills. To the left was the Crocker rampart: and on a clear evening, the serrated crown of Mount Kinabalu could be seen, remote and enormously intriguing.

At seven p.m. a Sergeant or Corporal would come across from the office, salute the D.O. smartly, and give his report. Night after night it was the same old formula.

"What news, Sergeant?"

"There's nothing, Tuan."

"What, nothing?"

"No, nothing."

There was just a suggestion of Gilbert and Sullivan in this nightly performance. Sometimes, though, there was a slight variation, such as:

"Wasn't Kampong Keningau burnt to the ground today?"

"*That,* of course, Tuan."

The D.O.'s house faced the other way. In the hollow below it everything was green and exuberantly alive, with the exception of a large durian tree. The local natives had a tradition that when the durian tree died, government would fall. By 1941, the tree stood stark and leafless: only a few scraggy epiphytes gave any semblance of life to the decaying trunk. Few knew the story, and certainly no-one paid any attention to it. Life was comfortable and pleasant — war-torn Europe was very far away. In its way, North Borneo was a colonial administrator's dream — a friendly, backward people, an honest government staff, plenty to amuse and adequate fuel for self-esteem.

Yet, sometimes, in the soft evening light, the quietness and timeless beauty of it all gave such an impression of unreality that one felt that if a village dog chanced to bark too loudly the scene would shatter and nothing would ever be the same again.

Young Dusun girls with rice trays. Hill rice is grown in the hills between Marudu Bay and Kinabalu.

Crossing the Padas River.

Clinic at Kampong Remidi.

The annual market at Sipitang. Baskets of Damar (resin) were carried by natives for long distances taking 10 or 12 days to sell at the market.

Chapter 5

1942 PRISON

At first war with Japan seemed a remote possibility — this, in spite of declared and even published intentions — then it became probable: and finally inevitable. Nevertheless, the attack on Pearl Harbour left our small community completely stunned. One generous donor to the China Relief Fund expressed everyone's thoughts when he said "I say, man, what is going to happen to us?"

Very suddenly, the local people seemed to matter very much. Here we were, a handful of Europeans, occupying the key posts of a government run by a chartered company with ultimate responsibility, of all things, to shareholders. We conducted most of the big business, owned most of the large rubber and tobacco estates. The alert and competent Chinese community was comparatively well-to-do. But when we looked at it closely — as now we did — the vast bulk of inland and sea-going natives had acquired from British rule little beyond a peaceful existence and a decent system of law largely administered by themselves through native courts. This, of course, was a very great boon, as everyone was to learn. Happily, there was a substantial feeling of goodwill for the British. The Europeans were in danger, like everyone else, and they quietly stood their ground. The Resident, West Coast, had lived all his adult life in the country, and he and his wife Benita were held in very high regard. In the Interior, the District Officer, "Bukit" Hill, was the antithesis of what one would imagine a colonial exploiter to be — quiet, fair, gentlemanly; indeed, it was doubtful whether a single native was ready to raise a hand against him. The government was benign to the point of being colourless, and perhaps many people were not entirely averse to a change: but fortunately there was no bitterness in the sentiment. The Chinese did not fail to recall the reported horrors of Nanking. They were very afraid.

One day a hostile plane flew over the Jesselton area and dropped pamphlets urging people to kill the white man. Many (including myself) regarded this as in very bad taste. I saw one pamphlet: a man in a Chinese peasant's hat and with upraised dagger in his hand was chasing a well-dressed scoundrel across the page. "Tikam orang putch! Stab the White Man!"

At Christmas, four polo teams collected at Keningau for a last fling before the impending occupation. A Keningau team, including surprisingly enough the District Officer and myself, won all our matches. We had chosen our supporting players well.

At last they came — 25 of them. I received the news from Hedley, the assistant District Officer, Tambunan, towards the end of an urgent 61 kilometre ride to attend the Malaria Research Officer's wife at childbirth. The A.D.O. stroked my pony on its neck and said "They're here. Landed at Weston. And now they are in Beaufort." We both laughed. Then I said, "See you", and continued on to Timbau. It was rather a trying night: a first baby with the mother in her late thirties. It was an assisted delivery, shortly after midnight, with the Research Officer himself giving the ether anaesthetic. As I fell asleep I wondered about their future — what a time to acquire a brand new baby!

Next morning at breakfast I broke the news of the landing. Shortly after morning-tea, I left the family and rode back to Tambunan for lunch with the A.D.O. Several native Chiefs and Headmen were with him, having "a final drink". After lunch Hedley announced a scorched earth policy of not allowing good Scotch etc. to fall into enemy hands. It was a patriotic move, but after an hour or two, quite a formidable business. I asked for a haircut. A policeman was called and he was given a full glass of Black Label. "Down with it, and give Tuan Doktor a Japanese haircut!" This seemed to be enormously funny.

In the cool of the evening, I left for Keningau. The pony, Mouree, carried me over the six kilometres of plain in good time. It was dark when I reached the hills. Small groups of natives including some mata mata and their families, were streaming homewards along the bridle path. Some exchanged greetings; some stood silently to one side as they often did. I had never taken notice of this before.

Late at night I came to a deserted rest house. I unsaddled and stretched out on the bamboo floor. Next morning, I pushed on and was met near Kitau by Health Inspector Tundau, a good, hardbitten Kwijau. Tundau was excited. "Tabe, Tuan! Did you hear there are only 25 of them! Why don't we wipe them out?" He was so earnest I could not help laughing. I said "Tundau, there are thousands more behind them, very close." It stood to reason this must be true — 25 was too insulting altogether!

We rode on to Apin-Apin, had a swim and then cantered along twenty-three kilometres of plain to Keningau. I watched my pony closely. It was eager, knowing it was on the way home, with rest and feed coming up. Fortunately, the future is hidden. It was fated to be killed and eaten by the Japanese.

Many of the medical staff had parents and relatives on the Coast and in the confusion and worry of the invasion a few had left their stations and hurried home. I thought freedom for us government officers at least was limited to a few days. On the afternoon of my return, I drafted a short farewell letter to the Dressers and Health Inspectors in all Interior Districts. The contents seemed innocuous enough at the time, but the letter led to some rather unusual experiences. For me, the first half of the Japanese war was to become essentially a private affair. My circular to the Interior staff indicated that the Japanese were taking over the country. In British North Borneo, without adequate means to resist, the position had to be accepted. Most probably, the Medical Department would be permitted to function as usual. The news from Europe and Africa could scarcely be better at this stage. Good news could be expected locally in perhaps twelve to eighteen months.

A sense of shame possessed us. The enemy had come in very small numbers and we had offered no resistance at all. Our small volunteer force was suitable only for maintaining public order and was disbanded about the time of the landing at Weston. The West Coast European women were sent to the rest house in Tenom and I visited them there. A gramophone was playing and drinks and packets of cigarettes were on the tables: the scene was classical imperial puppetry.

January 1942 passed slowly. More Japanese troops moved into Jesselton. They created an impression by running five kilometres to the Customs, working all day, and running back to Batu Tiga in the evening. The Resident, West Coast, and the Commandant were taken off to Brunei. Under duress they agreed to maintain the Administration and police force until the Japanese could take over. The hope was to maintain a buffer between the local people and the invaders. With civilian lives and immediate welfare at stake it was a hard decision — sensible and realistic. But in a short time the Kempei-tai (Military Police) moved into Jesselton Police Station and commenced its deadly work of fastening its eyes and claws on various members of the public. It was surprising how quickly and effectively it ate its way into the community. Some of the younger government officers were not prepared to surrender their freedom without trying to do something about it. A New Zealander, Sam Timberlake, District Officer, Kota Belud, and a wild colonial boy if ever there was one, was soon in trouble. On leave in England he had volunteered to help the Finns against the Russians. Later, the R.A.F. would not accept him as a pilot because he was colour blind, and so he joined the army and was sent to Egypt. A few days before General Wavell's offensive he was recalled to Borneo and resumed his work as District Officer, Kota Belud. Still imbued with military spirit he set about giving about 30 natives and Chinese some training in irregular warfare, and he was eager to demonstrate his prowess. The Japanese were a little too smart for him, and presently he found himself in Jesselton with the difficult task of explaining his intentions to a group of equally eager Nipponese. For once in his life he proved reasonable. Later, out in the fresh air, he joked, "When I saw that bunch of hombres I wasn't half so keen!" Everyone heaved a sigh of relief when he was freed.

Others besides Timberlake were restless. I had a letter from a planter suggesting going to Sarawak to join in the fighting there. The letter passed right through a Japanese occupied area. Why I replied I do not know. I felt I should. In a delayed and very cautiously worded reply I indicated no interest in his proposition. Nevertheless, the possibility of escape did exist and offered an alternative life-style, and I hid an escape kit, including gun, rifles and ammunition, in a village not far from my house. It seemed possible to get away to the East Coast via Pensiangan. The telephone line ran beside the bridle path and could easily be destroyed.

On the evening of 30 January the District Officer walked across to see me. My houseboy brought two beers and we sat down glumly beside them. Instructions had been received for me to go to Jesselton to see the Japanese authorities about the letter I had written to my staff. I was asked to bring the office copy. It was as simple as that — all I had to do was do as I was told. I considered attempting a get-away, but somehow or other, it didn't seem the thing to do. I borrowed $50 from the office, packed a few things and went to bed. Next morning I went by bus to Melalap and caught the train. At 4 p.m. I reached Jesselton. Almost immediately I was called to Kempei-tai headquarters in the Police Station. I was shown upstairs and ordered to sit at a table. The evening sun shone through a window straight into my face. Four representatives of the new regime came in and sat opposite me. There was Mr Ino, Chief of Military Police; Sakai, former Jesselton shopkeeper and well known locally as a resident spy, now in uniform and wearing a sword, but still with an atmosphere of dried fish and paper umbrellas about him; Lieutenant Koyama, already nicknamed "The Boy King", as the man who had captured the country; and finally, an edifying example of the genus quisling, specifically Indian. I had never seen him before.

I was asked my name, my age, and who had paid for my education. Then I was handed a copy of my famous letter.

"Did you write this?"

"Yes."

Ino's response, through Towkei Sakai, was scarcely encouraging. "When people do things like that, we always cut their throats." Mr Ino proceeded. I had insulted the Japanese Army by not being present at an official luncheon at Keningau given (under instructions) to the Japanese. I explained that at the time this took place I was in Beaufort and was informed of the luncheon neither by the Japanese nor anyone else. The reply was "It doesn't matter. It's a very great crime."

Sakai asked what other letter I had written. Apart from official correspondence, I denied having written any letters. Sakai stated bluntly that they had proof to the contrary. Thinking of my reply to the planter, I continued to deny writing any other letters. Sakai waved a sheet of Japanese characters in my face. "We have absolute proof!" he shouted. Mr Ino went to the door and shouted downstairs. Within a few seconds there was a clatter on the stairs and in came a group of Kempei-tai guards. I was dragged from my chair and forced to the floor. "It is because of things like this that the natives are not happy with us," cried the former trader.

Four soldiers began to beat me with rubber truncheons. I tried to rise but could not do so. I turned partly on my right side and extended my left arm to protect my chest and abdomen. Each soldier selected his own field of operations and went to work on me. The discomfort and pain of each blow seemed to increase as the beating went on. Finally, the truncheons were withdrawn. My left ulna was cracked and my left side from shoulder to ankle was severely contused.

Mr Ino then took a more personal interest. He commenced by taking off my shoes, straightening my ankles and stamping on them. He dragged me to my feet, tore off my coat, threw it on the floor and jumped on it. Then he tied my hands behind my back and commenced slapping. His fury increased and he lost control. He kicked and thumped and, much to my astonishment, he put his fingers in my mouth and proceeded to stretch that orifice! Next, he picked up the shoes again and rubbed them all over my face. Then he tried to pull my ears off. What an exhibition of temper!

Sakai was still at the table, thumbing his sheets of paper and saying "We have absolute proof!"

Ino resumed slapping and ruptured my left eardrum. Then he looped some rope round my neck and fastened it to my wrists. He took my necktie and knotted it round one of my ears.

Sakai said "When we have finished you can go back and tell the natives what we have done." Actually, I was willing to leave with the story immediately. No such luck, however. Instead, I was driven out on to the road with truncheon blows. On each side of me were Jap soldiers with fixed bayonets, with another soldier behind holding a loose end of rope. We proceeded past the railway station to the fish market and then turned left twice to the centre of town. There, I was halted. Mr Ino and Lieutenant Koyama appeared in a car. Ino waited for a crowd to gather and then swaggered across to confront me. His hands on his hips, he gave a big grunt of contempt.

I could see what was coming, but failed to recall any precedent in medical literature for coping with such an emergency. Mr Ino thereupon administered a public slapping. I stood perfectly still and my head did not move a fraction either way under the blows.

The Chinese watched the incident in absolute silence. Indeed, some of the townspeople turned away. For this I was grateful.

Finally, Mr Ino shouted "Habis!" and the soldiers marched me out of town towards Batu Tiga. As we approached the hospital turn-off at Karamunsing I had hopes of turning left, but on we went. Finally, we marched up the drive leading to Government Cottage. Near the top of the road we passed a Jap guard. I was checked. "Bow to Japanese soldier." But by this time I was in no mood to bow to anyone. They seized me and forced my head down between my knees to all the soldiers in turn.

There was a small hut about 22 metres from Government Cottage. I was tied to a post in front of it. My hands were brought together behind the post, tied tightly with fine cord, then lifted upwards by another cord thrown over a projecting beam. This threw my head forward and it was then drawn back to the post with a cord tied tightly behind my neck. Then rope was wound round and round from neck to ankle, completing my attachment to the post.

Before darkness, I was already feeling the strain. Four guards sat in front of me and every time I slipped down slightly, one got up and beat me with a stick until I forced myself upright again. One or two already knew some Malay and they told me several times I could go back to Keningau next morning. Anyway, I thought, there is a limit to this.

The slipping-down and beating sequence continued till about 9.30 p.m. when "The Boy King" arrived with several N.C.O.s and about 80 soldiers. Over their uniforms they wore camouflage nets covered with leaves and twigs. Lights from Government Cottage lit the scene dimly and a stranger sight I had never seen. Koyama addressed his troops and his sentences rang through the darkness.

When Koyama departed, another officer drilled the soldiers for nearly an hour, marching them up and down in front of me. After a fashion they were impressive. Eager, determined little men, they were exhilarated and inspired by their amazing victories. Finally, the soldiers went off singing. An officer came across to me and said in English "I am sorry you are tight. Japanese custom. You no gentlemen. Tomorrow you go back."

After this, the guards resumed their attentions. One tried to pick a gold filling from the front teeth. Another took a stick and hit me across the testicles until I fainted. This was repeated twice, after I had been brought to by having tinfuls of water thrown over me. Finally, no amount of beating or slapping could force me upright again. The Japs chattered amongst themselves and then untied the rope binding me to the post. I sat on the ground and worked my wrists. I was wet through and began to shiver.

The soldiers now took my wrists and bound them separately and then together with fine cord as tightly as possible. A cord was thrown over a branch and my wrists yanked upwards so that my forehead was forced down to the wet ground. Time passed very slowly. Three soldiers clad only in loincloths appeared. Their appearance was classically savage and the unusual sight frightened me for some reason. The cords round my wrists hindered circulation: as my hands began to swell they bit deeply into the skin. My left side was aching and my arm was uncomfortable, but the pain from the wrists was intolerable. The Japanese had a reputation for toughness and I was anxious to give a reasonable demonstration of fortitude. I bit the grass to stop myself crying out.

However, as time went on, I found myself constitutionally incapable of bearing this pain in silence. I began to groan and grunt and crawl around a little, a few centimetres that way, a few centimetres this. The soldiers asked "Sakit-Kah? Is it painful?" and pointed to their wrists and put them behind their backs and pretended to groan.

In the early hours of the morning they untied my wrists and bound my legs together and let me lie in a pool of water near the post. They said "Tolong jangan lari — don't run away." And then most of them sat with their backs against the side wall of the hut and dozed off. I noted they were bitten by mosquitoes — with luck, sporozoite-loaded.

I rested my left arm across my chest and rubbed it gently until feeling came back. I killed mosquitoes and gave a Jap a short Malay lesson. He tapped his head and asked "Nama apa? What name?" I almost said "Kelapa" — meaning coconut, but I was living and learning. "Kepala", I said. About five o'clock a soldier sitting near me lit a cigarette, and immediately dozed off. The burning end got closer to his trousers as his hand fell, and finally touched the cloth. I kicked him gently with my foot.

In the morning I was taken to the verandah of Government Cottage and tied, sitting, to one of the posts. I was filthy, my white clothes wet and plastered with mud. Presently, Lieutenant Koyama came and sat opposite, on the cement floor. There followed a most interesting interlude. "The Boy King" was younger than I was, about 23, and just over 150 centimetres. He was dressed in green khaki, with his shirt open at the neck, and he wore leather sandals. His head was shaved. He was elated by his country's successes, and delighted with his own effort of capturing the West Coast Residency. This was the man who had landed at a small village in enemy territory, had cheekily telephoned district headquarters for a train — and had got it. If roles had been reversed and he had been British he would have become a folk-hero immediately and forever. Koyama looked the picture of health and youthful confidence. He was immensely race conscious and obviously a determined soldier who welcomed the present hostilities. Possibly he had never before had personal contact with a European. He knew a little English and tried it, speaking very slowly; but after a time he had to call a Malay-speaking Banggi Island fisherman to interpret. "Your clothes come from hotel. A thief — a kuli — stole $50." Then he said "My parents are very sad because we fight the English."

"Yes. Before, Allies," I said.

"Japanese soldier, small. Strong hearts. Hearts are big." He repeated this several times, finding difficulty with the words. "You are a doctor. Why a soldier's heart?"

"I am a doctor, not a soldier."

Koyama asked me my rank; this, by pointing at my lapel and indicating his own designation. I shook my head and said that I had no army rank. Through the interpreter, Koyama pursued one line of questioning for fifteen minutes. How many Japanese troops were there at Weston? Had I received a letter from anyone telling me the number of soldiers at Weston? How many soldiers did I *think* there were at Weston?

"I don't know."

The Banggi fisherman said "Tuan says you must know. You are an officer, not a doctor."

"How could I know? I haven't been to Weston since the war started."

"Tuan says you must speak what is in your heart. How many soldiers do you guess are at Weston?"

It was difficult to take this seriously and several times I laughed. Koyama smiled, but was not amused. He said it was foolish of me to write the news and even more foolish not to admit it. I suddenly realised what Sakai's reference to "other letters" meant. We were isolated in the Interior district and occasionally the District Officer, Keningau, sent round news bulletins to government servants, each person signing after reading, so that the Orderly knew who had read the news and who had not. One day, returning from Tenom, I had heard some BBC news over the wireless at Melalap and had written a summary for the medical staff: actually, before the Japs entered the country. Somehow or other they had heard of this.

Koyama reverted to the strength of the garrison at Weston, and then referred to the difference in size between Europeans and Japanese. He said all Japs had strong hearts and were full of fighting spirit. Though their bodies were small, their hearts were strong, and therefore they would win every time.

"Tuan says he gets $60 a month," said the fisherman. "How many do you get, the Tuan questions?"

"$650, with $32 for the horses," I replied.

Koyama grew angry. "You big before. Now kuli. Must work." The Jap struggled in his memory for English words. However, his meaning was transparently clear. He motioned as if using a hoe.

I said, "A doctor's work but no other work for the Japanese." By this time Koyama wasn't the only one in earnest. I had grown up in a small country society saturated with the history of World War I.

"You must work now, the Tuan says. Before, you were rich, now you are poor" said the fisherman.

"A doctor's work, yes. Other work, no."

Koyama said, "You think light. Think deep."

"The Boy King" was becoming irritated. He once again said he was full of fighting spirit. Of this there was no doubt whatsoever. His eyes had narrowed, his small fist was pressed against his heart, and he further showed his determination by clenching his jaw and tightening his lips. If someone had picked him as the most determined soldier in the country I would have agreed. Koyama spoke to the fisherman, who translated. "Yesterday everyone saw you being beaten. You must work as a kuli, not a doctor."

"A doctor's work only," I answered, without much enthusiasm.

"No work, no food" said Koyama.

"The Boy King" stood up and told me my clothes were coming. He spoke to the fisherman, then walked away. The clothes arrived and I was taken to a bathroom. The left side of my body was already black, my left arm and face swollen. I had a shave and a bath and dressed in clean white drill. Shortly after, I set off for town, escorted by a soldier. The portmanteau (suitcase) was heavy and I had difficulty with it. The soldier put a stick through the grip and lent a hand. I could not have carried it five kilometres.

Koyama overtook us in a car and ordered the soldier inside and myself onto the running-board. We proceeded to the Police Station where I was put in one of two small lock-up cells on the ground floor.

Much to my surprise, I had lunch and a glass of beer at the hotel opposite in the company of a Sikh policeman. Then for the next five days I was given practically nothing to eat.

Monseigneur Wachter visited the Kempei-tai. I learnt later that, speaking of the treatment meted out to me, he asked the Chief of Military Police, ''What sort of people are you?'' It was an essay in self-destruction: the brave Austrian priest did not survive the war; and Father Theurl died with him.

My cell was about 240 cm by 300 centimetres, with a barred window, high up on each of the front and back walls. In the centre of the door there was a small peep-hole covered with an iron grill and wooden door. When the peep-hole was open I could see the guardroom in front of the cell and, through windows, the road leading to town, with the padang beyond it. When it was closed, there were only four walls, a sanitary pan, and a very low plank bed, plus a little of the external world through tiny cracks around the peep-hole door, to be seen.

For the first three days local policemen kept guard in front of the cell. One, a Dusun from Impin's village, Sunsuran, expressed sympathy, and an Indian N.C.O. asked if I wanted to escape and then turned abruptly away. A steady stream of informers and persons for interrogation went in and out of the building.

Of the Jap guards who took over from the local police two were quite friendly. They knew a little English and Malay, enough for prison conversation. Very quickly I tagged several guards with nicknames without realising that, in doing so, I was following an age-long prison practice. One small fellow became Red Tape. He seldom spoke and was forever writing, bundling up papers, and closing the peep-hole door with irritating efficiency. ''The Gorilla'' was tough, heavy, ugly and a bit of a clown. In the evenings he often walked along the road on his hands, presumably for exercise. If any local saluted him, and he happened to be upright, he would bow low, then relax his shoulders and let his arms dangle down in front of him, and walk about in this unusual anthropoid manner for some minutes. His boots had separate compartments for the big toes. One guard was unusually virulent — ''Hydrophobia''. He frequently presented his profile at the grille, then allowed his head to fall back, his eyes to roll, his cheeks to blow in and out, his lips to imitate ocean rollers beating against a cliff. Quite clearly he was indicating, ''I dislike you very much''.

A man of some importance was bespectacled Hirosumi Smidzu. About 35, he seemed to be an all-purposes clerk. He told me he was a ''doctor of indirect medicine'' before the war. He was detailed to ''investigate'' me.

On the third day in prison, I was taken to another room. Smidzu and two ''secretaries'' were seated at a desk mounted on a high rostrum. I was forced to kneel in front of them. ''The Boy King'' appeared and spoke energetically for fifteen minutes: then left, thank heavens.

I was asked my name, my age and who had paid for my education. Then Smidzu asked how I knew there would be good news in eighteen months? Three times he asked, three times I replied that I did not know. I was guessing; and three times the ''secretaries'' wrote down my answer.

The ''Doctor'' then switched to world events. He said ''Do you realise we Japanese have conquered Hong Kong?''

''Yes,'' I replied.

''Do you realise we Japanese have conquered Saigon?''

''Yes.''

''Do you realise we Japanese have conquered Manila?''

"Yes."

The following were dealt with similarly — Sarawak, Brunei, Macassar, New Guinea, Siam, Malaya, Singapore, Sumatra, Java and Burma. The "secretaries" and the "doctor" wrote down everything. Finally, place names in the Far East having been exhausted, Smidzu asked "Do you realise we Japanese have conquered Hong Kong?"

"Yes," I said with some surprise.

"Do you realise we Japanese have conquered Saigon?"

"Yes".

The "Doctor" went through the list again. Then there was a discussion in Japanese. Finally, Smidzu looked at me and said thoughtfully "Do you realise that we Japanese have conquered Hong Kong?" This was carrying the business a bit too far. Somewhat testily, I said in Malay, "There is no doubt about it, the Japs are very strong."

The effect of this was simply astonishing. The "doctor of indirect medicine" sat bolt upright. He asked me to repeat my statement, which I did, though with considerable reluctance. Smidzu looked sharply at his "secretary" and all three commenced scribbling rapidly. Finally, they stood up, bowed to me, and left the room. The "Gorilla" appeared and took me back to my cell. Fortunately, he didn't decide to do this exercise upside down. There is a final straw and that might have been it.

Smidzu spent much time at the peep-hole. Often he asked me what I was thinking about, and spent hours trying to read my mind. Several times he must have succeeded, for he went away having written down nothing. Then he tried a new approach. He pushed in a pencil and paper and asked me to write down what I was thinking. I declined this invitation to trouble. Smidzu accused me of being an Army officer and of inciting my patients to revolt.

One night he tried a confidential approach. He said he had a headache from teaching Chinese and Malay schoolboys Japanese. The Chinese were quick but Malays were slow. They could not remember anything. This upset him. Other worries beset him, he could not sleep. Now, about this twelve or eighteen months business, how did I know?

I replied to some charges brought against me. As for inciting my patients to revolt, I pointed out that, except for one short visit to Tenom and Beaufort, I had not left the government grounds at Keningau since the Occupation. I had had malaria and was convalescent. Furthermore, at the outbreak of war nearly all patients at Keningau Sick Rest House had absconded and there remained only a Murut woman dying of dysentery and an elderly Dusun with paralysis agitans — scarcely suitable material for rebellion.

On the fifth day I was told I was to be executed on the morrow. I was questioned from early morning. Smidzu said I was going to be shot. He was anxious to get as much information as possible beforehand. He prefaced nearly every question with "Angkau mau mati? Boleh kaseh bunoh. You wish to die? We will kill . . ." Occasionally he said "Kau mau bunoh - kah? You wish to kill?" I criticised his Malay: without much feeling, it must be admitted, because I did not care tuppence whether Hirosumi Smidzu of Kyushu spoke Malay backwards, forwards or upside down.

Koyama was active. At intervals he selected a soldier for a dressing down and was very noisy about it. Several times he struck someone over the head with his sword. The sound of the impact was disturbing.

About midday, the "doctor of indirect medicine" came to me and said, "You my friend. Tomorrow you die. Tonight anything you wish to eat. Makan besar — big meal."

I had been troubled with colic since the night at Government Cottage. I therefore said, "Two bottles of beer will do." Smidzu showed an unnecessary irritation; unnecessary because, after all, it was the doctor of direct medicine who was having his life cut short, not the practitioner of the indirect art.

Smidzu was firm. Only cold water but plenty of it. Finally, I asked him to select the dinner himself.

In the afternoon Smidzu entered the cell with three soldiers. They stamped about, shouted, and were generally fierce. The fighting doctor was questioned about his firearms. I admitted to possessing a .22 Winchester, a single barrelled shotgun and a .500 Savage. There were officials records at Jesselton and Keningau, all in Jap hands.

"Where is your revolver?"

"I haven't got one."

"Hydrophobia" struck me with his rifle butt. "Revolver ada" he spat.

"Tid-ada — I haven't."

Smidzu said, "Officer must have revolver."

I was forced about the cell with hands and rifle butts while I continued to deny owning a revolver. "Hydrophobia" stamped on my retreating feet and finally tripped over the bed and landed on his bottom. He became livid with rage.

Next came a polite Chinese clerk who spoke Japanese and English fluently. He said "Sir" when he spoke to me. "The Boy King" came to the peep-hole: I was lying on my plank bed and took no notice of him. He slammed the peep-hole door petulantly.

Shortly after sunset, a Chinese servant from the hotel brought the "makan besar". It was a good meal and Smidzu himself poured out the cold water. "You my friend. Jangan susah hati-na! Don't be downhearted." I obtained a semblance of enjoyment in satisfying my metabolic requirements, such as they appeared to be.

About 8 p.m. Mr Ino came to the peep-hole, opened his mouth widely and pointed down his throat. For a moment, I thought the Kempei-tai Chief was indicating my destination, but then realised it was only a friendly inquiry about dinner.

I settled down for the evening. For a time I tried to think objectively about tomorrow's event. A public affair, presumably. My memory played rather a trick when it brought back a recollection of photographs which a Shanghai policeman had shown me in 1938 — Communist boys tied to posts in a kneeling position, with tongues protruding from their mouths. Cords had been tightened round their necks with sticks. I had some razor blades, but dismissed the idea of suicide: there should be no doubt but that I had been killed by the Japanese. Such an act would probably help our side a little and, with luck, some day, some time, there would be retribution. (I still believed, or rather felt, that each individual was of some importance in war time.) I had slept little the previous four nights. My thigh was tense and throbbing from extravasated blood. The fractured arm gave little trouble, but when I jarred the limb I felt the slightly sickening pain. Hearing was practically absent from my left ear. A crop of small boils had appeared on the skin over my sacrum. Colic and tenesmus completed my unhappiness. These matters served one good purpose — they lessened the natural fear of departing this life and made me more resigned.

The electric light in the ante-room threw a beam down on to the back wall of the cell just above the bed. Padre Collis had brought some books to the prison and the Japanese allowed me to have two of them — one, Damon Runyan's *More than Somewhat* and the other, Somerset Maugham's *Of Human Bondage*. Damon Runyan's book seemed the more appropriate so I selected it. When lying on the bed I could place the book in the beam of light by holding it at full arm's length vertically. The blurb on the cover contained press comments praising it as an extremely funny book. Apparently, reviewers had laughed until their sides ached. I read for several hours with interest, but did not laugh once. Afterwards I slept. At 4 a.m. I shaved and had a near-complete wash in the remaining contents of the water bottle. After dressing, I slipped a razor blade into the fob pocket of my white trousers without any clear reason beyond the thought that perhaps humiliation in public would become intolerable. Then, to improve Runyan's book, I wrote my Will and a last letter to my mother between some lines on a middle page. A record is a record, and maybe it would survive.

About 4.30 a.m. an alarm clock went off in Mr Ino's room above. The Chief got up and stamped about, then he lay down again and everything remained quiet until dawn. I expected them to come for me about six. The hangings I had attended before the occupation had taken place about that time. But the guards did not come and the hours passed slowly.

Breakfast and later lunch were brought from the hotel. In the afternoon several high-ranking officers came and had a look at me. One had a moustache like Lord Kitchener.

Days passed. A Javanese continued to bring meals from the hotel. One morning I gave him my dirty clothes and said "Take these to the dhobi and bring them back clean." Thus it came about that a European in the Kempei-tai was receiving first-class meals from the hotel and having his washing done by a laundry. I began to buck up. I spent some time at the peep-hole watching the townsfolk go by. One day there was a sports meeting on the padang. A squad of British-trained native police attended; they looked very smart as they went by, led by a European officer. Koyama, always immaculate, often stood talking on the edge of the road. Passing locals saluted him or bowed. He returned all acknowledgments, even from children. He looked and acted the part very well.

One morning five Japanese officers got into a car and went round and round the football field. They knocked off for lunch and resumed shortly afterwards. This continued for three days. I wondered at the patience of those in the back seat.

The clothes worn by some of the Japanese visitors to the prison were unusual. One be-spectacled, middle-aged man sported a white topee, khaki shirt without a tie, a white coat with gold buttons, white shorts, black socks with suspenders and tennis shoes. He had white gloves, a watch on either wrist, and carried a cane walking stick. Apparently, white gloves were regarded as the snootiest articles in a gentleman's equipment.

At night, officers frequently caught soldiers in various misdemeanours. A furious dressing-down usually resulted. Oft-times, the officer concerned welted an offender across the face with his sword. The noise frightened me.

I saw little of Ino, but one afternoon the Chief appeared outside the building. He hadn't shaved for days and was wearing a jersey with blue and white horizontal stripes. He lifted up the front of the jersey and drew clawed fingers from the mid-line outwards towards his loins. His head was forward, and he looked up and down the street and slowly scratched, his two elbows moving in and out together.

On the afternoon of 10 February, guards came into my cell, bound my arms behind my back, and sent me round the town again. Two native policemen carried a notice, written on a cloth in Chinese characters, over my head. They stopped at the same corner as on the previous occasion. A crowd collected to read the notice; after which I was taken back to my cell, and the placard was fixed on the fence in front of the lock-up.

The same afternoon I was at the peep-hole when a limousine pulled up outside and, to my very great surprise, out climbed John Savage and his houseboy, Sangkai. The pair unloaded a bag of golfsticks and much other luggage. I wondered had Savage been promoted?

My friend went upstairs to the Kempei-tai office. I lay down on my bed and listened for the rum-tum-tum of truncheons. I dozed off and finally was awakened by knocks on the partition between the two cells. "Kell, Kell!" I checked there were no guards outside, bid Savage welcome, and asked, "How did you know it was me here?"

"Who else could it be?"

I guessed — quite correctly as it transpired — that Savage was in gaol for cracking jokes.

"Derwent!"

"Yes, John?"

"How long have you been here?"

"Ten days, I guess."

"What? Ten days! You mean to tell me that you have been in a cell for ten days?" Savage was incredulous, and I could not help smiling with self-satisfaction.

Koyama learned that Savage's houseboy, Sangkai, received $15 a month. He appointed him prison sweeper at $20 a month. Sangkai, just over four feet high, was far from Jap-happy. Savage's luggage was left outside his cell and Sangkai passed in his requirements and transferred things from cell to cell. Savage wanted something to read and I sent him *More than Somewhat*, first tearing out the two pages containing my Will and last letter.

I soon had Savage's story. The Japs had surprised him in bed very early one morning. He asked them to wait downstairs while he dressed, which they did. Later, he offended them by commenting on the temporary nature of their occupation. When they came too far south the Russians would give them what-ho from the north. That night the local Chinese gave a party for the invaders, as tangible proof of esteem, and sent them home drunk. At midnight the Japs attacked Savage with fists and swords. Next day, they congratulated him on holding out longer than anyone else in Borneo. Like myself, Savage had concealed his rifle, thinking it might be of use later on. The Japs asked him "Have you a rifle?"

"No," answered Savage.

"Is this your rifle?" they asked, producing one for inspection.

"Yes," said Savage: for there it was! It was very amusing.

The time now passed much more pleasantly. I enjoyed telling Savage something for a change — about food from the hotel, how to get his laundry done, how to bathe at 4 a.m. from his water bottle, what to do about the pan, and so on. We conversed by throwing our words, as it were, out through the bars of our own cell to the ceiling of the ante-room which reflected them downwards through the bars of the adjacent cell. When either of us saw a guard coming, we scraped a shoe on the cement floor. At first, every guard entering the ante-room was greeted with a loud scraping sound as we both drew our shoes across the cement. The matter was reported to "The Boy King" who ordered us to cease conversation forthwith. Koyama had a way with him that made prisoners slightly apprehensive: as soon as he had gone, we arranged to maintain silence for two days as a goodwill gesture. However, that night we resumed. Most nights, there were no guards in the ante-room for an hour or so, and advantage was taken of this. By nature, I was rather nervous, and hence found Savage positively garrulous at times.

"Derwent!"

"Yes, John."

"That's a pretty potent sigh you've got."

This seemed an unnecessary observation; moreover, Savage himself was soon emitting the most sustained sighs ever heard in prison. Strangely curious, he applied his face to the grille or door crack for hours on end. When he saw anything of interest, he tapped on the wall, and I got up and had a look. I was still licking my wounds and spent hours each day on the broad of my back, and was often disturbed by statements of this nature: "Derwent, take over for a moment will you? I want to use the pan." I had an idea.

"John!"

"Yes?"

"Don't spend so long at the grille. You'll have the pattern sunburnt on your face."

Savage had little prison sense. He weighed 95 to 100 kilograms and almost pulled down the back wall of the prison in his efforts to look through the high back window.

One night there was a hullaballo, and guards appeared with a Chinese drunk, and hurled him into Savage's cell. The drunk was vociferous.

"Tuan! Tuan! May I sing a Malay song?"

"You shut up or I'll crack you one. Warder, warder!"

Savage was being unreasonable. After all, he wasn't in a private room at the Savoy. The two of them were still at loggerheads when I fell asleep again.

Another time a carpenter was working outside and Savage couldn't quite see what he was doing. He asked me to investigate. "What is he doing? Can you see?"

"Yes, he's making a guillotine."

I knew I had scored a bull because Savage commenced his reply rather irritably, "I know that. What I really want to know is this — is it a double one?"

One day "Red Tape" appeared at my peep-hole and levelled a revolver at me. The little Jap was frightened, perspiration on his brow, face pale, licking his lips in obvious distress. Suddenly, he quite deliberately altered his aim and pulled the trigger. Sand or powder spattered against the wall. Koyama was outside superintending the execution of this joke. Another guard did the same thing to Savage who, at the time, was lying down enjoying a malaria rigor. That night he said "I was feeling so miserable my only fear was that he would miss."

There was one unforgettable day; the occasion of a Japanese festival. We heard a weird chanting in the distance coming closer and closer. Presently, a dozen Japs appeared carrying on their shoulders a platform decorated with palms and flowers. They were naked except for coloured cloths on their heads and loins. They set down the platform in front of the Kempei-tai headquarters, then danced round it while guards threw bucketfuls of water over them. There was laughter and shouting. Then more chanting came from the direction of Batu Tiga and along came another band bearing a second decorated platform and put it down in front of the building.

Two prisoners, two platforms. I concluded that the Japs were going to put me on one platform amongst the palms and flowers, Savage on the other, and carry us both round town, perhaps to be pelted with refuse from the market.

Some of the clowning Japs came into the ante-room and inspected us. Then "The Gorilla" came with a bunch of keys, opened my cell and walked in. He shuffled about, inspected my belongings, then went out, slamming the door to, without locking it. I stood tense, with a queer mixture of fear and hopeless anger; I felt that I just could not face a public humiliation of this nature.

"The Gorilla" unlocked Savage's cell, went in, came out again and did not lock the door.

Presently the Japs picked up their platforms and set off towards town, singing and laughing. In half an hour they were back and more water was thrown over them. Then a Jap with a drum was put on each platform and off they went again, with drums beating. This sort of thing went on all afternoon and, finally, to my unutterable relief, they returned towards Batu Tiga.

Savage must have felt very much as I did; that night he said, "If they had taken us into town, at a given signal we could have dived on to the road, head first."

I considered this incident was my worst experience of the war. I was really afraid and felt like a cornered animal. Such can be the effect of imagination.

Hirosumi Smidzu, practitioner of the indirect art, did not visit the cells as previously; but one day "The Boy King" sent him down. He told me that the "Commander" had said that I must work as "tukang sapu" or sweeper of the prison. I said no. Hirosumi Smidzu disappeared upstairs. Presently he was back again at the peep-hole.

"Very difficult. Commander orders."

"A doctor's work, okay," I said. "Other work, no." On this small matter my mind was made up. There was no way in the world that I would do a kuli's work for Koyama. Smidzu tapped the pencil on his teeth with vexation. "If Commander order, you must obey. Misti obey." I repeated my refusal and Smidzu went upstairs again.

After several such exchanges, during which I became more and more depressed, the doctor of indirect medicine made a very fine ethical gesture. He said "If Commander orders, must obey. Understand? Ini chakap sedja, chakap sedja. This is only talk. Only talk." He repeated this with some earnestness.

"Well, if it's only talk, I agree to become the prison sweeper."

Smidzu was pleased and ran off upstairs. Nothing further was said about the matter.

One day I was privileged to hear Savage's defence of his actions in Kudat. Koyama accused Savage of being very "jahat" (bad) in his speech. Savage admitted that at the beginning his "chakap" had been very "jahat". He added in Malay "But when I understood correctly I wasn't bad any more." I treasured this statement and marked it down for future reference. Everything sounds a little funnier when spoken in elementary Malay. Savage had understood correctly after being smacked across the head with a sword and having a tooth knocked out! Neverthele, I was grateful that no-one was present when I had to defend myself against various charges. It was necessary to fall back on the most childish explanations for things not requiring explanation at all. It was a reversion to kindergarten level.

One night there was a knock on the wall. "Yes?"

"Derwent, I've been thinking things over. I don't think they'll shoot you."

"Well, that's fine!" I laughed outright. I was really amused at the trend of Savage's thoughts.

"I think they might have done so at the beginning, but not now."

On 25 February, I was taken to a school behind the Kempei-tai headquarters. On one wall was a large map of the Pacific with red arrows radiating from Japan along the lines of advance of the Invincible Imperial Forces. From Java there was a heavy arrow directed at Port Darwin. Mr Ino sat at a table, with a polite Japanese-speaking Chinese clerk as interpreter. I sat in one of 50 schoolboy seats. The Chief searched ponderously for other possible crimes. At times he appeared slightly baffled. He alleged that I had tried to stir up rebellion in the Interior. I had stated that the Japanese ill-treated women and children. If the local people refused to co-operate with the Japanese they would become downhearted and return home. Japanese planes were made of bamboo. The Allies had bombed Formosa and would presently be attacking Japan itself. And so on. I defended myself to the best of my ability against these grave charges.

Ino said one thing through the interpreter which raised this investigation to a high psychological level.

"The Chief thinks it possible that you have a double personality. Do you think so?" No, I didn't think so, I barely had one. Finally, the interpreter said "You will be court-martialled in a few days."

That night I told Savage what was happening. About 9 p.m. a clerk came from the office above and asked "What is bamboo?" Apparently, the Chief was working late.

Early next morning I was called upstairs to sign my name to sheets of "evidence" against me. It was all in kanji. Ino signed and then held out the pen. In Malay, of which Ino knew next to nothing, I asked what it was I was signing? Ino dipped the pen in the ink and held it out. There was no mistaking what he meant. It was now merely a matter of whether or not I could fix my signature to the "evidence" before Ino fixed his signature on me. And so I acted, with seconds to spare. The matter was serious. Any sane person would realise I did not know what I was signing. And I had to get out of this madhouse at all costs.

The same morning I was led from my cell again and my arms were lightly bound together behind my back. I was taken to the railway station by a soldier and a corporal. Koyama followed closely. As the train drew out "The Boy King" stood at attention and saluted with great intensity. His eyes, his lips, his clenched jaw — everything about this little fanatic advertised his fighting spirit. I was off his hook and swimming away, and in this small victory I could afford to be magnanimous. I stood up and slowly gave him ten degrees from the waist. I smiled slightly. I think he was aware of this, though he kept his very narrow eyes fixed on the soldier. I had my private opinion as to what would happen to Koyama. Somewhere further south, this spirited but inexperienced youth would meet something decidedly more lively than a small group of ageing civil servants and a peaceful unarmed Asiatic public: he would then shout and scream at his uniformed followers, belt some of them with his sword, put on his white gloves and charge with the whole yelling menagerie straight into a stream of machine-gun bullets. Banzai!

Chapter 6

1942 TO MIRI — THE TRIAL

The Corporal, the soldier and I had a carriage to ourselves. The soldier, Tada, soon became friendly.

"Do you remember me?" he asked, speaking in Malay. I did not.

"What? Don't you remember, you were tied up and we beat you."

"Oh, yes! Of course!"

Tada was delighted. He said in English, "You, English gentleman", and ostentatiously removed the bullet from the breech of his rifle. He offered me a cigarette. All Koyama's soldiers studied Malay, but Tada had a better knowledge of it than the others; to this, he added some English. A tough, friendly little adventurer, he liked talking to people, and languages apparently came easily to him. He patted his rifle and said "Very good. Shoot straight." He handed it to me; I inspected it, and then sighted on various objects through the window.

The Corporal was possibly a clerk in civilian life. He was tall and rather slight for a Jap. He spoke not one word to me throughout the trip. Several times he knelt on the carriage seat and waved vigorously. When villagers waved back he was delighted, and resumed his seat with a look of satisfaction on his face: for he could see the locals were happy under the new regime.

We reached Beaufort. The Japs seemed at a loss where to proceed. I had no such doubts. I was very thirsty and pointed to the Club; when the Corporal went off to explore, Tada and I immediately went to the club verandah. We were joined by several rather dejected-looking Europeans. The steward served beer and I had a picnic lunch provided by Mrs Sykes, the District Officer's wife.

In the afternoon the three of us crossed the Padas river and went by motor trolley to Weston, a small village on Brunei Bay. The garrison consisted of a dozen soldiers and an officer, quartered in the small railway station. Here I was seated across a bench and then fastened to railings with an incredible length of rope. Sleep was impossible: there were millions of mosquitoes and I could not slap them. I spent the night watching the guards on duty. All had Malay handbooks which they studied diligently. After dark some Malay youngsters appeared and hung over their shoulders, laughing and teaching them words. For several hours the soldiers repeated two sentences. "Prumm-pang chantek ada-kah? Are there any pretty women?" "Prumm-pang" was the peculiar Japanese rendering of "perampuan". The second was "Boleh kasih sahaya-kah? Will you give me?"

The Malays didn't produce any beautiful women, so the Japs created a diversion by grabbing them by leg and thigh. The youngsters turned away laughing. One middle-aged Lance Corporal studied Malay earnestly for ten solid hours. It is doubtful whether he learnt three words. Occasionally, he looked sideways at me with the greatest disdain. His features were the strangest I ever saw in a human being.

We left by launch for Brunei at 4 a.m. The sea was calm. I was given a cane armchair on the after deck. As we went along I considered the possibility of overcoming the two soldiers. Far in the distant hills was the Christian village of Pa Sia. Tada was strong and capable of giving a good account of himself; the Corporal, however, was not impressive. The rope fastened to my arms was tight enough to restrict free movement. This, plus the fact of being left-handed, and recovery from my left-sided injuries being incomplete, made reliance on punches very hazardous. A weightier consideration was that I could not recall ever having hurt anyone with a punch in my life. That left only my white pig skin shoes. I actually and seriously spent several hours studying the relation of the soldiers' chins to the floor from which I contemplated delivering the kicks, and the position of their rifles. It was a strange business. Tada was obviously a good, jovial sort of fellow: and there was nothing about the gentle, benign "clerk" to inspire murderous thoughts. In fact, there was little chance of making a getaway. The Malay crew and their families now lived in Jap-occupied territory. The launch was useless without fuel. Inland, malaria was hyperendemic. Anyone who helped me would probably find themselves in the Kempei-tai.

About 9 o'clock Tada produced a loaf of bread and a tin of condensed milk. He sliced the bread, opened the tin, and spread the milk, all with his bayonet. He handed me a slice of bread and milk, and also the bayonet to inspect. I took a mouthful of bread and ran my finger along the blade. When Tada turned away I tingled all over.

In due course the launch entered the Kuala and made up river to Brunei, the capital and seat of the Sultan. We went to Kempei-tai headquarters. When I saw the local Chief, my heart sank: Mr. Ino all over again, perhaps slightly worse! However, after a time the Chief called me over and went to considerable trouble removing the rope binding my arms. Then he shouted for food. I fed on rice and Chinese cabbage, and soup with the skeletons of small fish in it. Then I was taken to the prison and locked in a large, comfortable cell. To my joy and surprise, in the cell opposite were two Europeans — Humphreys, the Resident, Labuan Island; and Anderson, the Resident, Limbang. a division of Sarawak.

After dark, Malay policemen opened the cell doors. We bathed and then gathered round a table in the corridor between the cells. The Residents produced a bottle of Black Label Scotch with ostentatious nonchalance. Both had had experiences similar to my own. Anderson gave an amusing account of his capture. A company of camouflaged Japs encircled his house and came up the hill in short, cautious rushes, while he sat drinking a whiskey and soda, and watching the performance. He had his houseboy put out extra glasses, and when they finally burst in, he asked them to join him. However, they soon made it plain that they were in charge of proceedings and that included his liquor cabinet! Humphreys was resolute and very serious about the war. The problem of escape and contending with the enemy was very much on his mind. I met him later in Kuching and he did not change throughout the war.

After weeks in a cell together, the pair were in good health and spirits. The Japs supplied no food at all and forbad them to communicate with anyone outside. They lived on smuggled foodstuffs, much of it from the local hospital where a Canadian doctor was still working. They gave me $25 which fitted into my fob pocket much more comfortably than the famous razor blade.

Next morning the Corporal and Tada and I continued on to Miri in the back of a truck. We followed the beach over 110 kilometres to the oil-fields at Seria and then went on to Kuala Belait, where we lunched at Kempei-tai headquarters. I sat at a table amongst the security men. The Japs were in merry mood and offered me everything that was going, including some delicious meatballs from a tin. One patted me on the shoulder and said "A very great mistake has been made about you ."

After lunch I was taken to the former Residency; to the O.C. (Officer Commanding), the Corporal delivered an envelope containing the papers signed by me in Jesselton. The O.C. passed them round to other officers who read them and regarded me with interest.

These Japs were of a much better type than I had met previously: well-dressed, confident, even impressive. It stood to reason that somewhere behind this spreading crowd of enthusiastic rice farmers, urban workers, and fishermen, there were well-educated, competent and formidable men. A nation capable of building a battle fleet is capable of anything.

After long delays, we crossed the Belait and Baram rivers. As we entered Miri, collapsed oil tanks and much damaged machinery could be seen. The Miri Kempei-tai headquarters was in a two-storey weatherboard building. I stood against the wall of the office on the second floor while the Corporal reported to the Chief of Military Police. This gentleman was slighter than either of the Brunei or Jesselton Chiefs, unshaven, with a set of prominent teeth and a slight stoop. He appeared equally ruthless. A Malay policeman told me to sit on the floor but I remained standing. Tada noticed this and brought over a chair. As Tada and the Corporal were leaving, the former came across to me and shook me warmly by the hand. "I am returning to Jesselton. Another day, eh?"

Several hours later, I was taken to a prison near the river mouth. It contained three roomy cells with a broad verandah. A high, barbed wire fence surrounded it, and included various outhouses comprising a kitchen, lavatory and some sheds in which prisoners apparently fed. Under a mango tree was an open cement cistern. Near the entrance was a small Guard House.

The Japanese soldiers took my bag, hat, coat, belt, socks and shoes to the Guard House, and locked me in the cell furthest from the river. On the floor was an empty cigarette tin, nothing else.

Seconds later, there was a knock on the wall on my cell. Not Savage again, surely! A cigarette appeared through a crack and fell to the floor. I spoke in English and Malay, and finally discovered that there were two prisoners in the next cell, both Japanese.

I settled in easily. My cell had five windows. During daylight hours I watched oil company barges going to and fro through the river mouth. Nearby, amongst some trees, a squad of Japanese signallers trained for eight hours daily. Just outside the compound was a house belonging to a Malay family. One morning the mother put on a gramophone record. I nodded and smiled and thereafter the woman kept the instrument going several hours daily.

After a few days in prison my clothes were filthy from lying on the floor. Hordes of voracious mosquitoes made sleep difficult. Twice daily I was allowed out to the lavatory. I walked barefooted across the ground and came back dirtier than ever. I was not allowed to bathe or shave.

One night, about midnight, two guards came in with coffee. One said "You know Tolstoy?"

I doubted I had heard correctly. "What's that?"

"You know Tolstoy? Peace and War?"

"Yes, Tolstoy. I know."

"You know Anna Karenina? Good."

"Very good."

"You know Thomas Hardy?"

The two soldiers showed a knowledge of Mark Twain, Honoré de Balzac, Galsworthy and Maeterlinck. One had read Renan's *Life of Jesus* and, astoundingly, Anatole France's *Crime of Sylvestre Bonnard*. I was so surprised that every time a guard showed any inclination to talk I questioned him regarding his excursions into literature. A fair proportion of the soldiers had at least heard of the outstanding literary achievements of other nations. The majority had studied English at what they termed "Middle School".

Three times daily two dixies were brought to the prison and given to the Japanese prisoners. When one of these had finished, his dixie was brought in to me. There were two compartments, the upper containing soup; the lower, cold rice. By the time the soup reached me, the Japanese had extracted nearly all the vegetables and fish. To aggravate matters, one guard often disallowed requests to go to the lavatory, denied drinking water and was generally disagreeable. One morning this soldier opened the door and came in with the dixie but without the usual spoon. I asked for it: but the guard gave a demonstration of eating with his hand. I seized the dixie, walked through the open door and put it down on the verandah. I then returned to the middle of the cell. After a pause the soldier went out and locked the door after him.

At mid-day, much the same performance was repeated.

In the evening the door was unlocked and the soldier came again and put the dixie down in front of me. "Spoon" I said.

The soldier shook his head and said "Spoon — nai."

"No spoon, no eat" I said.

The soldier pointed at the dixie. I found the spoon dug into the rice in the lower compartment, and commenced eating. The soldier rubbed his hand across his upper abdomen and asked "Hungry — kah?" I was hungry but could not eat normally under these circumstances. I closed the dixie and put it near the door.

Late that night, I was asleep on the floor, with the cigarette tin serving as a pillow. I was awakened by something pressing on my chest. The same soldier was standing over me, treading down with one foot. I rolled to one side and stood up. The soldier shoved me against the wall, laughed and then went out.

By the fifth day, with intermittent teasing of this nature, I had had enough, and called for a pencil and paper. I wrote a formal complaint to the Chief of Military Police, asking for permission to change my clothes, have a bath, to be given a blanket, mosquito net, food and better treatment generally.

Several hours later the guards came to my cell, gave me my bag and told me to put on my hat, coat, belt and shoes. My cell was closed and we proceeded to Kempei-tai headquarters. I thought all this had resulted from my letter, but it soon became evident that this was the day of the court-martial. Several officers spent some time examining sheets of evidence.

I sat near the head of the stairs. I took very great care to acknowledge every passing Jap. This had its amusing side. Officers were studying the Fighting Doctor's misdeeds, and here in person was the unshaven, unwashed villain of the piece observing all the courtesies meticulously.

My prospect being not over-bright, I spent quite a time considering the problem of contending with Kempei-tai and military interrogation. Obviously, it was essential to avoid giving offence, particularly by "thinking lightly". I resolved to stick to the truth, even to admitting error on unimportant matters: and to use a minimum of words. The Japanese had all the evidence before them, and with no barristers to argue for days on end, it was clear that the court-martial would be brief. The impression created in the final confrontation was all important. Two things seemed relevant — the understandable desire of the Japanese to be accepted as civilized people and to be treated with respect, and a similar desire to be regarded as awesome members of the most powerful military machine in history. So there it was: sincerity; humility. If possible a faint trace of awe. Definitely no levity. In this way, I defined my theoretical approach to a difficult problem; and then smiled at my own futility.

The Military Court sat about 3 p.m. in a small room overlooking a basketball court. An Air Force Officer was in charge. He appeared to be of strong character and above average in intelligence and general appearance. Another officer with a moustache wandered in and out of the room, leaning for periods on a window-sill, listening. At times, he seemed to be amused. There were two interpreters: one, a Eurasian who, poor fellow, said little throughout; the other, a middle-aged Japanese civilian named Ida, a planter before the war. Ida spoke both English and Malay, but seemed to be more at ease in the latter.

Tea was served. The Air Force Officer passed a plate of biscuits to me. While we munched, I was asked my name, age, whether single or married, the age of my parents and where I was educated. I was not asked who paid for my education. Perhaps the officer guessed this, being considerably more worldly-wise than either Mr Ino or Hirosumi Smidzu, Practitioner of the Indirect Art. Then Mr Ida asked

"Are you an army officer?" Everyone put down their biscuits.

"No. I am a doctor."

"Have you ever been an army officer?"

"No, not at any time."

"Did you ever wish to become an officer?"

"I have never been interested in anything but medicine."

"Why did you write this letter, the officer asks?"

I was half-expecting this question. I explained that the Jap landing had produced the utmost confusion. Many worried government servants had run away from their offices, even from their wives. Two members of the medical staff could not be traced. As District Surgeon, I was afraid that more would run away and so dislocate the whole medical service. I had written the letter so that the staff would settle down and continue work as usual. I gave a brief description of telephone and bridle path communication in the Interior of Borneo and drew a rough map. For a time the officer was fascinated by the chaos the Jap Army had produced in the heart of nowhere. "You Japanese are very patriotic. The British are the same. We were ashamed we could not resist the Japanese when they came. You were too strong. All we could do was to hold out hope for the future."

I felt that Ida was helping me to some extent. Perhaps he had had European friends before the war. My last statements appeared to go down very well.

Mr Ida continued "It says here that you urged people to fight the Japanese. You are a doctor. Why did you do this?"

"Mr Ida, could I see the letter which has caused this trouble?"

The letter was handed to me and, word by word, I pointed out this sentence to Ida: "In this country, where we have nothing to fight with, we must just accept the position as it is."

More care should have been taken in composing this sentence. However, it was in basic English. Mr Ida said "Yes, it does say that." He read it again, and then he and the Jap officer spoke together for some time.

"The officer asked, "Did you write this letter to calm your staff? Now, is this so?"

"Yes, exactly" I said, with a feeling of relief.

A little more Japanese. Then, "The officer wants to know, did you have anything else in your mind when you wrote this letter?"

The Air Force Officer had spoken to Mr Ida with great intensity. I looked at him before replying. Previously, the man had been calm and self-possessed, but now he looked at me as if he would liquidate me on the spot if I admitted any ulterior motive.

"I had nothing else in my mind," I said.

While the officer did up two of his coat buttons and calmed down, Mr Ida and I sipped our tea. This habit of expressing determination and fighting spirit by gross facial contortion was disconcerting to prisoners; for, at one and the same time, it inspired both nervousness and amusement — and the latter had to be concealed at all costs.

The various other charges against me were examined with some expedition. The officer actually laughed when he came to an alleged declaration of mine that the Japanese tortured women and children and practised rape. "You didn't say that!" How could anyone say that of a civilized people! The question of Japanese planes being made of bamboo was dealt with as follows: Mr Ida said, "It says here that you told people the Japanese planes were made of bamboo".

The officer was turning over a page of the papers in front of him. He paused, and for ten seconds fixed his eyes very objectively on an embarrassed prisoner. No questions.

Finally, the officer folded up one or two kilograms of evidence and walked out. That was that! No truncheons, no stretching of the mouth, no ropes. Mr Ida turned to me. "The officer says, shortly we will let you know what is going to happen. Now, there is another matter." He lowered his voice and spoke gravely. "The Chief of Military Police says you have written rudely to him. He is most upset."

This was serious. No M.P. broods over anything for long; in my experience they were men of action. "I did not mean to be rude, Mr Ida. The letter was written quite politely."

"The M.P. says you complained of everything. You have hurt his feelings."

"Mr Ida, in prison I had no mosquito net, no blanket, no bath and little food."

The interpreter became quite exasperated. "You do not seem to understand, doctor! Sometimes things must just be like this! You must be satisfied." This had gone on long enough. "I understand now, Mr Ida. I will not complain again."

The interpreter went to the Chief's desk. Fortunately the matter rested. I was taken back to the prison. I handed my hat, coat, belt, socks and shoes to the Corporal in charge and wandered forlornly to my cell.

As the days passed, my discomfort increased; no haircut for two months, no bath, shave or change of clothes since leaving Brunei. The nights were stuffy and the mosquito population seemed to double every evening. One day, when returning from the latrine, I stopped by the cement water tank. In it was 30 centimetres of yellow water and hundreds of mosquito larvae and decaying mango leaves. I climbed in and washed my hands, feet and face; then I walked across the roots of the mango tree and along a cement drain leading towards the steps of the prison. At the end of the drain I stopped. My feet were wet and several metres of dirty grey sand separated me from the steps.

The sentry saw my dilemma. He put down his rifle, came over and bent down in front of me and offered his back. I was taken by surprise. "No, no! It doesn't matter. Tid'apa!" I said.

The sentry insisted. So I got on his back and was carried to the steps. I gave the sentry a sincere bow and said "aregato". It was an extraordinary little incident.

The Malay woman next door became progressively more sympathetic. Once when the guard was away, she said "What sort of people are these, Tuan? I don't understand. Be patient and Tuan Allah will see that everything becomes as it was before the short ones entered the country."

Some days after the trial, the two Jap prisoners and I were called from the cells. I was given my hat, coat, belt, socks and shoes to put on, and then handed my bag. The prison was closed and all the guards left. With the Jap prisoners I went by taxi to Kempei-tai headquarters. The Japanese were very much down in the dumps.

Before long two senior officers arrived, and one of the Jap prisoners was called into the room where my court-martial was held. The door was closed. Presently, distinct sobbing could be heard. Ten minutes later the prisoner came out and sat on a bench near the stairway. The other Jap prisoner was then called in, and a short time later he too broke down, sobbing. When he emerged, he went over and sat beside his friend. Heads bowed, the pair looked utterly miserable: Understandably so, perhaps; they had been sentenced to death. I patted one on the knee and said, "Don't worry."

I waited with some impatience. At eleven o'clock I joined the Kempei-tai staff at morning tea and ate a cake. When I returned to the office, the Chief M.P. called me across and spoke to a Chinese interpreter. The interpreter said "The Chief M.P. wants to know if you agree to become the doctor at Kuala Belait? You will work amongst the local people."

"I do."

The Chief M.P. was smiling in a friendly fashion.

"The Chief says you will be paid wages and will work in a hospital."

"Thank you," I said.

"Here is your bag. Have a wash and change your clothes it you want to."

I went into a room with a washbasin and mirror. I lathered for ten minutes before using the razor; even so, the operation was painful. When I came out again, the Chief M.P., through the interpreter, said, "You are now free. You can go anywhere you like."

I didn't quite know what to do.

"The Chief M.P. says to go for a walk now."

"Thanks very much."

I was nonplussed. Miri was new to me — there didn't seem to be anywhere I wanted to go. The interpreter said "Go down into the street and walk about. Come back here later."

I went down the stairs and, taking pot luck, I turned right and walked up the street. I felt as if I was convalescing after a prolonged illness, uncertain and a little unsteady. I had gone perhaps 80 metres when I heard shouting. Three figures were at a window of the Kempei-tai building, waving. One shouted "Don't go too far that way. Go this way."

I turned and walked slowly back. I passed "The Spiro Nightclub" and came to a Chinese restaurant and entered. The old shopkeeper greeted me politely and showed me to a table upstairs. No-one else was present. "What do you wish to eat?"

"First a beer, Towkei. Is there any?"

"Perhaps I can get a bottle. I will see."

"After that, a large plate of fried rice. Have you any, Towkei?"

"Native rice, no, Tuan. I'll give you Siam No. 1. It's splendid to eat." The old man went off. A European dropping in for a meal was something of an event these days, but he showed no surprise. In a few minutes he was back again with a bottle of Tiger beer and a glass. I poured out the beer and looked at the bubbles for a moment. Then I took a long cool draught. Having had little to eat for ten days, I was ready for the fine meal the Towkei put down in front of me. After I had finished, I paid for it, and then strolled back to the Kempei-tai.

Some hours later, the Chief M.P. and the interpreter took me across the street and down a small lane leading into the centre of the Chinese section of the town. We turned into an old, unpainted dwelling house, and went upstairs to the back verandah. I was shown a room. "The M.P. says you can sleep here. You are free but must come and see us at the Kempei-tai when you have time."

The Chief spoke again to the interpreter.

"The Chief asks if you were born in Australia?" He pronounced it "Oss-tray-lee-ah". "Yes."

"The Chief asks if Australians will be friendly towards the Japanese?"

"Once we were allies. At present, we are at war. Perhaps this will pass."

"The Chief says the Americans attacked Japan and the Japanese were forced to fight. The Japanese are peaceful and wish to join Australia in what you call prosperity."

They departed. In going, the Chief gave a bow and saluted. I did not know what to make of him. Certainly, his office wasn't crowded with informers and unhappy Chinese for interrogation.

It was a very strange room given to me. A huge fourposter bed occupied half the floor space. The net was down and the bed had not been made. Partly covering the untidy sheets was an eiderdown. The room was crammed with articles of every kind — tables, chairs, brooms, violins, gramophones, window blinds, bathtubs, commodes, and swollen sugar bags. I was pleased when several Chinese oil company clerks arrived and introduced themselves. They called for coffee and soya bean cakes from below. One said "They are very bad people, sir. They have beaten many Chinese. There was one Chinese here who owned some land. He had papers to show it. When the shorties landed here early in the morning — it was still dark and raining, my how it was raining, man! — well, he was frightened and ran away to the jungle. Quite natural, is it not? Many people ran away. Well, when he came back, it seems another man had settled on his property, and he won't get off! So he goes along to the M.P. and he puts in his complaint. 'Where is the other man?' asks the M.P. So he gets this other fellow and brings him in front of the M.P. 'It seems you two have been quarrelling!' They admitted it, because it was true, wasn't it? And then the M.P. called a lot of shorties and they gave these two Chinese such a hiding. They beat them and beat them! Both of them! They hit them until they were nearly half dead! ''Now get out and don't quarrel any more!'' said the M.P. One had his legs broken and he couldn't get away anyway, could he?''

The Chinese laughed at this, as was their wont.

''Which M.P. was it?'' I asked.

''Why, this one now. Just a minute ago he was here.'' The coffee was delicious and I enjoyed it. I asked who normally occupied the room. ''Oh, that fellow! He hasn't been seen since. He was a looter and ran about grabbing everything. The Malays call it 'rampas'. Anything at all he took, especially if it was European. Finally, the M.P. grabbed him.''

''How do I get a bath here?''

''Just give a shout to the people down below.''

''Would you mind giving a shout for me?'' A visitor obliged. Presently, the good-natured Chinese left, and soon I was sitting in a small tin tub in a slightly bigger bathroom. The walls were as black as ink. I baled hot water over myself and felt fine. I turned in early and had the best sleep for weeks.

In the morning I was called to the Kempei-tai and was told I was going to an ''hotel''. I sat about waiting for hours. At lunchtime I set off for the Chinese restaurant, but was called back and ordered into a waiting car.

''Where are we going? What about my luggage?'' I asked the interpreter.

''Oh, that! You had better bring it quickly. Don't waste time, please.'' I hurried to the looter's room, collected my things and returned to the car. An hour later we started off. In another hour I found myself in a private room at the end of an empty ward in the Oil Company hospital. An armed sentry was stationed ten yards away. I wondered what had happened to the patients.

About 7 p.m. I was summoned to the Medical Officer's quarters. I was introduced to Doctors Harada, Ito, Tanaka and Ivanaga. They were friendly and I was pleased about this, but conversation was difficult. Two wore only loincloths and slippers — so attired, and with shaven heads, few would have guessed they were practitioners of the direct art. After a while conversation took a political turn. One said ''Japan - must - fight. You rich - not many. Japan poor - plenty people. Australia and New Zealand gentlemen - not want - friends - with - Japanese.'' Another added ''Australia is very weak, very weak, you understand weak?'' They knew something of my recent history. When one said ''You wished to fight Japanese soldier before. Not now.'' I felt embarrassed, but they were amused at such eccentric behaviour. After about an hour I left them and was pleased to get to bed.

Early next morning soldiers paraded outside the ward. Dr Ito conducted the parade. He looked smart in a new uniform, polished leggings, and a red sash passing over one shoulder: dignified and quaint was a fair description. He seemed a good citizen. Later in the morning Dr Harada visited me. He was middle-aged and reserved. ''What do you think of Japanese victories? Singapore, Java, Manila and many more?''

''We are rather surprised you have advanced so fast.''

''Ah! You are surprised?''

''Yes.''

''Well, we Japanese, we also are very surprised.''

I was impressed by this admission. I said, ''Why has Japan been fighting China so long? The Chinese haven't a military reputation like Japan.'' Harada put considerable emphasis on his words when he replied. ''Chinese soldiers, very brave, very brave indeed. We kill - kill - kill and still they fight. We kill more, still they fight. They have not good weapons. Chinese soldiers, very brave.'' I looked at Dr Harada with respect. This was the only time I ever heard a Japanese say a good word for the Chinese.

On one occasion Dr Ito noticed that I had left some rice on my plate. He made a gesture of distaste, drew a picture of a loaf of bread, said ''pang'' and pointed down his throat and chewed. I nodded; yes, I liked bread. Thereafter I received two small bread rolls and a cup of tea two or three times daily. As a rule, the Japanese orderly overlooked one meal a day. Once Ito came in after the normal meal time and asked (using signs) had I eaten? I shook my head and said ''Pang-nai.'' Ito pulled me by the sleeve, pointed to the kitchen, and made a series of slapping movements. He tapped me on the chest and pointed to the kitchen again. Obviously, he wanted me to give the cook a slapping.

Dr Ito gave a most amusing resumé of the war. He knew little English and no Malay, and, after trying me in German, he drew a picture of five large ships and three little ships. Then he said ''Pearl Harbour'' and beat his fists on the table, shouting ''Bomb! bomb! bomb!'' He indicated a number of towns like Batavia, Rangoon and Macassar, and gave them ''the works'' one after the other. ''Bomb! bomb! bomb!''

This business was infectious and I felt like drawing a map of Japan and banging the table and shouting ''Bomb! bomb! bomb!'' However, I had learnt the value of reasonable restraint.

On the third, fourth and fifth days I was told to pack my bag because I was being taken to Kuala Belait immediately. Twice I sat for hours outside an office waiting for a bus. On the third occasion I was taken to the Kempei-tai. In the office was a group which included Mr Ida, the interpreter, and Mr Fukui of Sandakan, the very man Abdul Majit, the leper, had decided to assassinate.

Fukui shook hands with me. He looked very concerned. ''What *have* you been doing, doctor?'' he asked. I smiled and shrugged my shoulders. Fukui added ''You are accompanying me to Belait. I am returning now and will soon be leaving for an unknown destination.''

Presently I found myself engaged in conversation with Mr Ida. ''Mr Fukui tells me he knew you very well before the war. He said he once had some drinks with you before lunch at a friend's house. He was very impressed.''

I was tired and not quite with it, and could think of nothing to say. In a few weeks everything had changed. Conduct, values, words and meanings, all were different. I felt Mr Ida's eyes upon me. ''It is very kind of you to say so, Mr Ida,'' I murmured.

The interpreter leant over and said confidentially, ''Fukui tells me he is leaving very soon for an unknown destination.'' I drew in my breath, very much as the Japanese do. I felt exhausted and could not control a sigh.

On the way to Kuala Belait, Fukui was polite, with but a touch of distance in his manner. We crossed the Baram River and settled down to wait for the car which Fukui had ordered from Belait. It didn't come, of course. As time went on Fukui began to look more and more upset. He walked up and down with a mixed air of injured self-importance and exasperation, saying ''But I ordered it to be here, and they promised! Oh, these people, you never know what they are going to do!''

Fukui was telling me exactly nothing.

A few days later, in Kuala Belait, a Chinese clerk gave me a Japanese news sheet produced by ''these people'' some weeks previously. This is what I read:

''JESSELTON WAR NEWS   5th February, 1942
DR KELL'S CASE

Why does the arrest of Dr Kell want the Public Judgment?

He is one of the worst anti-Japanese men who tried to agitate the mind of the people.

Since he is a doctor, his words are believed by the public. By means of his occupation and rank, he stirred the minds of the submissive, steady and honest hearts of the natives in the West Coast by telling lies everywhere.

The following propaganda was broadcast by him to the natives of the Interior:

'The English Army is now bombing Formosa, therefore, it will not be long that the British and Americans will attack Japan.'

Now the Japanese have almost become the leaders of the new Asia, and nearly completed their mission: even then, Dr Kell tried to bluff the public in the front. We must hate this sort of conduct, that is selfish as well as cunning. He thought that this is an opportune time and a chance to talk all the nonsense.

He is a doctor. Why should he hide his rifle, revolver, gun and ammunition — such a good lot.

In reality he is not at all a doctor, but a real fighting man: the way he kept the arms and ammunition shows it. By using these arms he tried to render a bloodshed amongst us Asiatics.

The propaganda was a well made one that almost everybody believed it. The Native and the Chinese now understand what Japan stands for, and begin to like them very much, and the kind treatment given them by the Japanese Military is known everywhere. Representatives of Natives and Chinese came and apologised and said that they must always take Japan as their only leader, and swear from their very hearts that they are to co-operate to make a New Great Asia.

It is now clear why Dr Kell was taken into imprisonment. He is the real enemy of the Asiatics. Dr Kell has gone too far and against the order given. The offence is so great. It is also said in the public, and letters are pouring into our office from every place asking that he should be shot, but, in spite of this, the Japanese Military, who is the leader of the Asiatics, do not try to punish him so severely until today. We cannot say what will happen to this man in future. It is our motto to treat everybody very kindly and also to be on the side who act rightly and we must punish those who go in the wrong way, whether big or small.

Chapter 7

KUALA BELAIT 1942

The District Officer, Kuala Belait, found quarters for me — semi-detached, a bedroom and sitting-room, with a kitchen, bathroom and lavatory across a small cement-covered backyard. I soon realised that I had fallen amongst very good people. My neighbour, Abang Ali, was married, with three children, affectionately nicknamed the Crying One (Si-Menangis), the Laughing One (Si-Ketawa), and the Crustacean (Si-Ketam). The latter had reached the crawling stage.

The Government Sanitary Inspector, Chong Fah, helped me settle in. He became a firm friend from the word go. He begged and borrowed the basic domestic requirements and engaged an old Hailam cook who complained angrily about the high prices and the absence of everything Europeans were accustomed to eat. A Ceylonese named Di Alvis knocked on the door, came in, shook hands and said "Well, doctor, we are still the same old British citizens."

Ten years previously Kuala Belait had been an insignificant Malay village closely invested by sea, river and coastal swamp. Then a vast underground lake of oil was discovered nearby. Fields opened on either side at Seria and Miri; Chinese traders arrived and Kuala Belait became the shopping centre for Seria. A 16 kilometre strip of asphalt road connected the two places.

A line of clerks' houses, in which I now lived, lay in the centre of the town area. The town consisted of a small main bazaar, a Chinese village, a Malay village, company workshops and quarters near the river mouth, a hospital, a Post Office and Wireless Station, a Police Station and a cinema. For a small town, there was an extraordinary number of clubs: every section of the community had one.

There were two missions, Church of England and Roman Catholic. In the former, furnishings had been smashed and soldiers had used two corners of the building near the entrance as latrines. One day I wandered in and had a look. There was an air of historical familiarity about the shambles.

Along the beach were the former European Club, the Residency, the Forestry Officer's home, the rest house and three cottages for company clerks. The ex-Forestry Officer's home, now occupied by the Military Police, was already referred to in Chinese as the House of Terror.

Every part of the town was within a kilometre of my house. Between the government clerks' houses and those on the beach was open land recently planted with coconuts. Often domestic cats could be seen tormenting grey land crabs in the grass. On the outskirts, as far as Mile 2, people were busy felling jungle, digging drains, and opening gardens. The new land was still very sour.

Township of Kuala Belait.

The first day, there was a conference. Present were Dr Hashimoto, full to the eyebrows with samsu; Mr Fukui; several other Japs and myself. Fukui acted as interpreter. I was instructed to act as Medical Officer to the company staff, to government servants, and to the public generally; salary, $75 a month plus $5 laundry allowance. No servants. I could accept fees from well-to-do civilians, providing they were Chinese. Towards the end of the conference Hashimoto woke up and was most affable.

For the first ten days, I worked in the Out-Patients Department in the company hospital. The Senior Dresser was a Sikh named Balwant Singh, in his early fifties. He spoke English very well and made it plain he did not welcome the Occupation. Under him was Kim Sing, small, cheerful and friendly. There was also a Sikh technician, Chundra Singh, rather frightened by events and inclined to suspect the change might be permanent.

The first working morning a Jap sat down at a table with Balwant Singh and myself and tried to follow the conversation. In the afternoon he introduced himself as Dr Kitagawa. "I am the Health Officer" he said, bowing and smiling. "You must meet my Chief. Come, if you please."

We were half way to the sea shore when Dr Kitagawa stopped and said "I like you very much". He bowed and laughed, and we continued on to the former Residency. I waited on the kitchen verandah while Dr Kitagawa went inside. In a few minutes he returned. "Mr Saito is busy. He will come soon."

We waited. Nearby, an orderly was breaking up a wardrobe for firewood. Finally, Mr Saito came out to farewell a visitor. Then he re-entered the Residency, deliberately ignoring a call from Dr Kitagawa. Snubbed, we returned to the hospital.

Next day we had more success. The three of us sat down at a table in the covered way between the kitchen and house. We were joined at tea by the cook and orderlies.

Saito was middle-aged and tall. In peace time he was a brewer, a good public-spirited man. Dr Kitagawa knew enough English to interpret. A sackful of European male evening wear was brought out; then magazine illustrations of white men attired in dinner jackets and tails. I was asked to fit the pieces together into conventional evening dress. Before I left Saito invited me to come to the Residency whenever I wished. Dr Kitagawa said, "We are sorry. A big mistake has been made about you."

When Mr Fukui left for his unknown destination, I gave him a letter, addressed to Keningau, asking for my belongings to be sent. At least, it was an optimistic gesture.

The Civil Dispensary was opened in the former Government Servants Club and I transferred to it. The building was single-storied; in front of it was the football field, behind it land planted with coconuts. The staff consisted of a Malay Dresser, Hussein, and a Malay Attendant, Sayed. The government midwife, Mrs Tan Pan Siong, opened a Baby Clinic in one half of the Dispensary; assisting her was a native midwife, Pangiran Hitam, a perfectly delightful person.

The Sanitary Inspector, Chong Fah, called on me daily. One evening he said, "Doctor, all government servants must attend school to learn Japanese. Anyone who cannot speak it in a year is going to get the sack. The order seems to include you. Anyway, why not come along? It will pass the time."

The "Jap class" was held every evening in the Chung Hwa School. A young Military Policeman, Kato, was the teacher. There were thirty-five students — Chinese, Malays, Indians, Eurasians and myself. Ages ranged from 10 to 50, with an I.Q. range even more extreme. Kato wrote the Katakana alphabet on a blackboard and the class ran through it twenty times every lesson. Ah, ee, oo, eh, or. Kah, kee, koo, keh, kor. And so on. Then Kato wrote a Japanese word in Katakana, and read out its meaning. The students made notes in Chinese, English, Romanised Malay or Jawi. A clerk from Malabar employed a script resembling the contortions of an earthworm. On the third evening, Kato asked me to write the Jap word for "distant" on the board, and was very enthusiastic when I managed it correctly.

The official opening of the Japanese brothel opposite the Chung Hwa School excited great interest. Wreaths of flowers and yards of ribbons decorated the building. Carpenters had converted the upstairs rooms into small cubicles by means of three-ply partitions; downstairs there was a small room like a ticket office in a cinema. Scales of charges were one dollar for ordinary ranks, three dollars for officers, five dollars for privileged civilians.

In the evening a curious crowd gathered outside. As I went past to "Jap class" two of the girls took off their skirts in front of the open door. One smiled and waved her dress to her audience in the street. The young girls were from Taiwan (Formosa). The authorities were shipping boat-loads of them to forces in South East Asia. The Belait people benefited greatly from this arrangement: I never heard of a single assault on a local girl by a Japanese soldier.

One Sunday night, Dr Kitagawa knocked at my door. He said, "We will visit a Chinese friend." We set off along the road. The moon was up and Dr Kitagawa said, "The moon, it is very beautiful. Do you not agree?" We came to a house surrounded by a high palisade. Inside, the midwife and her husband made us welcome. We sat around a table laden with Chinese wines and makan "kitchee" (small eats). Dr Kitagawa was extremely jovial. After several drinks he complimented his host on his wife's appearance. An hour later, he decided to show his admiration of the opposite sex in a practical manner. He stood up and reaching for his coat, said to me "Now we will go to the prostitutes."

He took me by the arm and was bowing farewell before I managed to splutter "But I can't do that! I am the doctor here!"

Dr Kitagawa's face registered incomprehension. "What?" he asked. "What did you say?'' Our host repeated my words. Dr Kitagawa laughed outright. ''Ah, I am a doctor also. Doctors understand. Come along.''

I sat down resolutely and drew Dr Kitagawa towards his chair. ''Let's have another drink first, doctor,'' I said. I filled my colleague's glass two-thirds full of neat Ngo Kah Pi. ''Here's fun'' I said. I knew there was venereal disease amongst the Taiwan prostitutes: the old gonococcus was having a ball! I had seen some very frightening slides. Indeed, I had recommended that several girls go off duty, on worker's compensation.

Conversation was resumed. I watched Dr Kitagawa's glass: as soon as the level sank appreciably I filled it up again. Dr Kitagawa gradually responded to this treatment: so indeed, did I. Every time I filled his glass my colleague, showing perfect manners, reciprocated. At midnight two medicos rose unsteadily and thanked their host. Outside, the fresh air hit us like a hammer. Dr Kitagawa made the distance to a known destination. My distance was fortunately significantly less than his: in a short time I was in bed at home.

Next morning Dr Kitagawa arrived at my house looking as if he had never had a drink in his life. ''I am sorry . . '' he said, as he sat down laughing. I gave him a bottle of underground stout. Before long, he face was quite red.

Dr Kitagawa was a rare and refreshing character. He was genuinely polite, laughed freely, liked everyone he met, did little or no work and wasn't morbidly sensitive. He made no effort to impress anyone and everyone liked him. He left the coat of his uniform open, disclosing a singlet which he never bothered to change. To him the war was fine. You sail into a harbour, occupy someone else's house, use the furniture for firewood, get the best of food from looted shops and spend the day meeting the perfectly charming local people and drinking tea with them. A few more like him and the relatively sticky Europeans would soon be forgotten. He shaped up as a greater menace to our cause than a company of bloodthirsty soldiers.

Beri-beri was prevalent on the oil-fields and Dr Kitagawa rightly prescribed rice-bran tablets known as Wakamoto pills; before long he was known as ''Dr Wakamoto''. Unfortunately a Departmental Chief at Seria.heard of this homely nickname. He called his staff together and shouted angrily to an interpreter. The latter turned to the assembled clerks and said ''Everyone who has referred to Kitagawa as Dr Wakamoto is to receive a thrashing. All who have done so please come forward.'' No one was injured in the rush to confess.

One afternoon Dr Kitagawa and Balwant Singh called for me. We motored out to see some Indian P.O.W.s from the 21st Punjab Machine-gun Regiment at Seria. There were 212 in all, billeted in kongses built for oil-field labourers. There were four Europeans including the O.C., Lieutenant Hodges. He and 75 men had surrendered at Kuching. The Japs had bayoneted the wounded in front of their eyes. A composite force of Sikhs and Moslems, these chappati-and paratha-consuming Punjabis were unaccustomed to eating local or limed rice and received scarcely any fruit, vegetables, fish or meat. Dysentery had broken out and soldiers unable to work were being beaten. Feeling was running high. Hodges spoke to me of escape but it was clearly impossible with so many men sick.

Balwant Singh and I visited the P.O.W.s several times, taking what presents we could. On one occasion I stayed for lunch. The four Europeans had practically no cutlery and flies swarmed over everything. I took tea from a marmalade jar. Over 80 Punjabis were off duty due to starvation and most of them had beri-beri, failing vision, sore mouths and scrotal dermatitis. Several dozen were down with dysentery. Water supply and sanitary arrangements had broken down. Some toilet wells were choked with maggots. Many Punjabis said they preferred to die like soldiers in an attack on the Japanese guards, and had to be restrained.

After rounds, I was invited to tea by the Jap N.C.O. in charge, a young man named Wada, who systematically beat the unfit P.O.W.s and traded their sugar and tea rations for his personal requirements. To be in a position to help the P.O.W.s at all, I could not refuse. I sat at a table with Wada and the guards and sipped well-sugared tea. Wada was affable. We spoke of the fortunes of war, of Fujisan, of patriotic suicide and photography.

I saw the Jap authorities about the P.O.W.s, entering a plea for every-day necessities, religious books for both Sikhs and Moslems, medical supplies, bedding and mosquito nets. I asked that they be allowed their own vegetable garden, suggesting that only fit soldiers were capable of doing the work required of them. Shortly afterwards I heard a rumour that sick Punjabis were being transferred to hospital and I mentioned this to Balwant Sing. "Laugh it off!" was the Dresser's answer. He had just informed Dr Hashimoto that if the unfit Punjabis were not admitted for treatment, they would die. "Then let them die," said the Chief Military Surgeon.

Much to my surprise and delight, my clothes and two medical books arrived from Keningau, thanks to "Bukit" Hill. This made life immeasurably easier.

My daily life settled down much as follows. I got up when Kuki arrived around 6.30 a.m. and had a cup of tea. Dr Kitagawa had given me Shaw's *Collected Prefaces* to his plays, and *How Green was My Valley*, by Richard Llewellyn. I read till 8 a.m., then bathed, shaved, and put on a white suit. I had very tough bristles and my few remaining razor blades had to be sharpened repeatedly in a tumbler. The tap water was coloured and my white clothes soon took on a yellow tinge.

After breakfast I went to the Dispensary. Here, the shelves were almost empty. Not a single stock mixture could be dispensed. There were a dozen pairs of dental forceps, and these outnumbered, almost twice, all the other surgical instruments put together. There was some catgut and twenty-odd metres of horsehair. Dresser Hussein bought a thermometer from a Jap soldier for one dollar. One valuable piece of equipment was an enema syringe.

With nothing to dispense except advice, it was a busy morning if I saw 20 patients. Usually I was home by 11.30 a.m. I then changed into shorts and read until tiffin. Sweet potatoes and rice formed a large part of my diet, and I put on weight rapidly. I read till 5 p.m., when Kuki turned on black coffee, plus a tapioca cake of three coloured layers, each with the consistency of thick glue. It wobbled if I happened to move the plate, which I often did just to pass away the time.

After tea, I skipped exactly three hundred times in the courtyard. I dislike this type of exercise very much and persisted only because it occurred to me that I might have to cover ground quite smartly at some future date if I was to survive. After that, a bath, and then "Jap class" for an hour. The walk home from the Chung Hwa School with Abang Ali, Chong Fah or Chundra Singh was the best part of the day.

Dinner came at seven — this only after a battle with Kuki who wanted it at 5 p.m. After that, almost nothing. Reading was difficult, the glass of the single oil lamp blackening rapidly due to poor quality kerosene. Often I sat alone in the dark for several hours; at other times I sat on the front steps talking to Chong Fah, neighbour Abang Ali or other government clerks. One evening I went down to the beach and sat on the sand in front of Kempei-tai headquarters. No-one objected. After that, I often walked along the beach after dark, looking out to sea. A forlorn hope, of course, was an Allied landing party. Most nights, Japanese vessels were anchored offshore, all lights blazing. Apparently they were not in the least bit concerned about Allied submarines. It worried me. These were oil-fields — why weren't they receiving Allied attention?

At 11 p.m. or thereabouts I went to bed. My capacity for sleep varied greatly.

Breaking this monotonous routine were occasional calls to patients' homes. It surprised me that the Japs said nothing when I took my first trip beyond town limits. A Chinese came to the midwife with a story of a complicated childbirth at Kuala Liang, nearly 28 kilometres eastwards. He said the baby's head had been delivered about midnight, since when there had been no further advance. The midwife hired a car and off we went. After one breakdown, we eventually arrived, to learn that the baby had been born as a breech presentation at 7 p.m. the previous night and all was well.

For babies, particularly, the town became increasingly inhospitable. Due to malnutrition, breast feeding could not be maintained. Infantile beri-beri and dysentery were prevalent. In the Register of Deaths under ''Duration of illness'' such entries as ''Half an hour'' or ''Two hours'' were common. Many parents did not seem to know when their children were critically ill. I was frequently called to see a restless, pallid and cyanotic baby, crying weakly, tossing its head from side to side and bringing up most of the food offered to it. Often, it was too late to do anything. In the Malay village a woman nursed a wizened little creature with the wrinkled skin of a man of eighty. I asked, ''What do you feed it on?'' The mother, a pleasant woman, laughingly said ''Only sugar water, Tuan. What else is there?'' There was no happiness in her laughter. Day after day the child took its sugar water, clung to its smiling mother like a strange little animal, and for some reason did not develop cardiac beri-beri like many others.

Twice within a week I saw babies already dead, still being nursed by uncomprehending mothers. Indeed, babies became a liability in many houses and some were given away or sold.

The Baby Clinic did not flourish. The small supply of tinned milk was soon exhausted, and there was nothing to give beyond advice. No people are more devoted to children than the Chinese, yet they repeated and laughed at this joke about the dispensary scales — ''You can weigh your baby each week to find out how fast it is going downhill.''

One day there came a sudden cry from the Out-Patients. ''Here comes the M.P.!'' I went to the window, as several patients rushed out of sight. Kato the Second came swiftly on a bicycle, leapt off and ran in shouting ''Come quickly, Doctor! Hyaku!''

I mounted a patient's bicycle and followed Kato to Kampong China. Kato-san, on a house to house visit doing a survey of sewing machines, had entered a dwelling to find a baby in convulsions. He was so startled that he forgot it was a Chinese baby and did not matter. Mopping his face, he told me how frightened he was: he had never seen anything like it before.

On another occasion I was summoned urgently to see a pregnant woman ''half-dead' 'from loss of blood. As I approached the woman's house, a crowd of agitated Hakka women in the road shouted ''Yi-sang Loi! The Doctor comes!'' From the house itself came wails of despair. I pushed my way into the bedroom through a jostling crowd. Pandemonium reigned. There were eight women standing on the bed itself, forming a circle around the patient, whom they were holding upright and shaking vigorously up and down. Simultaneously, raw ginger was being rubbed on her limbs and face. The poor woman had fainted: there was blood everywhere. Blood was being shaken from her like water from a cloth dampener on to an ironing board. The friends were persuaded to leave the room, with some difficulty. Ruptured varices were the trouble and these were controlled by sutures.

Some days later, the bleeding recurred and the performance in the house was repeated almost without variation by relatives and friends, as if the first incident had been merely a dress rehearsal.

One of our regular out-patients was a Chinese woman with cirrhosis of the liver. Once a fortnight she was carried to the Dispensary sitting up in a large cane laundry basket suspended from a carrying pole by ropes. On each occasion pints of fluid were tapped from her abdomen and off she went full of gratitude and slightly breathless from the ordeal.

As stocks of opium ran low, chronic smokers came to the Dispensary like blowflies, begging for licences or restoration of cut rations. Their illnesses were always severe and nothing equalled their inventions, pretences and persistence. One, noticing the consideration with which the Chinese woman was treated, hired her friends to carry him to the Dispensary in the cane laundry basket. When I proved unco-operative, he paid off the carriers and went home on shanks' pony.

One evening, I received an invitation to the Residency. I arrived to find four Japs, including Mr Saito and Dr Kitagawa in the lounge. They had just received home mail. Photographs of pretty women were circulated and there was free comment and hearty laughter. Dr Kitagawa had several photographs of his baby. They were magnificent and he was delighted. Presently he said to me "We and Mr Saito will go to an Army Officer's house."

This we did. I was introduced to a Lieutenant and we sat down at a table on which were bottles of whisky, gin, brandy, greenlight, curacao, port, sherry, benedictine, even claret cup. In fact, a good selection of drinks normally consumed by well-to-do planters. An orderly served everyone with weak Chinese tea.

Dr Kitagawa said "The Officer, our host, says Anzac cobbers are good, but Americans are very bad." He burst out laughing. The Officer shouted "Orang Australia — bagus! Australians are just the stuff!''

The Lieutenant was approaching his forties and looked very tough. The three spoke together and then Dr Kitagawa addressed me "You gave me stout. Mr Saito knows stout. I enjoyed it. When I returned home I was very talkative.''

There was further laughter. Then the Lieutenant picked up a bottle of port and poured some into my tea, then some into his own. Dr Kitagawa and the Resident poured whisky into their cups. Then everyone drank a toast.

Dr Kitagawa said, "Do you like whisky?''

Before I had time to reply my Japanese colleague poured some into my tea and port.

The party continued in this fashion. The Japanese picked up bottle after bottle and poured indiscriminately. An orderly was active with the teapot, topping up with this benign beverage as the impulse seized him.

It was an extraordinary party. After a time the Lieutenant began to shout and bang the table in mental anguish. He complained that he had not been home for five years. During this time he had not seen his parents, his wife or his children: he had been too busy killing Chinese. Normal human sentiments were now eroding his fighting spirit — at least when he was full.

When Dr Kitagawa and Mr Saito decided to visit a lady friend, I rose and made my excuses.

Next morning Dr Kitagawa came to see me. "Did you see your lady friend last night, Doctor?" I asked inquisitively. "We did not. Mr Saito was drunk. He put the car into a ditch. We walked home, using our legs.''

He lifted his singlet and scratched his stomach, and laughed heartily at the recollection.

In May, I made my final visit to the P.O.W.s at Seria. Wada was driving them hard. Lieutenant Hodges asked me to appeal, as a doctor, to all partly fit Punjabis to muster for work in order that those more seriously ill should be able to rest. This I did to the assembled Punjabis, with Lieutenant Hodges translating into Hindustani. As I half expected, the address did not find favour with the Japanese guards. A few days later an order was given that everyone visiting the P.O.W.s camp had to have a pass. I applied at the Residency, through Dr Kitagawa. The latter was upset: the Japanese had to be very strict now; no pass could be granted to me. Balwant Singh would do all the necessary visiting.

In mid-May, two soldiers died. By the end of June, deaths numbered 22, and there were 80 cases of severe beri-beri: so it was reported on the grapevine. Then suddenly treatment improved and better food was given to the survivors. Balwant Singh was refused a pass one week after me. Subsequently, apart from casual contact, Kim Sing remained the sole means of communicating with the prisoners. Some months later, the four European P.O.W. were transferred to Kuching, the capital of Sarawak.

Two Japanese doctors frequently called on me, having appointed me as their English teacher.

One was Takahashi, a graduate of the Imperial University of Formosa. He was a decent fellow and I respected him; even grew to like him. He was a first-class swimmer, and had apparently been engaged in research in physiology before the outbreak of hostilities.

One evening during puasa (period of fasting), he was in my room when the Malay family next door started saying their prayers. Takahashi was interested, and I explained about the annual period of fasting during which meals were taken only in hours of darkness. When Takahashi had grasped what I was saying, he said slowly "The Malays are a third-class people. They are first-class idiots. They do not know science."

A few days later I returned his visit. The Japanese showed me his highly prized sword. It was 400 years old and had a sharkskin-covered hilt, and was as sharp as a razor. Takahashi said it had miraculous qualities. If ever bent in battle, it was placed on a mantelpiece overnight, and in the morning, lo and behold! it was straight again.

"Science cannot explain it," he said.

Takahashi was a man of more than average character and competence. But I saw two rather disconcerting instances of his medical work. Neither gave a fair impression; of this, I am quite sure.

One day I had to go to the hospital and I found him in the operating theatre with Dr Kitagawa, both scrubbing up. Kitagawa finished and then put on his cap with his clean hands, which touched his hair. Takahashi gave a shout of anger and slapped his careless colleague. He then put on his own gloves without further scrubbing.

Another time, I went into a ward where he was doing a post-operative dressing. The patient, a soldier, was lying naked on the bed with his hands behind his head. In the centre of an appendicectomy wound there was a gauze ribbon pack. Takahashi and two assistants scrubbed up, put on gowns and gloves, and then Takahashi removed the long piece of gauze ribbon with a pair of forceps. A deep clean cavity was revealed. Takahashi then repacked the wound tightly with fresh gauze. This unusual procedure must have been painful, but the patient's face showed not the slightest change of expression. Speaking slowly, Takahashi said, "Appendicitis is a disease of civilised people. It is very common in Japanese Army."

I remarked "This soldier is a very good patient."

"Why?"

"He bears pain very well."

Takahashi took off his gloves and raised a closed fist above his head and stood over the patient.

"If he cries — oosh!" he said, bringing his fist downward to the patient's face.

At the New Year, 1943, I was invited to visit the Japanese doctor in his new quarters, recently acquired at Balwant Singh's expense. During the course of the evening the question of "geisha girls" came up. Takahashi said Europeans had the wrong idea: they were not prostitutes but "social entertainers". He admitted that there were prostitutes in Japan and asked me whether there were any in Australia.

"They have been reported from time to time," I said.

"Do medical students go to the prostitutes?"

"Good heavens, no!" I said.

"Then, if they do not, how do they make love?"

It was obviously absurd to tell a Japanese doctor that Australian undergraduates were entirely chaste. I thought for a moment and then said "Well, doctor, they make love to their friends' friends." Takahashi was intrigued with this answer. He repeated it in English very thoughtfully, and asked me to elucidate further. I explained that it was a point of etiquette not to make love to your friends' sisters or daughters or aunts, but acceptable to do so to the sisters, daughters or aunts of their friends. Distance added some semblance of respectability.

Takahashi was intelligent, and the explanation made a curious appeal to him. "That is very interesting," he said, stressing the adverb. "Very interesting, indeed." Then, "How, in what way, can a girl be asked?"

"You meet them socially."

"But they are high and cultured. How can you know which girl will say 'Yes' and which will say 'No'?"

"That's the most baffling problem in Australia. One can only guess."

"Guess! Make a guess? I see." He laughed heartily, and added "At a time like that one must make many jokes. It is necessary. Science plays no part." Presently he said "People feel better in cold climates, yet in hot countries they are more immoral. Why is that?" I laughed. "I suppose it is easier to make love under a coconut palm than on a heap of snow!"

Takahashi enjoyed this conversation immensely. So did I. He was anxious to improve his English and just before I left he asked "How can I get a Russian girl who speaks English fluently?"

I almost sighed. "I don't know, doctor. I've tried saying 'Abra kadabra' one hundred times, but that doesn't work! Perhaps, with luck, a Russian circus will pay us a visit."

Dr Yujima was a cut below Takahashi. His English was laborious and he was forever talking politics. "Before, Japs go to America, now shut out. To Australia, now shut out. To China, now shut out. All countries, shut out. This means we must fight." On occasions he qualified as a first-class bore.

He was crazy about muscle development and had a disconcerting habit of ranging himself beside me and comparing our respective heights. He often felt his own biceps, triceps and quadriceps. One morning, in my sitting-room he suddenly reached down and felt my calf. The action annoyed me, and presently, when he suggested a trial of strength — elbows on the table, hands gripping (Indian wrestling I believe it is called) — I accepted the challenge at once. I rather fancied myself with my left hand and so placed my left elbow on the table, leading Yujima to do likewise. We locked grips. In quick time I had his forearm flat on the table. This was a thoughtless mistake. Yujima took defeat badly. He said my forearm was too long. I offered him a book to put under his elbow to eliminate this advantage; but Yujima took my right hand and made me put my right elbow further away so that I was immediately under a great mechanical disadvantage. Then he put his shoulder behind his arm, gripped the leg of the table with his left hand, and began shoving ferociously. Clearly, national as well as personal honour was involved. Yujima's teeth were showing and his eyes popping out of his head. With an eye on consequences, I struggled for a minute or two, then threw in the sponge. "You are too strong, doctor" I said. Yujima was delighted and bowed to me. I felt quite angry at having to make a diplomatic surrender. But several days later I felt better. He appeared in front of my house mounted insecurely on a pony. Right in front of my eyes he was thrown over the pony's head and landed on his backside.

Yujima came to see me the morning he left on transfer. "You have Manson-Bahr. I want please."

He found the highly-prized text-book on tropical medicine among my books. I protested: "Doctor, it's the only one I have. I need it."

"Manson-Bahr — very famous. You give it. I must have."

"It's the only book on tropical medicine I have. I want it."

"I am sorry, I must have. I cannot give you anything."

I stood silent. The Jap doctor was in a hurry. "I must have", he repeated. "You write."

He opened the front cover. I picked up a pencil and wrote like a petulant child. "It's a gift — to Dr Yujima".

"Jap class" did not maintain popularity. Chundra Singh alone was a model of diligence and he reprimanded youngsters for chattering, telling them he could not concentrate. At night, he wrapped wet towels around his head and slogged on into the midnight hours, wearing himself out in the process. One night, Tokyo radio beamed congratulations to him for his diligence. He thought about this publicity, and about 48 hours later suffered an attack of what appeared to be delayed shock. Others were not as keen as he and attendance fell. After repeating "Open! Open! Cherry blossom — lah! Open!" several hundred times I had had enough of it. To make up the numbers police were ordered to attend and class started all over again on the "Ah, ee, oo, eh, or" business. Townsfolk joked, "Everyone can speak Japanese except those who go to school!" All the best students stayed at home, and so I followed suit.

The first Japanese propaganda film came to Kuala Belait and I went to see it on a free ticket from the anti-Japanese cinema manager. There was a loudspeaker in front of the cinema and through it came an almost deafening recording of "Land of Hope and Glory". The voice sounded like Clara Butt's and could be heard all over the main bazaar. Amongst the audience I picked out two Frenchmen who had recently come across from Saigon to work on the oil-fields at Seria. I went through some French in my mind and then slipped along between two rows of seats and tapped one of the Frenchmen on the shoulder.

"Monsieur, parlez-vous Anglais?"

The Frenchman looked surprised. "Un peu, Monsieur", he said.

I pressed on in my schoolboy French. "Je suis le docteur dans cette ville. Si vous voulez venir chez moi — tres bon!"

The Frenchmen were sitting amongst a crowd of Japanese: having delivered myself thus, I returned to my seat quickly.

On 6 September 1943, one of the Frenchmen, Monsieur Leblanc, knocked on my door and introduced himself. I knew practically no spoken French but M. Leblanc could struggle along in English, with a little spoken or written French thrown in if he got into difficulty. Very soon I realised I had met a live wire. He asked if I could come to lunch at Seria. Certainly! "Don't you 'ave to get the permit, Monsieur le docteur?"

"No, indeed! Do you think I am a prisoner, monsieur?"

We went by truck to Seria, where M. Leblanc and his friend, M. Dijoud, lived together in a spacious bungalow. They were very comfortable, and to my very great surprise had a good supply of Moroccan and Australian wines, the gift of a sympathetic French Navy to two compatriots in an awkward predicament. It was scattered all over the floor of the spare room, and I looked at it in amazement.

M. Leblanc and M. Dijoud were employees of the Shell company in Saigon. A few months after the outbreak of war, the Japanese approached the government of Indo-China for skilled men to help repair the partly destroyed oil-fields at Seria in Brunei. No volunteers were forthcoming. One night M. Leblanc and M. Dijoud received orders to be ready to leave on the morrow for a place they had never heard of before. The prospect seemed dangerous and they protested, of course; nevertheless, they were sent across the water to the Land Below the Wind, accompanied by a small detachment of impressed Annamites and a French-speaking Nipponese known as Monsieur Igashii.

Within a few days of arriving at the oil-fields the Frenchmen were severely reprimanded by the Jap authorities. "Hurry up! Be quick! You haven't built any oil tanks yet!" This wasn't fair.

The pair complained: "But you haven't given us any tools or screws or anything!"

"Ah, screws! You want screws?"

"Yes, we must have screws", said M. Leblanc emphatically.

The Japs obtained some screws — seventeen of them — and gave them to the Frenchmen.

At this point in the story M. Leblanc exploded "Docteur, in one tank 20,000 screws is nothing, nothing! And they gave us *seventeen*!"

After several drinks, an excellent five course lunch was served, including such exotic items as tinned artichokes. A long siesta ended when servants re-appeared with Moroccan wine. It was a pleasant gathering and the two hospitable Frenchmen insisted that I stay for dinner. Why not? We were joined at table by M. Igashii. He entered the party with gusto. His French was not particularly fluent, consisting in large part of "Comment on dit?". But he was susceptible to atmosphere, and soon was toasting the King, the Emperor, La France, The Bear, even Chiang Kai Shek. I could not remember who was Governor-General of Australia, so I proposed a toast to Ned Kelly. French, Japanese and Australian elbows and tastebuds met the challenge very well.

After an enjoyable evening, the Frenchmen drove me home. The government staff and their families were startled by the hearty Gallic farewells.

M. Leblanc was a delightful person, lively and full of fun. He was no bigger than Napoleon but very strong, with a grip like steel. When he took my hand and shook it vigorously I had difficulty in maintaining the even tenor of salutations without manifesting distress.

One morning I saw an aspect of M. Leblanc which impressed me even more than the strength of his grip — this was the length and breadth of his upper jaw. M. Leblanc entered my quarters, opened his mouth and indicated a tooth which he wished to have removed immediately. It was so far away that I could scarcely see it. I said, "M. Leblanc, I must tell you. This is a job for the Japanese Military Surgeons."

"M. le Docteur, first, you understand? First I went there and they sent me to the — Officier de Hygiene Publique, is it not? He looked and sent me to the Sikh Dresser. No-one has done anything! I still have it. The Sikh said you would free it for me."

Somewhat reluctantly, I took M. Leblanc to the Dispensary, telling him I was pleased to attempt my first extraction. Having no dental syringe I used a 5 cc. syringe with a fine hypodermic needle which bent like a bow at the slightest pressure. Thus equipped, I had great difficulty in producing adequate anaesthesia. The Dispensary possessed a surfeit of dental forceps. The Dresser sterilized the lot and laid them out in a line on a table. M. Leblanc inspected them and then was persuaded to sit down on a chair. He watched me select an instrument with a beak like a parrot. I said "Now please stop talking, M. Leblanc, and open your mouth," I pushed the forceps along the Frenchman's jaw and after a little manoeuvring was able to satisfy the patient that I had clamped it on the right tooth.

"Prenez la garde, Monsieur", I said, then pulled. M. Leblanc leapt up shouting, "Monsieur, it is *full*, it is *full*. . ."

The Malay staff were surprised by the fuss made by M. Leblanc. He paced up and down the Dispensary speaking very rapidly in French. He didn't seem to have any inhibitions.

"Sit down, Monsieur Leblanc, please!"

I made two further attempts to produce anaesthesia. Finally, with one arm locked around my Gallic patient's head, I managed to drag the terrible tooth from its socket. As it released its hold, M Leblanc indicated with a vigorously down-pointing finger that his right eye was also being extracted by the forceps. After it was over he walked about briskly, holding his jaw and saying "Ah, it was not good work, it was not good work!" However, next day he was thoughtful enough to send word by M. Igashii that he was no longer in extreme pain.

On Monday morning, 5 October, Messieurs Leblanc and Dijoud appeared at my door for the last time. "We are going back to Saigon," they cried, smiling happily. They put down a box packed with blocks of scented soap, needle and cotton, tins of artichokes, etc., and a large bottle of eau-de-cologne. M. Leblanc and I had our first drink of Mr Red with lots of water, but M. Dijoud declined to adulterate his poison. After drinking it and another, he said he could not stay for lunch but declared he would like to drink a toast with me. It was a neat way of asking for a third drink, and so it was done with considerable enthusiasm, and then M. Dijoud departed briskly. He did not look at all well and was apparently worrying more than was good for him.

M. Leblanc and I talked about everything under the sun — Saigon, "les sauvages", shooting, the conflict in Cambodia, and so on.

Speaking of native women, M. Leblanc asked me what native girls who taught Europeans to speak the native dialect were called. "Long-haired teachers" was the term, I informed him.

"That is not very good", said M. Leblanc. "The French call them — how is it? Skin-of-the-bottom dictionaries."

I burst out laughing. "Why? Why a name like that, Monsieur?"

M. Leblanc gave this homely explanation. A keen young French Administrator gets an attractive girl to teach him the native tongue. On, say, Saturday afternoons, as he and his teacher lie together in bed, he may idly test his vocabulary on various things he can see — the window, the wall, the mirror and so on. Presently he sees something for which he does not know the native name. He then reaches across and pats his charming teacher on the bottom and says, "Cherie, what is the name of that?"

For lunch I had to borrow several plates, forks, etc. from my neighbours. At such short notice Kuki did very well, turning on rice and curried fowl, then sago with gula malacca and coconut milk. But the curry was brought in in a ghastly old black pot which was deposited in the centre of the table. M. Leblanc seemed hypnotised by it.

During the course of the meal, he remarked that British people thought that the French subsisted largely on frogs.

"But isn't that true?" I joked. "I thought that just as we sit down to curry tiffin on Sunday, so the French collect around a bowl of frogs!" M. Leblanc went into a torrent of French and waved his hands about. For a time he was quite unable to remain seated at the table.

"M. le Docteur, I have eaten frogs only four times in my life! *Four times!*"

"Then you stand condemned out of your own mouth, M. Leblanc."

Just before leaving M. Leblanc handed me ten dollars, saying it was for my "assistant" for helping with the tooth extraction. Then he looked perplexed and kept on repeating "Que c'est difficile, que c'est difficile. Comment dit-on ca?"

Then suddenly out it came. "I will not give it to you, I will lend it to you, and if you cannot meet me again you can give it to a poor man." He put his hand in his pocket and then handed me a roll of Japanese money amounting to a hundred dollars. At the first sign of protest, he said "You must keep it. I have seen how you live. That pot!"

He put his hand across his eyes to blot out the sight of it. Then he took my hand, crushed it vigorously, and was off. It was a sad moment. I would miss the pair.

I called to M. Leblanc from the window, "When did you say you were leaving?"

"Tomorrow! At sunrise."

"Who said so?"

"The Japanese. They told us to pack urgently tonight."

"Then good luck and thank you, M. Leblanc."

Six weeks later two jaded Frenchmen left the oil-fields for Saigon.

Subedar Makhmad Anwar, I.D.S.M. (Pathan) 1927–1945 of the 2nd Bn. 15th Punjab Machine Gun Regiment.
A professional soldier who valued his oath of allegiance more than his own life.

Chapter 8

KUALA BELAIT — TO BRUNEI

Entry into the "co-prosperity sphere" soon led to a number of changes. Merchandise disappeared from the bazaar overnight. Club life ceased. People left their houses in the evenings with increasing reluctance. Free expression of opinion became a thing of "British times". Friends underwent a sharp metamorphosis into acquaintances. Down in the House of Terror, carpenters constructed two small cells, boarded to the roof, with doors so small that prisoners had to crawl in and out. The M.P.s built up personal files on everyone who excited their attention. To the "headquarters" came a stream of quislings, opportunists, informers and, at night, a truckload of prostitutes.

With a fluctuating garrison of 500–1,500 soldiers in the background, several M.P.s and a few tough orderlies were enough to control the oil-fields.

The arrival of Hamada, brother-in-law of Sakai, the Jesselton towkei, as interpreter to the military police and also teacher at "Jap class", was a significant event. He spoke Japanese, Malay and English and understood a deal of Chinese. Born and bred in the country, he was soon at home in Kuala Belait; he understood the local people and was more dangerous than a score of M.Ps fresh from Japan. For a long time, he did not actually lay hands on anyone in public; then one day he gave the old Court Clerk a slapping.

The military police functioned independently of the Courts. Even here, power was gradually taken from the Magistrate. All Court papers were sent to a Jap Chief Police Officer in Brunei: he perused them and jotted down sentences. No appeal was allowed. He gave one man seven years for stealing 500 grams of rice.

Summary punishment was given any place, any time, by any Jap — slaps, kicks, a ticking-off or a standing-at-attention for hours under the tropical sun. More severe assaults were just frequent enough to make everyone apprehensive. On one occasion, two tailors were taken from their shop, manhandled severely and thrown off the wharf into the river. Again, a well-known pacifist, an Indian, was taken to prison and beaten until he soiled himself.

Some "incidents" had their amusing side. One morning the military police entered a clerk's house, gave him a thrashing and said, "You know what that's for?".

"I don't. What is if for?"

"You're Ramm, aren't you?"

"No. My name's Rumm."

"Rumm! I say, we've made a mistake."

The military police went away laughing; presently, Ramm copped it!

I made a point of being meticulously careful in acknowledging Jap officers. However, one with a birthmark on his neck like a map of England was not satisfied and sent a Company clerk to demonstrate the correct method: but the very low bow and simultaneous salute requested was too much to expect of anyone in public. For several weeks until this hallmarked officer left for an unknown destination I always carried a book under my right arm as an excuse for not saluting. The walk to and from the Dispensary became a minor hazard of every-day life.

One morning, there was a military truck parked beside the road. A Jap soldier with rifle and fixed bayonet leant against the driver's door talking to someone inside; otherwise the street was deserted. As I approached, the soldier straightened up and stood at attention, facing me. Something was doing. Five metres from the soldier I halted, stood at attention and bowed. The soldier entered the truck and drove off. Surely it was a deliberate test! If I had failed, presumably I would have had an exciting morning.

Another morning, I left the Dispensary on a bicycle. Turning into the road, I met tough Colonel Okawa. I nodded and said, "Konnichi wa". This was received with extreme disfavour; as I rode past, the Colonel contorted his face angrily. A patient was just quitting the Dispensary. The Colonel assaulted him, knocking him up and down the path; after which the patient returned to the Dispensary for further treatment. The colonel had sent me a message!

In time, the minor and major acts of brutality came closer to every home. Uneasiness, then actual fear, came into the town like an unhealthy emanation from the coastal swamps. Finally, nearly all windows and doors were closed at sunset and few people came into the streets.

In early November, rumour had it that the Ibans or Sea Dyaks living in the hill-country behind the oil-fields intended running wild on the night of the coming full moon. "There is no government now!" was a cry that passed from lip to lip in bamboo longhouses. News of small, armed parties moving about the Ulu caused some uneasiness on the coast.

On that fateful evening, the full moon rose above the jungle-covered interior. There were dark clouds in the sky and sheet lightning flickered on the horizon. Some townsfolk stood in the road laughing at suggestions about possible happenings in the next few hours. The nimble-minded Chinese take a delight in frightening each other.

I went to bed early. Shortly after midnight the Dresser knocked urgently on the side wall of my quarters. "Doctor! Doctor! The Ibans have amuk'd. They are killing Chinese it seems. The M.P. says we must hurry."

I dressed and went to the Dispensary for what first aid equipment I could find.

The M.P.s had received word of an "ayau" (headhunting disturbance) at Sungei Liang at 10 p.m. They immediately went into conference. At 3 a.m. the relief party left Kuala Belait in two ex-A.I.F. (Australian Imperial Forces) trucks. A light rain was falling and I crouched with others under a tarpaulin in the back of the second truck. The Slapper, a small M.P. who adored emergencies, was at the wheel.

Shortly before dawn the party reached Liang. A small hut of bark and branches had been hastily erected near the sandy track. In it, lying on a broad slab of timber, was a young Chinese woman named Helen. Her face and right shoulder were roughly bound with bloodstained strips of torn up clothes. She was pale and shocked and lay sighing and tossing her head to and fro.

Morphine was given and as gently as possible, Helen was moved into an open woodshed nearby. I took off her rough dressings. The girl's right arm had been amputated some centimetres below the shoulder. The parang used by the assailant had also touched her right cheek. Her eyelids and the corner of her mouth were paralyzed. Dressings were applied and Helen was made comfortable with blankets and bottles of warm water.

Before long, Helen's mother was brought in on an improvised stretcher by four peasants. She had spent the night with two whimpering children in the jungle. Her left shoulder blade had been cleft. I quickly closed the gaping wound with sutures. While I was so engaged my patient was sitting up and the M.P.s questioned her. I had to ask her not to use her hands in conversation.

Frank Chin, a small, sturdy Chinese, lived nearby. Years ago, he had been interpreter on a trans-Pacific liner. Because of his accent he was known as American Frank. He spoke to Helen in as comforting a voice as I have ever heard. From him and others, I got this story.

Helen's father, Ah Pin, worked for the oil company, finishing up as Chief Clerk. He retired just before the War. With his provident fund he paid his debts, bought some land at Sungei Liang, built a house and set about establishing a farm. Soon, with a few cattle, an area under sweet potatoes, a pig sty and a fish pond stocked with carp, he and his family were fairly comfortable. They employed a servant girl and an Iban handyman.

About 5 o'clock the previous evening, the family were in the kitchen eating when the Dyak entered with a parang in his hand and attacked them. The family had been uneasy about him for a day or two suspecting he had been chewing certain jungle leaves which disturb the mind.

The children scattered, much as do the kahawai when a marlin drives in amongst them. The mother and two children escaped through a tiny window at one end of the kitchen. Helen received one blow from the parang. She fled through the door and down the hill: but while crossing the swampy ground at its foot, she collapsed. A sister hurried on and summoned Frank Chin. He came and applied a ligature and assisted Helen to where I first saw her.

Frank now armed himself with a shotgun and several cartridges made from fireworks and returned to help the rest of the family. As he ascended the hill he could see a small girl standing beside the body of her father, petrified with fear. In front of her, flourishing a parang menacingly was the Iban servant. Where was her father's gun hidden, the Iban was asking. The girl could not answer a word.

Frank knew the Iban well and for a moment had difficulty in accepting him as the killer. The native saw him approaching and walked off slowly towards the jungle.

On the hillside was an old truck. Frank tried to start it but without success. The evening shadows were moving down the hillside and spreading from the hollows; he gave up the attempt and took the girl back to his house. A friend left by bicycle for Kuala Belait to obtain medical assistance and to inform the authorities.

Hamada, Kato and compatriots did not remain long. They refused to take the injured woman with them but said they would send a bus and arrange admission to the Company hospital.

I went to Ah Pin's house. Ah Pin's body lay prone a few metres from the front door. One of many blows had divided his spine. His eldest son lay at the foot of the back steps, his body resting on his amputated hand. The servant girl was found face downwards in an irrigation stream. Parang blows had rained upon her back.

In the kitchen, two tables were set for food. The rice was partly eaten and several chopsticks were scattered about the floor.

As the party stood in the kitchen, considerably shaken by this scene, the silence was broken by one of Ah Pin's daughters saying, "Dia masok (he came in) — cut! cut! cut!".

It was after mid-day before the two women were admitted to hospital. Helen had a bad time for three days, then began to pickup. Her mother suddenly collapsed and died on the fourth day. Several hundred dollars were found hidden in her pillow and were given to the eldest surviving son.

Helen asked to be shifted to the Dispensary and, later, when she had improved sufficiently, she was transferred to Brunei Hospital. Those slain were given a Christian burial in Kuala Belait. The surviving children came to live with Chong Thau, the wireless operator, next door to me.

One night, three weeks after the Sungei Liang ayau, six Ibans entered a Chinese kongsi at Sungei Bera on the edge of the oil-fields. They asked for salt and tobacco, then suddenly drew their parangs and attacked the Chinese about to oblige them.

The following morning, I went to Sungei Bera with the Military Police. There were two headless bodies on the ground in front of the kongsi. The attack had continued after death. Inside the building an elderly Chinese lay dead on his bed. About 22 metres behind the kongsi, on the very edge of the jungle clearing, was another headless body.

The Military Police gave a remarkable demonstration. With a long tape measure they measured the length and breadth of the rough bamboo shack, the position and width of the doors, the dimensions of various rooms and the beds therein. They determined accurately the distance of each body from the building and also that of a hand which lay in a wheel track some distance away. They asked me to submit a similarly detailed report on the wounds received by the slain.

After this second attack, the Ibans became exceedingly unpopular. Most of the townsfolk had relatives living out in gardens and farms without any protection. Everyone took some measures of self defence. At sunset every house and every shop was converted into a miniature blockhouse by closing doors and windows. One government clerk carried a walking stick with a 20 centimetre long dagger inside it. My old cook walked about even at mid-day bearing a knob-kerry.

The Japs sent a detachment of soldiers to the Ulu Baram villages with full equipment, including gas masks and threatened to burn villages if headhunting continued. All Headmen were ordered to apprehend the six Dyaks on sight.

One evening, a clerk's wife and two of her children came and sat on my front steps. Speaking of the recent killings she said in English, "The Dyaks are not like us, Doctor. We Chinese cannot store trouble in out hearts. We must talk and out it all comes, and is finished with. But the Dyaks, they are different. They think and think and think and then suddenly they kill".

Christmas and New Year together amounted to quite a festive season. Half the worried town was three-parts pickled for days on end. For a week I lived very well, dining out several times. Lau Ham Chung, a young Chinese merchant living with his family in the bazaar above his shop, couldn't do enough for me. On Christmas Day, the Japs gave the government staff a half holiday. In the morning an Iban came to the Dispensary for treatment. He was a big, strong fellow, practically naked and lavishly tattoo'd with scorpions, crabs and stars. I asked, "What are you Ibans up to lately?".

The primitive was disarmingly frank. His reply, translated, was, "It's true, Tuan, the Ibans in the Ulu Baram are very naughty —lah!".

"Where is your village?"

"In the Ulu Baram, Tuan."

Everyone in the Dispensary burst out laughing. During the season, small groups of Ibans wandered round the town. The townsfolk regarded them with a mixture of interest, respect and frank hostility. At Sungei Liang the Chinese settlers collected nightly in a "fortress" with three fences round it and a tower from which constant watch was maintained. Having no firearms. the settlers armed themselves with giant bamboo syringes charged with a noxious mixture of pepper, banana juice, chillies and tuber root.

I had New Year's dinner with Di Alvis and his family, a few friends and an odd Jap or two, several kilometres out of town towards Seria. We ate very well and a great variety of alcoholic drinks were consumed — pre-war beer retrieved from underground, Japanese "bieru" and Suntori whisky and local liquors ingeniously fermented and distilled from meticulously discarded Kuala Belait fruits. I was driven home in style, in a vintage car, referred to by a cheerful Eurasian adept at belly dancing as Farting Fanny. As we passed the House of Terror, Di Alvis' children, sitting in the back seat, were singing, "God save the King" at the tops of their voices.

Frank Chin came to live in a dilapidated dwelling not far from my quarters. He refused to work for the Japs and was having a lean time. I had opened an abscess for him recently and on Christmas evening went along to see how he was progressing. I found Frank sitting cross-legged on the floor studying an illustrated English work on Chinese characters and sat down beside him. Together we went through several pages, Frank explaining the compounding of ideographs from fundamental characters. The only light was supplied by a single coconut oil lamp. In the shadows on the far side of the room five young children were sleeping on the floor. Frank's mother-in-law brought in coffee. Frank showed the character for "mountain". From it were derived — to go into retirement, rugged, pheasant, crossroads, etc. "Crossroads" was formed by combining the character for "mountain" with that for "divided". Frank asked, "Doctor, do you know the local Chinese nickname for Mr Churchill?"

"No. What is it?"

"We call him Hu Kit Nye. Word by word, it is 'mountain, lucky, you', or just 'Lucky Mountain'."

On 10 January 1943, I was advised that Dr Graham, the Canadian Medical Officer at Brunei, had obtained permission for me to go there to operate. Next morning I rose early. I packed carefully in case I did not return.

To his own grief, Sezuki, a Japanese shopkeeper in the main bazaar, had been appointed Resident by the military police. He met me at the bus, shook hands cordially, handed over a pass, then introduced a fellow passenger, Tuan Okana, of the Transport Department.

Just outside the town we passed between two lines of local people engaged on compulsory labour, this time clearing out the deep drains skirting the road. Armed guards were present. There was a look of abject misery on the face of old Mr Yap, the Court Clerk, standing knee deep in mud.

On arrival at Brunei, Tuan Okana took me to the Chief of Military Police and then to the hospital. An attendant showed me to Dr Graham's quarters. George Graham came out. His face was pale and strained. We shook hands and went into a sitting-room. Immediately, the Canadian gave a detailed account of the patients he had for operation. Then, lowering his voice so much that I had to lean forward to hear, he gave the war news up to the time when all wireless sets had been confiscated.

That evening, the only other European in Brunei, an Englishman known affectionately as Old Bill, obtained permission to come for dinner. He had a vast paunch and no sooner had he met me than he put his arms around it, lifted it up and put in on the table. "There, Doctor Kell! What do you think of it? It should be good because it's cost me 10,000 quid already!"

It was a very good introduction. In a few seconds he was downing a friendly measure of locally brewed brandy. Bill was an "old timer", full of tales of the country. He did not stop all evening. In his time he had seen remarkable sights — a tapir walking across Brunei golf course (its occurrence is generally denied); a Dyak palang (sex aid) made from the springs of an alarm clock; a Chief Police Officer going home from his office standing on his head on the bonnet of his car! He added a story to the medical legends of Borneo. A government doctor was intent on becoming rich. Every patient seeing him was asked bluntly, "Ada wang? Have you got any money on you?" If they answered "No", he shouted, "Then get to hell out of here!". A simple story, but the way it was told I thought I had never heard anything quite so funny.

As he left, Old Bill advised, "Keep your pecker up you two kids!".

"Cheers, Bill, careful of the crocodile on the causeway!". It was a delightful evening.

I stayed in Brunei ten days. I slept in the X-ray room, bathed in the toilet nearby and had my meals with Graham. The hospital was new. Facilities and supplies were still fairly good. Indeed, the medical storeroom seemed like Aladdin's Cave.

In order to prolong my stay, we operated every second day. The first operation — removal of an eye — was an unforgettable experience for me. Graham wasn't particularly keen on surgery; one of the pre-war staff was pro Japanese and two Japanese doctors came in to watch. Suddenly, when about to begin, I felt as nervous as a kitten. The only pair of scissors available to me was long, heavy and blunt-ended and I could not hold the damn thing steady as I used it to snip the conjunctiva around the cornea. I put down the instruments, went across to a basin and slowly washed my hands; then I returned and completed the prefectly simple operation. Subsequently, all was well; but the incident brought home to me something of the strain under which I have been living during the past year.

George Graham was an extremely good fellow, a winner if ever there was one, immensely popular amongst the staff and townsfolk. He was about 180 centimetres, slightly built, with dark hair, greying at the temples. His features were fine and very pale as a result of the present indoor existence. In speaking, he seldom raised his voice above a low, serious monotone which I, with ears which had not yet regained their normal acuteness after Mr Ino's regrettable display, often had trouble in following. He had more than his share of the tough, medical sense of humour which casts a kindly light over the world of patients and all their ingenious miseries. The Japs had given him gratuitous permission to keep a Malay girl if he wished; but, being married to a dietician from Medicine Hat (Canada), he did not avail himself of this sporting concession: that was his story anyway! Certainly, there were no hairpins or plastic flowers lying round the place.

One night, the Canadian opened the back door and admitted two Malays. They came across to me and shook me warmly by the hand. One was Daud, driver to a Jap V.I.P.; the other was Pangiran Mohommet, the Brunei wireless operator. The latter told us news he had been able to obtain by clandestine listening-in, and he had an intent and very appreciative audience. They were a brave pair and risked serious punishment if caught in our company.

Graham stood in high favour with the Sultan of Brunei. One afternoon, he and I were summoned to the Istana. The Private Secretary showed us to a large polished table on the first floor verandah. In a glass-fronted cabinet was a magnificent display of Brunei silverware. On the walls were swords, krises, food covers and other decorative pieces. Further along the verandah was a throne with coloured curtains draped about it.

Presently the Sultan joined us. His attire acknowledged the Malay love for brilliant colours. In his early thirties, he was slightly built, with an aquiline nose, large, humorous eyes and a scanty, rather whimsical moustache. He was not happy about the Japanese invasion. Rather than do nothing, he became deliberately busy — he gambled, drank and made love, fulltime! He commiserated with Graham about the loss of his personal possessions, including a car which had been turned upside down in the river by the Japanese. Graham told the Sultan that his salary did not reach him, but I don't think this impressed the Sultan who never personally handled any money at all. After 15 minutes conversation we accompanied the Sultan to his private office. The Sultan removed his coat and opened a gap in his shirt between two buttons. Graham applied his stethescope to the small area of golden brown skin so revealed. For some seconds there was dead silence; then the Sultan burst out laughing, "There's nothing the matter with me! I only called you to have a talk. Now, tell me, when is Mr Pengilly coming back?"

Mr Pengilly had been the Resident, Brunei, when war broke out.

Before we departed, the Sultan had us examine an old retainer who, worried by events, had been consuming too much Chinese wine. Graham advised him to give up drinking.

The Sultan asked, "But why?". Graham faced the matter bravely. He explained how, due to malnutrition, excessive drinking could lead to cirrhosis of the liver. He became graphic in describing this disease; it progressed slowly, with the liver contracting and getting harder and harder, until finally, the blood could not percolate through it and fluid collected in the abdomen. His Highness looked alarmed and patted his faithful retainer on the shoulder. I remarked that the process sometimes took twenty or even thirty years: at this everyone in the room began to breathe more freely.

As we drove back to town, I said to Graham, "You were looking decidedly pale as you described the ravages of cirrhosis. Have you got any personal worries about it?".

The Canadian laughed. "I like that!" he said. "And what about you?"

"If your description had gone on any longer I would have fainted", I replied.

Finally, my stay in Brunei came to an end. George Graham and Old Bill's company suited me down to the ground: as did luxuries like a full bookcase and electric light. Sitting in a corner of Graham's lounge, like one of the lost Elgin marbles, was a refrigerator. He went to it and we had one for the road — a banana brandy and cold water — and then I was called to a car which took me to the police station. After a three hour wait, I entered the bus and returned to Kuala Belait. Back "home" without drugs, equipment or hospital facilities, I resumed my civilian practice.

Helen returned from Brunei hospital and came to live with my neighbour, Mr Chong Thau and his wife. She attended the Dispensary twice a week and was treated like royalty. She was a charming girl and usually dressed in Malay-style with floral sarong and white baju. It was obvious from the way people spoke to her that they still found her attractive. Through the window of my bedroom I often saw her sitting on a box in front of the kitchen next door, while Mrs Chong Thau did her hair. Helen had a very straight back and her long hair reached almost to the ground.

One afternoon a son was born to Chundra Singh. I was called in. Chundra Singh was dressed in a long white coat and his eldest son, a quaint little miniature Sikh, stood beside him.

"Why didn't you call the midwife?" I asked.

"I never call a midwife, Sir. As for the Japanese doctors, they know nothing."

The labour lasted only two hours and when everything was tidied up Chundra Singh and I sat down at a table at the foot of the bed and had tea with salt and cakes and boiled eggs. Chundra Singh had been under a strain. "Oh, Sir, my wife is a wonderful woman!", he exclaimed. "she feels it coming, cooks the meal, attends to the children, sets the table for afternoon tea and when everything is ready, then she says, 'Well, here I am'."

Chundra Singh told me that Balwant Singh had been sacked. "One of the doctors threw him out. He has gone to his garden at Mile 3. Now he will have to live like a poor man, without luxuries like drink. Someone must have been digging at him."

Chundra Singh lived in a world where nothing was straightforward. He was quite a character round town. He was tall, with a dark beard and brown knees; everything else visible about him was snow white — turban, teeth, shirt, shorts, stockings and shoes. He walked quickly and his mind was in a constant state of turbulence. Apart from a few quislings, I could see no enemies except the Japanese in town. But for twenty minutes, Chundra Singh told me of feuds existing between local Indians and ended with this extraordinary statement, "When you see two Indians co-operating, you know they are Dyaks. It's certain they are not true Indians. They must have Dyak's blood in them: or white man's blood."

Various Indian clerks were contending one against the other for promotion in what appeared to be a battle royal. Chundra Singh mentioned the hatred which existed between an oil-field quisling and Balwant Singh.

This surprised me. "But I saw them today, talking and joking together like old friends!"

Chundra Singh almost shouted, "Sir, that means nothing with Indians! Now, I'm here talking to you about everything. But I may be out to do you the very greatest harm!"

I smiled. When with Chundra Singh and indeed with many others, I listened rather than talked: but now I said half jokingly, "Chundra Singh, yesterday I heard a Chinese say, 'If you are walking in the jungle and happen to meet an Indian and a cobra, you always kill the Indian first.' What did he mean by that?"

Chundra Singh hesitated. "What does he mean by that? Nothing, probably. Sometimes these Chinese don't know what they are talking about. Now yesterday a man said something most peculiar to me. I have written it down to see if it means anything. We'll see."

Mrs Chundra Singh sat up in bed and called, "Does doctor want any more tea?".

A fever broke out in the community which was no concern of mine. The M.P.s granted a licence to a group of Chinese to conduct a gambling farm. Over the Chinese New Year there was heavy gambling. Kuki lost $20. "It doesn't matter," he said, "it's only once a year." I gave him $5 to try his luck again. In half an hour he had lost that too.

A clerk on $100 a month threw away $1,000 at a single sitting. The Malays took to the tables almost as readily as the Chinese. Those most affected by the gambling fever were said to be women, children and paupers! Housekeeping money was lost in the farm. Husbands and children still had to be fed. Divorces, separations and robberies sprang up in the community like weeds. Some families shed every bit of jewellery they possessed: the only limit was complete bankruptcy.

One night there was a furious little man in the House of Terror. The Chief M.P. had parked his bicycle outside a shop and someone had stolen it: tyres commanded a good price. To demonstrate anger, the M.P.s went to the farm and knocked the towkei-in-charge about amongst the closely packed tables.

Hwa Hwi was a popular game based on 36 numbers and simple enough for housewives, children and paupers to understand. The winning number was selected by the manager of the gambling farm 24 hours before being made public and written on a piece of paper. This was then enclosed in a packet and hung on the wall in public view. The manager released a "chai" or tip, such as "two men in a canoe", which in a vague way gave a pointer to the winning number. The public backed their fancies and on the following mid-day the packet was opened and the winning number disclosed. Nearly everyone was ruined once again.

The Chinese, particularly, found Hwa Hwi well nigh irresistible. In the tantalising packet the winning number was invisible to ordinary eyes: perhaps there were eyes in the spirit world capable of seeing it? Some housewives gave spirits of goodwill a chance to pass on information as follows: they chalked the 36 numbers in a circle on their kitchen table and in the centre, they imprisoned a cockroach or centipede under an empty jam tin. Exactly at midnight, they raised the tin and watched to see which number was trodden on by the insect as it ran away! The cemetery attracted a regular pilgrimage of determined bettors. Some gathered beside a grave at midnight and over it shook a tin containing 36 numbered slips of paper. The first slip to fall out was thought to bear the next winning number and they bet heavily on it. Others went further: they put small offerings of rice, wine and paper money on to a recently made grave, lit joss sticks and spread 36 numbered cards on the mound. They forced a bamboo tube down into the coffin,then killed a cock and allowed its blood to trickle down the tube into the coffin, to the accompaniment of prayers. The expectation was that the dead person's spirit would emerge along the tube and in some manner indicate the card bearing the next winning number.

Similarly, the supernatural entered more and more into everyday affairs. Freedom was gone, only imagination could not be restrained. Anything out of the ordinary was held to symbolise something. One patient had some hens which began to crow in the morning. He said, "We Chinese do not like that. It means that times are very strange, does it not? We always cut off their heads and eat them".

A dense cloud of white moths appearing in the padang drew excited comment. And Kuki reported seeing a waterspout in the sea towering over and threatening the House of Terror. In Brunei Government Offices, a strange monkey went beserk one night and knocked down a Japanese flag. The native midwife described two amuk monkeys which came into Kampong Melayu. "Their skin was absolutely white, Tuan Doctor," said Pangiran Hitam. "These are monkeys that are never, never seen anywhere except in big jungle. They were not afraid. They looked straight into people's eyes as no monkeys ever looked. A white skin — that's true!"

I personally pinned my faith on the Southern Cross, which crept across the evening sky in a low arc for a short time each year. I said to myself, "When next the Cross and pointers appear, the Anzacs will come." I felt that with a little co-operation from General MacArthur and Lucky Mountain, this could be true.

One morning I noticed two clerks cheerfully giving a curious signal to each other. Each raised a hand high and then let it fall in an undulating curve towards the ground, at the same time moving the fingers rapidly to and fro. It was intriguing to watch. Presently, I learnt that Lucky Mountain was reported as saying, "Before the leaves of autumn fall we will be attacking on all fronts." The imagery in the sentence made a strong appeal to the people of this evergreen land in their present mood. It couldn't be a rumour; it just couldn't.

Several times the doors and windows of Ah Pin's house at Sungei Liang had been found open after the house had been closed on the previous night. Accordingly, Frank Chin went to the house, locked all doors and windows and sprinkled ashes on the floor and back steps to retain footprints. Just before sunset he hid himself downhill from the house and kept watch. He saw nothing unusual. When it was dark he walked up the the hill to inspect. The back door and several side windows were open. There were no footprints in the ashes. He called, "Come out! Come out! Or I'll shoot!".

No one answered. Darkness quickens susceptibilities. The Chinese have a belief that metal of any kind has protective powers against evil spirits. Frank had a gun in his hands, some coins in his pockets and there was wire on the door; therefore, he had no cause to worry. From the very nature of what was happening, he felt that the spirit of Ah Pin's dead son must be playing childish pranks. He went into the deserted house, called the boy's name several times and then said quietly, "Why not leave them alone? You are troubling us and we are very worried people. Please don't cause any more trouble of this sort."

Frank told the story with evident sincerity. He was level-headed and had taken a better stand than most against the Japanese. I, therefore, was moved by the atmosphere of this curious little tale: for a long time I sat thinking of it. Memories of the "Ayau" were still very fresh. Before I went to bed I had to make a deliberate effort to sweep them from my mind.

On 22 February, all reasonably fit Punjabi P.O.W.s paraded on the padang in front of the Dispensary. A large Japanese flag was stretched across the baseball scoreboard and there were other smaller flags around the field. Diminutive Jap officers rushed about amongst the tall Punjabis, arranging them, well spaced, in square formation. Subedar

Makhmed Anwar and Jemedar Mohammed Hasham stood in front of the troops with a senior Jap officer. Both Punjabis were regular soldiers, with over 20 years of Army life behind them.

Suddenly, the order to stand at attention was given, in English.

For fully two minutes the Punjabis stood like statues. With the staff and a dozen patients, I stood in front of the Dispensary looking at them. It was a magnificent sight. Uniforms were extremely ragged, but it did not matter. Finally, after two minutes, a soldier in the back rank began to swat flies and a second scratched the back of one leg with the opposite foot. The soldiers were then turned to right and left, and when a Jap officer cried "Kirei", they saluted. A salute was given to the flag on the scoreboard.

A declaration was read to the Punjabis. The ceremony was in honour of those of them who had already died (that is, of starvation). The survivors were now "officially" free and at liberty to join the Indian Independence Army and to fight the British. Respect had been paid to their dead and all previous ill-treatment was expected to be forgotten.

This ceremony created quite an impression. Soldiers on parade could well be the most dignified thing in human affairs. British methods certainly produce a soldier who looks the part. The Punjabis were fine.

One morning, popular Ozawa-san of the Post and Telegraph Department appeared with a Japanese friend who had a black eye, swollen lips and several broken teeth. I examined him. Ozawa asked, "Dangerous nai — kah?".

It was difficult for me to keep a straight face. "Dangerous nai. What happened, Ozawa-san?

Ozawa himself looked the worse for wear, but with considerable zest he told his story. His boss, the Head of the Post and Telegraph Department, had come on a visit from Miri. They got drunk together in the canteen. Ozawa went off home and crawled round on the grass near his house looking for a pair of spectacles which he had possibly lost. Presently, he fell asleep out in the open and woke in the morning covered with dew and as cold as a frog. He went inside and noticed his boss's bed unoccupied; naturally he took no notice, assuming that he was spending the night with one or more of the Taiwan prostitutes. At 10 o'clock, however, he went in search of him. Canteen? — no; gambling farm? — no; at the prostitutes? — no. Finally, he found him in the House of Terror, sitting dejectedly at the breakfast table with the M.P.s. It appeared that he had wandered into the Police Station and had mistaken the Malay policemen for Dyaks and in self defence he attacked them. The Jap M.P.s were called and took him off to the House of Terror. There he gave further trouble, so the M.P.s — also drunk — gave him a frightful thrashing.

Ozawa asked, "Is he fit to go back to Miri today, Doctor?"

"Ozawa, send him back. He's not fit enough to remain here."

Ozawa roared with laughter. "Doctor, I visit you tonight."

True to his word, about 9 p.m. he did come carrying a bottle of rice wine under each arm and apparently as much again inside him. We sat down in my sitting room. Ozawa refused a corkscrew and pushed the cork into the bottle with his thumb. He was in riotous mood and held forth in a quaint mixture of three languages on his two favourite subjects — venereal disease and his cook starving him to death. "Selalu timun! Always cucumbers!", he wailed.

This became a sort of battle cry for the evening; every time Ozawa found himself at a loss for something to say, he cried, "Selalu timun!". His cook must have been a heartless devil to cause such distress.

About midnight, Ozawa began to cause me some distress. He had a picture in front of him of Europeans fleeing in every direction before the victorious Japanese. Quite thoughtlessly, he became far too descriptive about the cowardly white man: I became quite angry and, giving even less thought to the matter, I decided to teach him a lesson. I chased Ozawa round the table, intent on seizing him by the collar and pants and throwing him out. But to my annoyance, the little Jap showed considerable skill in upsetting chairs in the path of his retreat. Finally, he pulled the table against the door of the sitting-room and went out through the front door like a swallow emerging from an underground cavern at Pohun Batu. He stopped in the middle of the road and turned towards my quarters. I was now at the window laughing. He said, "Takut-lah! Afraid! Doctor is angry. What for? Everything is O.K., O.K. Sahaya pulang! Sayonara! (I'm off home! Goodbye)."

"Sayonara, Ozawa-san. Takusang no aregato. Thanks very much."

Ozawa then set off home. Suddenly he shouted, "Selalu timun!" ("Always cucumbers!") at the top of his voice, leapt into the air and sprinted up the road towards the corner.

On the evening of 6 March, the District Officer, "'Che Taib", received a letter from the Governor of Brunei marked "very urgent". It contained instructions that I was to proceed to Brunei as soon as possible. It was not necessary for me to bring any instruments. Taib and Di Alvis, who was with him, raised their right thumbs high as they left my quarters; apparently news, or rumours thereof, was good.

In Shop 26, there was a tailor's wife very sick with an empyema following pneumonia and I obtained permission to take her to Brunei for operation. A car was required. Abang Ali went down to Resident Sezuki's shop to inquire and found him lying on the floor dead drunk. Sezuki was roused, but all he could say was, "They must have a letter. They must have a letter." However, the patient's relatives obtained a car and borrowed some tyres for it.

Next morning, Sezuki took me to the House of Terror "for a pass". On the way he said emphatically, "Before the war everything was fine, Doctor". Poor Sezuki! He had been much happier before his compatriots "liberated" South-East Asia.

The M.P.s were waiting for me. I was given a seat and my personal file was produced — three piles of bulky manuscript, one 45 centimetres high, something like the paper one sees in butchers' shops. The No. 2 M.P. conducted the interrogation. On either side of him was one of the car drivers who administered routine beatings. Together, the M.P. and I went through notable incidents in my life, from birth onwards, then through the lives of my parents. Where had I worked in Australia? For how long? I had never been in private practice, but I had done short "locums" at three places in the country and I gave the names of these. They were copied down in katakana with inscrutable exactitude. The Japanese have no "L" in their language and, being a bit of a fisherman at one time, I threw in a fictitious name, "mola-mola", the name of a giant ocean sunfish common in offshore New Zealand waters, to see how the No. 2 would cope. He struggled with the word, rolling his lower jaw unconvincingly as if he had a pebble in his mouth.

After the interview, I left for Brunei. The tailor's wife, bent almost double, sat in the back seat beside me, two rugs round her and a man's felt hat on her head, looking like a frightened bird.

On arrival, I found George Graham very cheerful. I asked him, "What's the urgency?"

"There's none at all. Actually, I have had some difficulty in raking up cases. We might do Juga. Anyway, come over to the quarters. I've got some Tutong wine made from pineapples and bananas."

Juga, the Dyak, was a fine old character, open-hearted, exuberant and courageous. He had a chest like an organ and was facing starvation from pyloric stenosis. Graham was reluctant to operate, but every day Juga pestered the life out of him. Juga had a large endemic goitre and he wanted this out at the same time. We met him halfway and decided to tackle his stomach. The night before operation he walked the ward and after much discussion he found a Chinese with exactly the same symptoms as himself. They sat talking together until well after midnight.

Graham allowed a Headman and seven other Dyaks to witness the operation, saying to me, "We might need some friends upcountry at some future time!".

And so we struggled as best we could with Juga's innards and he ended up with a gastroenterostomy. The day after operation the Dyak's chest began to bubble ominously. On the third day we were still worried. On the fourth, he was smiling. On the sixth day he chided me for not visiting him before breakfast, then said, "Tomorrow, I am going home."

"What's that? Your stitches aren't out yet!"

"It doesn't matter, Tuan. They'll come out of their own accord."

Juga's Chinese friend with the same symptoms also came to operation. Two days afterwards, Graham, who was standing by a window, called to me, "Come and see some of your handiwork!". I went across and looked. Two labourers were passing, a long wooden pole on their shoulders; slung from it by ropes was a wooden coffin. It was a few seconds before I regained composure — the Canadian had caught me off balance completely. Some days later, details of this "bad result" filtered through to us. The very night of his operation, the hardy Chinese had got out of bed, ate what food he could find in the ward, then had walked down to Brunei town and had eaten a great deal more. Next day he was pleased, saying repeatedly in Chinese Malay, "Munyak babut, munyak babut, very good, very good"; but he was distended like a drum and passed away the following night. At least he had died with a full stomach.

To compensate, the tailor's wife survived operation for empyema first on one side, then the other. It was one of the best saves I have ever had.

One morning, a Japanese doctor asked me to see a young Japanese woman who was an in-patient. She seemed to be a typist or secretary. She had multiple ulcers on her legs and had been over-treated with neo-salvarsan and had developed chronic arsenical poisoning. It was a pleasure to attend her. I spent an hour in her room. She was good looking, friendly and her manners were perfect. She was perspiring under two woollen blankets and I had them removed and then prescribed an aluminium acetate lotion and extra vitamins. I remembered a clinical meeting a few years ago at which our professor of surgery had recommended intravenous sodium thiosulphate as the treatment of choice for acute arsenical poisoning. Whether it would do any good at this late stage I did not know. But the plain fact was that after inspecting some of it in an opened packet in the X-ray Department, I was too windy to give the dirty looking stuff into the veins of a Japanese subject, and passed the responsibility on to the quiet, non-committal Japanese doctor. What the eventual outcome was, I do not know; I hope she survived.

During this visit, the Brunei M.P.s allowed George Graham, but not myself, to visit Old Bill. Several Dressers were questioned about my movements. A loyal member of the staff showed us a copy of the daily report on our doings, sent from the hospital to the M.P.s.

These security measures of the Japanese worried me. But one night, shortly after I returned to Belait, a government servant came to see me and mentioned another Malay's name. "Tuan, don't say anything in front of him. I notice he says one thing to your face, another in the kampong."

In a short time everything became clear. A trusted person had "changed" and had turned informer. Day after day, we, his former friends, watched him cycle to the House of Terror.

My neighbour, Chong Thau, brother of Chong Fah, had become a good friend. He worked for Post and Telegraphs and occasionally, between sending messages to Brunei and Miri, he was able to tune in to San Francisco for a few minutes. On odd occasions, he stripped to the waist and did some gardening in the ground between his house and mine. I came close to my bedroom window and when the coast was clear, Chong Thau passed on such snippets of news as he had, at the same time continuing to cut the grass with his parang. Months before, he had given a few items of news to me in the presence of this informer. But there was one slightly balancing feature. Shortly after I arrived in Belait, the informer himself had had a secret wireless in his home for a short time and I myself had listened to it. Nevertheless, we now lived under added tension.

In March, the successor to the Emperor's special ambassador, the late Marquis Maeda, visited Kuala Belait. An order was issued that during his visit everyone must stay indoors, with doors and windows closed. These conditions were barely tolerable and I shed all clothes except underpants and still I sweated as I sat. Suddenly, there was a knock on the door. I answered: a Jap was on the step — a car on the roadside. "You must come", said the soldier.

I quickly dressed and went to the car. The soldier held the back door open for me and closed it as I sat down. The streets were deserted and every house was closed like a tin of salmon. As the car entered the Residency gates, an N.C.O. screamed and a squad of soldiers in new uniforms sprang to attention. The driver led a puzzled doctor to an armchair in front of the kitchen. Half an hour later, a middle-aged, rather portly Jap came out, sat at a bench and beckoned me over. He said, "I am Major Suga. I am in charge of all Borneo prisoners of war. Now, what is your name?" He opened a small notebook and perused it. He then told me to work hard and be content and obey the laws of the Japanese Army. "It is reported that you do not salute. You must salute all Japanese soldiers of whatever rank."

Suga spoke English well and did not seem to be upset about the adverse report he had received. However, he looked intently at me as he said, "You must appreciate that you are lucky to be alive".

"Yes, Major."

"What is your salary?"

"$30 a month."

"No. You are getting $75 a month. It says so here."

"Major, my salary was recently reduced to $30 a month. I'm finding it difficult to manage."

"You are only getting $30?" He seemed surprised.

"Yes." I did not voice the suspicion that the Kempei-tai mobsters were pocketing the difference.

"That is not enough. I will see to it."

Major Suga put the notebook in his pocket. "You may return now." Then he stood and turned abruptly towards the Residency.

No car was made available and so I walked home. However, the soldiers stood at attention as I walked through the Residency gates. It was a curious experience, walking home along the deserted road. My footsteps seemed unusually loud and I knew dozens of people were watching me through keyholes and cracks round doors and windows.

I was always pleased to see Dresser Kim Sing; the young Straits-born Chinese had a priceless gift for relieving the monotony of life in Belait. He was known in every house and escorted many patients to me, ranging from Kapitan China himself to broken-down rickshaw kulis: he was equally obliging to all and was an asset to the medical department.

A convivial soul, with an inexhaustible fund of good humour, he celebrated all festivals, whether European, Japanese, Chinese or Malay. Every amusing or absurd facet of human behaviour claimed his attention. He was Chinese, but spoke practically no Chinese at all.

One evening, I was busy on the nightly chore of cleaning the soot from the glass of my kerosene lamp when suddenly, Kim Sing appeared at the door. I was bored almost to distraction and was delighted to see him. ''Doctor, may I sleep here please? I have quarrelled with my wife!''

Under his arm was a basket of ''fruit'' (as he called it) containing three bottles of rice wine, called Mr Red, because of its colour. He came in and sat down. ''Doctor, today my dear wife most generously gave me the remnants of the housekeeping money, so for once, I set out to enjoy myself and to forget these horrible times. But when I came home some wretched fellow said I was tipsy! So I said, 'If I stay, he goes; if he stays, I go!'.''

''And he stayed?''

''He did. As I left my wife said 'Oh, let him go! He'll be back in half an hour!'. This hurt me very much, and so you can see I am determined to sleep out tonight!''

''Good show, Kim Sing!''

He went to the kitchen and came back with water and three glasses — Abang Ali had just come in to see what was doing. Kim Sing poured the drinks and then proceeded to tell us about the marvellous kachubong tree which grows on Labuan Island. Such were its powers that if anyone cared to do silly things near it (such as laughing in a silly fashion or dancing three times round it in the nude) and afterwards plucked fruit and squeezed a little of its juice into samsu, then whosoever drank this samsu would shortly come under its influence and repeat these same ridiculous antics exactly. ''It's the truth, or something like it,'' laughed Kim Sing. He ran round the table three times to illustrate his story and then took a mouthful of wine.

''I have heard of a case,'' said Abang, grinning broadly.

''Which wine do you prefer, Kim Sing? Mr Red or Mr White?''

''It doesn't matter a scrap, Doctor, so long as it makes you feel good. When on holiday I usually drink more of Mr Red simply because there is more of it. Nowadays, the poorer people are adding lime and tobacco ashes to their samsu. Why? Simply to accentuate the process of intoxication.''

Kim Sing settled back in his chair. ''When I was born, Doctor, I never thought I would live to see times like this. What trouble these shorties have caused! Take the fifteenth of the first month of the Chinese New Year just recently. It was full moon, of course, and we usually celebrate this fact with a makan besar (feast). But what? No meat, no eggs, no fowls, no fish, no samsu, no crackers. No fish! and there is the sea, but they won't let anyone go out on it! Co-prosperity! Di Alvis says, 'Now we have joined the rag and bones department of Asia!'.''

Chong Fah, the Sanitary Inspector, cycled past the window and Kim Sing chuckled. ''There goes a good man, Doctor. But when he first returned from the Royal Sanitary Institute with his diploma he was so strict that the townspeople decided public health wasn't necessary: not the men — it was the Chinese ladies! One morning they lay in wait with choppers and hoes — my! What weapons didn't they have! But our man smelt a rat, and so was able to survive. Bachelors are like that. When he acquired a wife he was much better.''

Listening to Kim Sing was a better way of killing time than cleaning soot from a lamp glass. I said, ''Tell me, Kim Sing, tragedy and comedy — are they far apart?''

Kin Sing drained his glass and put it on the table. ''An important question, Doctor! Let us take an example. This empty glass — well, it is a tragedy. And this bottle of Mr Red — it must be comic because it puts everyone in a good humour and makes them laugh. No doubt they are separate, but they must meet — like this!''

The inevitable happened: then Kim Sing resumed, laughing to himself as amusing thoughts passed through his head. "That Chinese kuli who was carrying a 90 kilogram bag up the sloping plank on to the lorry; halfway up and the lorry moved off! So down he crashed and broke his back. Very sad no doubt, but it has its funny side. Did you laugh, Doctor?"

"I don't remember doing so."

"Well, what about those twins you delivered? And the anak bumbong (breech) up the road here! You worked so hard and so did the midwife and what happened? Babies are too expensive and the poor mothers were forced to give them away! After all the trouble! And the M.P.s, when they wouldn't let you go up the river to that Chinese woman. 'It doesn't matter,' they said. 'It's only a Chinese and one more dead Chinese is not important.' Perhaps Europeans cannot see anything funny in that, but we Chinese can. It is so cruel and so absurd it makes us laugh."

"Have the other half, Kim Sing."

"Thank you, Doctor. You know, either the Chinese are silly or they keep on following former customs without thinking. Old fashioned Chinese girls don't commit adultery at all. You can scarcely speak to them, they are so shy! It's education that makes them modern. It seems that all the present-day Chinese are trying to be social, whereas all they are being is immoral!"

Kim Sing gave an account of housewives losing their money at the gambling farm and their method of balancing the budget. "I have seen the same thing in Singapore", he said. "Malay girls have strings of sovereigns down their bajus and powder and scent and lipstick and facecream — they want the lot and they get them! The husbands do not care. The poor fellows must have worries of their own."

Kim Sing went on in this way until eleven o'clock, then went to sleep in a chair. His last act was to pour Abang a drink saying, "Sir, I am not tipsy. See, I am pouring a correct measure!"

I borrowed a tikar (mat) from Abang and covered Kim Sing with a towel which Old Bill had given me in Brunei, and a strip of cloth which was a present from Sheik Kassim. Abang took off Kim Sing's shoes and the pocket philosopher was made comfortable for the night.

At 6 a.m. I woke him and persuaded him to have a cold bath. Then we sat in the lounge-room waiting for Kuki to serve some coffee. Kim Sing looked about the room and his fingers beat an irritable tattoo on the table. Where was his basket of fruit? Finally, he jumped up with a laugh and went to my room. Success! There was the basket of fruit! Glug. Glug. A few minutes later, he reappeared with 5 centimetres of Mr Red in his glass. "Just a little one of the dog that bit me, doctor!"

He settled down in the chair and resumed his inimitable discourse on interesting things. After some time, he got on to the fall of Singapore. "Some of the things people say about the Japanese are silly. An Indian told me that the Japs were kicking babies into the air and catching them on bayonets as they fell. Why, it is impossible. You cannot do it! A baby is not a football!"

"Of course not, Kim Sing. Have the second half."

"Thank you, Doctor. Why are you drinking coffee? What sort of a drink is that in terrible times like these?"

Presently, one of his children came looking for him so off he went to meet his wife.

About 4 p.m. I was standing at a window when I saw Kim Sing coming down the road at the head of a column of Punjabis. Why he was leading them I do not know. He had little or no medicines to give them, but he was a brave courier and the best friend they had. He was under 150 centimetres in height and every man of the Punjabis was over 30 centimeters taller. Dressed in white drill with a white panama hat on his head, he was strutting along with the peculiarly attractive gait and dignity of a penguin. Seeing me, he immediately lost all interest in marching about in the tropical sun. Opposite the quarters, he broke ranks and presently was seated in the lounge with a glass of his beloved Mr Red in front of him.

"Did you see their new shirts, Doctor, and Bata shoes? The Japs are being kind, with a purpose, of course. But just now the Subedar and Jemadar said to me, 'The British taught us to fight as they taught our fathers to fight. How can we be expected to fight against them?''.

Kim Sing's mind leapt from one thing to another with startling speed. In a few minutes he described how he came from a wealthy family and was sent to school in a Buick car with a chauffeur; how Father van Schloor tried to convert him to Christianity; how Dressers drank the hospital brandy when on night duty; and so on. Describing his father's funeral, he said that a Chinese priest, skilled at these things, breaks the bones with his hands ("crack! crack!" he said, laughing out aloud) so that the body can be doubled up in the coffin.

A sudden knocking on the door interrupted the story. With remarkable intuition, Kim Sing said, "M.P.s!" and lifted Mr Red and his glass from the table and put them out of sight.

Two M.P.s entered. We stood up and bowed. The Japs went immediately to the bedroom, turned back the bedclothes, opened the cupboard and came out again. They went to the kitchen and lavatory. It was barely half a minute before they were out of the front door again.

Kim Sing sat down. "I say! My heavens, Doctor, those people make me feel distinctly nervous. They are always interrupting our civilized conversation. Why can't they go home to Japan?"

In September 1945, after the surrender ceremony at Kuching the prisoners of the Prisoner of War and Internee Camp of Kuching were informed of their liberation. Among the happy released prisoners of war was Dr. George Graham (standing left) the Canadian medico who was my colleague at Brunei. Two Australian civilian internees are in this smiling group — Ivan Quartermaine and 'Kelly' Kirkwood, from Western Australia and New South Wales respectively (2nd and 3rd from left, front row).

Chapter 9

1943 KUALA BELAIT

In June, George Graham obtained permission from the Military Police for me to visit Brunei again. But being an enemy subject, he could not let me know. Nor could the Japanese Principal Medical Officer, since the Japanese telegraph authorities insisted that no Japanese could communicate with an enemy subject. In the end, with help from the Kempei-tai, bless them, this difficulty was overcome and I left Kuala Belait in the company of two Japanese businessmen. One had spent seven years in London and spoke English fluently. At the Lutong Crossing, he turned to me and said, "We have an exceptionally capable Medical Officer at Kuala Belait."

"I haven't met him yet," I answered, presuming someone new had arrived.

"I mean you."

We were approaching the eastern bank. After a long silence, he turned to me and said, earnestly, "You are doing great work for humanity."

I thanked him. He meant well, of that there was no shadow of doubt. He could not have had the slightest idea of whether I was good, bad or indifferent as a doctor.

It was dark when we arrived. Graham was not in his quarters and I found him in the wards examining a critically ill Chinese boy. During an attack of typhoid fever some little time ago, the boy's bowel had perforated: miraculously, he had survived this but now he had been admitted with symptoms of intestinal obstruction. Operation gave the only hope. The father, a fine old peasant, wept without restraint because the boy was an only child and both he and his wife were too old to hope for another. Graham had a way with him in these matters and presently the Chinese agreed to the operation. This was done under spinal anaesthesia and was not completed until the early hours of the morning. As Graham and I were removing our gloves, the wound was dressed and a white sheet was drawn up over the boy almost to his chin. In the glare of the theatre lights his features were strikingly composed. He said, "Trima kasih banyak, Tuan. Thank you very much." Everyone present was considerably affected. The very late hour, the strain we were under and the doubtful outcome all seemed to add up.

The boy spent a quiet night; but next day, drainage stopped and colicky pains returned. Without moving him from his bed, a tube was put into his small bowel above the obstruction; however, he passed away several hours later.

"A pity."

"Yes, bad luck."

Next day, the boy's parents sent Graham a small present of garden produce. Graham turned to me and said, "You know, this world will lose something when poverty is abolished — when and if it ever is".

It was a thoughtful remark and very, very true. After a time, I said, "I can remember treating people with pet dogs sprawled all over the bed and pills being carried in on silver trays. A Scotch and second halves from six till seven. How the rich suffer!".

Graham was laughing. "Did you enjoy it?"

He had had the same experience, of course. I said, "At least it was a damn sight better than this!."

During this visit, I got to know Graham well. The kindly Canadian was the perfect antidote to the violent element amongst the invaders. He seemed well suited for a fashionable physician's practice at home, yet he obviously enjoyed treating illiterate primitives like old Juga, the Dyak. In many ways he showed his courage. There was the time when, by threatening headmen, the Japs managed to apprehend the six Ibans concerned in the Sungei Bera headhunting affair. They were taken to Brunei prison, beaten and starved. One had his tongue crushed by pliers; another seen by Graham for an injury, was paralysed in hands and feet due to beri-beri. Graham wrote in an official report to the prison authorities, "prisoner has severe beri-beri and an ununited fracture of the forearm as a result of treatment following arrest".

I was amused to discover that, in spite of being trained in medical science, he was incurably romantic and read poetry, of all things, for the pleasure of it. Tennyson was his favourite. Often, in the sitting-room at night, he would say, "Here, listen to this", and then read out an agreeable passage. One evening, I showed him Shaw's "Preface to *Heartbreak House*" and commented on the beauty of the language and the portrait of the irate old reformer which emerged from it. But when I handed it to the Canadian, he become so exasperated with the radical subject matter that he could not continue reading.

One morning, His Highness, The Sultan, came into the operating theatre and advanced towards the table with outstretched hands. Crying, "Ah-h!" Graham raised his sterile, gloved hands high in the air: shaking hands was out of order! The Sultan watched the operation for a time then said, "Goodnight" in English to me and left.

On the morning of my return to Kuala Belait, I was summoned to the Brunei Kempei-tai office and questioned about all conversations I had had with Graham. The questions were simple but troublesome to answer. "Tell us, what have you been talking about?" "What else did you talk about?" And so on. I said that we had talked about medical matters and about poetry.

"Have you written any poetry?"

"No, not yet."

"When you do you must show it to us."

"Certainly."

Not many poets receive such a request before they have even taken up their quills.

At the end of the interview I requested permission to call on Old Bill. To my surprise, it was granted. I found him in one corner of the kutch factory, in charge of two vats in which gula apong was being made. Malays obtained the "tuak" or raw juice from the flowering stems of the nipah palms along the river. Bill boiled the juice down to a thick, ugly, treacly mass which he sold to Graham and others as sugar. A bathtub and two Javanese water containers were articles of equipment. The rear axle of a car was rigged up as a stirrer. "Occasionally, I toss in a Jap to thicken the mixture", said Bill, laughing as if he were in a pre-war club.

Between the two vats, Bill had rigged up a small seat and here he sat and thought away the days with the tuak bubbling lugubriously beside him. No doubt, he was making a small contribution to the co-prosperity sphere. It was a pretty pickle for a fine old adventurer to find himself in. Like Kim Sing, Bill could never resist a story. "Did I tell you about the Malay workman who fell into a vat of boiling kutch? His mates dressed him with castor oil and tea leaves and took him home. Hospital with you fellows? Not on your life! I went along to see how he was doing. Would you believe it? He was lying on the floor, all dressings removed. Beside him were four women busy chewing betel nut and spitting the stuff all over his burnt skin. He died, of course. It just goes to show you.''

''To show you what?''

''Why! Never to fall into boiling kutch, of course! You are dull this morning, Doctor!''

Back at the hospital, I packed my bags and Graham and I went into the dental room while waiting for the bus. I sat in the dentist's chair with my head back as if expecting the drill. George pulled up a chair and sat with his feet up on a bench. Conversation soon petered out and for a few minutes we sat in silence. A more forlorn pair of medicos it would be difficult to imagine! This must have occurred to Graham for he began to laugh and then added more seriously, ''Isn't it a bastard, this waiting, waiting, waiting!.''

I replied, ''It makes you wonder what the devil they're doing. Nothing we have seen can explain it. It stands to reason they must come. And then what? What do we do when the Allies attack? Go on tiptoe to an outhouse?''

Graham blew a column of cigarette smoke towards the window. ''A couple of locals say they'll take me up the river.''

I thought about this and turned towards him, smiling. ''What if you are in the theatre or the 'mid-block' at the time?''

Graham brought both his feet to the ground in mock irritation. ''Don't be so damn cheerful!'', he cried.

We both knew what had happened in an operating theatre in Singapore — the patient and all the attending medical staff had been bayoneted.

When we first saw them, they appeared to be a group of Japanese High School boys on a government-sponsored tour of the new overseas territories. They came dressed in white shirts and shorts and snow-white sandshoes and seemed subdued and a little mystified by the strange surroundings. Their ages seemed to range from 16 to 18 years and they all seemed very small and immature indeed. They settled down in some houses near the river mouth and at odd times, they were marched to and fro about the town and in the late afternoon they played baseball or volleyball on the padang. Then they took to running several kilometres in formation every morning at 6 a.m., passing in front of my quarters and then, after breakfast, drilling. They were stripped to the waist and there was one hairy Ainu amongst them looking like a black sheep in the flock. We then realised that the Japanese were turning these youngsters into soldiers. Next came uniforms and wooden rifles and they began to sing what was known locally as ''the Love Horse song'' as they ran and marched, just as all Japanese soldiers do. Occasionally they goose-stepped energetically. A few months later, they were issued with rifles and that was that — the transformation from normal, healthy teenagers, to professional killers was complete: at least at a casual glance.

The Malays, a sensitive and dignified people, have a flair for town planning amounting to genius. Most of their villages are like so many holiday huts scattered amongst elegant palms, with the shadows of moving fronds and patches of sunlight playing upon them; with, nearby, a river or seashore. Sometimes, like the village of Tambun in Marudu Bay, they are built in the sea itself, with an endless flow of tropic waves beneath the floor. And always they seem to be thousands of kilometres from the nearest commercial slum.

The Malay village in Kuala Belait had suffered from Sanitary Board planning, but close to the river, it was still unspoilt. I welcomed calls to it. The native midwife, Pangiran Hitam frequently accompanied me, walking beside me barefooted, talking of housekeeping and family matters. Amongst her people she was a respected practitioner with her bacha-bacha, berurut, bertiup and berhantu, i.e., praying, rubbing, blowing and expelling of evil spirits. Pangiran enjoyed quite a reputation for prowess in massage. One morning, just as we reached the edge of the palms on a visit, she told me of being called to the House of Terror. The Chief of Military Police himself required her services. He stripped naked, lay on a bed and ordered the timid, blushing midwife to give him a massage.

"I was so ashamed, Tuan Doktor!" she exclaimed.

"Perhaps he wants to keep you, Pangiran!", I said.

"Chelaka, Tuan Doktor!", she swore.

As we approached the house to which we were going, a young girl darted past us saying, "I am going to the shops," and off she went along a path leading to the main bazaar. As it happened, she was the patient, now recovered, whom I had been called to see.

Presently, Pangiran unearthed this reason for my being called. Three years previously, the girl's mother had given birth to a child; several nights later, as the cocks crowed on the change of tide, she had roused her husband and had asked him to get her some flowers. He was angry. "Flowers? flowers? How can I get flowers in the middle of the night? Go to sleep!"

A little later, she rose from her sleeping mat and walked from the house. Next day, two hundred people looked for her along the river and beaches. At night, the search was continued by torchlight, but without success. The Malays believed that a spirit called "puaka" had entered her body and had directed her steps towards the river; and there she had drowned.

Now, once again, the night before, the evil puaka had returned to the village and had taken possession of the young daughter while she slept; but she was seen leaving the house and was forcibly restrained by relatives. She fought and struggled to obey the power urging her to go.

Not for six months after the occupation was any serious attempt made to persuade local Indians into active collaboration. Then, one sultry afternoon, a delegation visited the Indian Association. Japanese speakers urged the Indians to assist in expelling the white man from Asia. Dr Hashimoto made what was described as a "hot speech". At the end of the afternoon an officer asked, "Is there anyone here who is still pro-British?". At this, M.P.s sprang to their feet and looked hard at everyone. In the resulting silence, someone sneezed and it sounded like an explosion.

Several months later another meeting was convened and everyone was urged once again to kill the white man and drive him out of Asia. Balwant Singh was called upon to make a speech. Later, he told me, "I didn't know what to say! I got up and spoke of general prosperity and said it was a good thing. No one could object to that!"

When the Japs raised the question of volunteers to fight for India's independence, the meeting resolved that a letter about physical standards required of volunteers be sent to headquarters at Kuching. This was clever and it shelved the question temporarily at least.

The next development was a procession. About two hundred Indians paraded round town with red, white and green flags. Some carried placards bearing slogans in English. "India is one and indivisible." "Fight the White Man!" "White Man go!" Cheerleaders leapt up and down urging everyone to exclaim. From the bazaar, the Indians marched to the House of Terror and gave rousing cheers; then, hot and fed up, they made towards the Company building near the river. As they approached the Dispensary, the medical staff, including myself, was standing at the door. Two cheerleaders were recent patients; many others had seen the only European in town professionally. Cheering died down, hats were raised, a few called, "Good morning, Doctor" and Balwant Singh grinned from ear to ear.

The best dressed man in the procession was Chundra Singh. He wore a royal blue blazer and looked like an Olympic athlete. Afterwards, for some reason or other, he came round to see me. He met Chong Fah ouside my quarters and brought him in too, looking under the house for possible spies before he climbed the steps. Kuki served tea and glutinous tapioca cakes. After a little general conversation, Chundra Singh said that what the Indians wanted was *justice*; other things too, including submarines and better salaries, but chiefly, *justice.* That meant self-government.

Chong Fah asked, laughingly, "But, Mr Chundra Singh, what about the 80 million Moslems?".

Chundra Singh threw all caution to the winds. He cried, "Man, listen to me. It is only British propaganda that says there are differences between Indians, Sikhs and Moslems. British propaganda made up all this business and now half the people are silly enough to believe it is true. As for the Moslems — you leave them to us. We'll soon straighten them out and turn them into gentlemen!"

Chundra Singh himself soon saw the humour in this. He cooled down and joined Chong Fah and I in showing amusement.

After Chundra Singh departed, Chong Fah, who had been standing at the window, took off his white helmet and sat down at the table. "Doctor," he said, "I would like to tell you that I do not agree with Confucius."

What a day! Asia was stirring with a vengeance! Chong Fah, one of the best friends I had, was now convinced that people should put nation before family. But unfortunately for him there were gentlemen in the House of Terror who did not agree with him: and from time to time, they jotted down notes about his views and activities. And about Balwant Singh they did the very same thing. In actual fact, the days of these two good people were numbered and they came to a terrible end.

Months later, a handful of Kuala Belait Indians actually joined the Indian National Army and went off for training. Two had been severely thrashed by the Japanese early in the occupation. Another was the mosquito collector who, day after day, rode round town on a bicycle just fast enough to stop it from falling over. He was a nice fellow, quite popular, a man who never harmed anyone or anything, and this went for mosquitoes too. When he left for Kuching no one said much against him, believing him to be sincere. He came round and shook my hand before he left and wished me good luck.

With July, came further trouble. Early one morning, an elderly Chinese came to see me. There was a boy in the Roman Catholic Mission suffering from constipation: would Doctor send the Dresser to give him an enema? "Yesterday I thought he had dhu mau thang, so I rubbed him with feathers wrapped in cloth and took out something like pig's bristles through the skin. Even so, he isn't better yet."

After breakfast, I went to the Mission. The boy was sitting on a platform under the Mission, legs stretched out in front, his arms behind, supporting him. He had the sardonic smile of tetanus and spasms were causing him to cry out. He was carried upstairs to bed and I obtained a supply of anti-tetanic serum from the Company hospital, on promise of replacement. A request was wired to Brunei for further supplies; I met the next three buses, but nothing came. Under treatment, the boy improved slightly, but the following day, spasms recurred on one side. In the late afternoon he was reaching with one hand towards the top of the mosquito net as if seeking something and he passed away shortly after sunset.

Earlier that same afternoon I had sent the Attendant to the Company hospital for a large syringe and needle. A patient had presented with a liver abcess so longstanding that it was pointing on the abdominal wall. Sayed returned and said I had to collect it myself. At the hospital, an orderly asked me to sit down in the waiting-room and this I did, for half an hour. Finally, I went to the operating theatre and explained my requirement to the Japanese doctor. I was sent outside and waited for another half an hour; then I was handed a syringe and needle wrapped neatly in iodoform gauze.

The following morning, I was called to the Company hospital and then to a pigeon-hole opening in the Dispensary. There were five Taiwan prostitutes sitting on a bench behind me as I bent towards the aperture. A bespectacled dispenser demanded the immediate return of the anti-tetanic serum and the syringe borrowed from the hospital. I explained my attempt to obtain serum, but the dispenser lost his temper and shouted that I was treating the Japanese like Kulis. Why must I ask for syringes? His anger increased and only the intervening wall saved me from a slapping. I was told that I would be beaten if ever again I asked for medicines or instruments from the Company hospital. My relationship with Japanese doctors had been good and this could only have been independent action by prickly subordinate staff.

On this occasion, I had difficulty in throwing off the tension which I felt. In the afternoon, still not settled, I received a call to an opium-smoker, living above the gambling farm. The old fellow's opium ration had been cut, due to dwindling supplies and he had decided to stage a demonstration to have it restored. As I entered his room, he was lying on the mat with opium pipe and lamp beside him, a picture of complete ill-health. When two Chinese came forward and started to raise the smoker from the floor, the wretched fellow pretended to be dead: and the two henchmen lifted him up and struggled around with his body, colliding with the wall and reeling backwards and forwards, dragging his flaccid legs across the mat.

Finally, I could stand it no longer. I left the room and went downstairs. In the farm, crowds of local people were tightly packed round the tables. I was forcing my way through when I found myself beside my poor old cook. The old man reached across to lay a bet and I tapped him on the shoulder. ''Tabe, Kuki'', I said.

If his open mouth meant anything, the cook was taken completely by surprise; but in a second he recovered. ''Ah, Tuan, I'm acting as another man's agent! It's not my money!''

I thought, ''Shortly it won't be mine, either.'' Then I said so and left Kuki laughing, like a horse.

A little later, the old fellow did me a very good turn. An informer reported to the Military Police that I was making a great deal of money (banana-leaf money, the Japanese notes were called) from private medical work. One afternoon, two M.P.s paid me a visit, one being Hamada, who had recently been promoted to full M.P. and was now wearing a sword. I met them at the door and Hamada said, ''We want to inspect all your belongings.''

I led the way to the bedroom. Hamada's companion was a new Chief of Military Police. The two Japanese sat down on chairs and I took a seat on the bed.

Hamada said, ''You must be very lonely now''.

''Yes.''

''You must remember it is only for the present. When the war is finished you will be sent home with a lump sum of money. Then you'll be comfortable.''

The Chief put questions through Hamada and I answered briefly. Did I ever go out? Yes, every day, to the Dispensary. Did I go out at night? Only when called. Did people visit me? No, not now.

''We want you to keep a list of all the people who visit you.''

Hamada went to a bedside table, picked up some books and went rapidly through the pages. Then he opened a leather bag containing hairbrushes and tested them for false backs. The Chief went through my clothes carefully, glanced behind the mirror and under the pillow and mattress. Beneath the bed he discovered an unopened bottle of "Superior Quality Stag Brand. Finest Great Age Lychee Wine"; a gift from the Customs Clerk. I offered them a drink, hopefully as one for the road, but Hamada replied, "No thanks, we don't drink." They sat down again.

"Jesus Christ must be very angry with Europeans."

"I am beginning to think so too."

"If you make a mistake you will never be sent home as long as you live. Have you a missus?"

"No."

"Do you keep a diary?"

"No."

"We are having you watched. A Doctor must stay on the premises. We will be coming again to inspect your house. Banyak terima kasih. Thank you very much."

With this, they went off. I was satisfied: they did not seem to be very excited about anything.

Presently, Kuki came in. He went first to the window and then, with a conspiratorial air, explained how the M.P.s had ordered their cook — a Hailam like himself and therefore a blood brother — to investigate my financial status through him. Kuki and his friend collaborated faultlessly: the M.P.s were told a harrowing story of how Kuki was never sure of his wages, how he had to scrape along from day to day, dependent on gifts from patients. This was true enough, but it surprised the Japanese. Kuki told of various accusations made to the M.P.s about how I was simply coining money.

"Don't worry, Tuan, they don't believe them."

"How long has this been going on, Kuki?"

"Not long."

"Why didn't you tell me?"

"It doesn't matter. We didn't want to bother you."

"Thanks very much, Kuki."

Kuki went to the kitchen. From the look on his face it was apparent he had entered into this intrigue with zest. A fine old man. Relations between us had been excellent ever since I gave up the silly business of account keeping. Kuki now took all my salary and all presents of food and fed us both. I kept the contents of little red packets often given by patients in the Chinese village and paid for the laundry, firewood and anything apart from food which I wanted. Even so, there were occasional crises when my pockets were empty and Kuki had lost everything at the gambling farm and had no money to buy food: he would then reveal his plight indirectly by railing against one of the town merchants. "Who could charge such a price and not be ashamed?", he would cry. I understood what he meant and his anger always subsided after I produced a few dollars from my hip pocket. After one such episode, when I was forced to offer some resistance to the old man, I said, "The trouble with you, Kuki, is that when you go to the gambling tables you put your money on the wrong number!".

With this, I scored a bull — Kuki was extremely exasperated. "I know! I know!", he cried. Then he broke from Malay into some remote Hainanese dialect and went off in a huff to the kitchen.

Soon after, Kuki fell ill with a real dog's disease — vomiting and diarrhoea. I visited him in the Chinese village. He occupied a tiny room just large enough to contain a bed and it was obvious he had no reserves at all. Over the next few days I gave him all the money I had and a few tradeable belongings. "Kuki, hide these in your house. If you ever have need, use them." I suppose they ended up in the gambling farm.

One morning, there was a short but amusing episode. There was a knock on the door and I answered and in came an excited Japanese soldier. He saluted and bowed and then shook my hands warmly. "I am going back to Japan!" he said. He was thrilled to bits.

"Yoroshii desu, very good", I said. Another bow and salute and he left my quarters, still smiling and shaking his head with pleasure. I had never seen him before. I presumed that he and his family had numbered Europeans amongst their friends. He had a long ocean journey ahead of him.

Three days after Kuki's admission of intrigue on my behalf, I was taken once again to the House of Terror. I was questioned at length about alleged contacts with someone from Labuan. This meant nothing to me and the fact that I had to persist in denials of meeting any such person rather worried me, since I did not know where it would lead. The new Chief of Military Police was heavily built and his face had strength in it. As he put each question through Sezuki, he leant over and studied my face intently. The range being almost point blank, it was most disconcerting. Before I left, he handed me a letter thanking me for my detailed report on the Sungei Bera Ayau.

One never knew what to expect. In the Kempei-tai you are within metres of the muscle-men and a slip of the tongue or an unpredictable change of mood in the Chief could activate them. The M.P.s were receiving constant reports about me and we all knew the main source. Yet nothing much happened. Sometimes, developments were bewildering. From time to time Japanese soldiers dropped into our Dispensary and requested examination and treatment. It was given to the best of my ability and with our very limited resources. One soldier gave me particular pleasure. He had epigastric pain and as he lay on the couch, pressing the upper abdomen here and there without finding a particular sore spot, I looked into his eyes and the diagnosis was clear — functional. A Son-of-Heaven had neurosis! Under tyrannical military compulsion, the Japanese had forced into them a little more courage and decidedly more determination than *most of the contemporary* human race. But the resultant teeth gritting violence is something we could all do without.

One morning, the Chief and his men came to the Dispensary and demanded a list of the names of every Japanese who had been there. We never saw any of these former Japanese out-patients again. However, presently, we acquired a new set of patients — members of the Kempei-tai itself!

Twice a week the soldiers of the Japanese Garrison at Seria piled into the back of ex-A.I.F. trucks and came to Kuala Belait to enjoy themselves at the cinema. For two or three hours they were packed like sardines inside a large hall made of bone dry timber and the real world outside was completely forgotten. They left their rifles at Seria, but carried short bayonets on their belts. The subordinate staff at the oil-fields had access to highly inflammable material and in every shop and house in town there were buckets and bottles. Parangs and changkuls (hoes) and garden forks were about the place in abundance. A Chinese hawker visited Japanese-occupied houses at Seria regularly selling peanuts, dried prawns etc., and at the same time he carefully counted the rifles in racks on the walls. Able-bodied Punjabi prisoners of war were also counted as they were marched to and from various labour projects. The oil-fields could be cut off from Brunei and Miri quite simply by destruction of unprotected boats and ferries at Lutong and Baram. Many of the Japanese soldiers were impressed North Chinese or Taiwanese. They carried only seven bullets in their belts, whereas soldiers from Japan itself carried twenty-two. They sat in shops chatting to the towkeis in Chinese and sipping coffee and eating cakes. There were no machine-guns, no artillery, no fixed guns or defences on the oil-fields and a Japanese plane or a warship was never seen. Blazing oil tanks could possibly attract Allied attention.

With the unsolicited help of a mere handful of bad-tempered, aggressive soldiers, the Kempei-tai was slowly provoking the district to rebellion. There are brave people everywhere and even frightened people can be driven to desperate deeds. The Chinese ladies had once got together to teach the Health Inspector a lesson and with luck they could be mobilised again, this time to join him in a wild attack upon the House of Terror and the dozen monsters in it. Five minutes would have been enough for a complete spring-cleaning. At least, that was the pious hope.

A Chinese living on a farm very close to Belait was an amateur student of history. Before Pearl Harbour he accurately predicted the outbreak of the Pacific War and gave as his opinion that New Guinea would be the limit of the Japanese advance. From there, they would be rolled back by Americans and Australians. The problem was — just when?

I learnt that in our small township a few resolute people were beginning to think seriously about these matters, just as they were doing so, quite independently, further north-east in North Borneo (*"Kinababu Guerillas"*). Everything hinged on the timing of any anti-Japanese move. One slip and all was lost.

Pressure came on fairly generally about town. The Punjabis sent word through Kim Sing that they were under heavy persuasion. Frank Chin was picked up and man-handled at the Kempei-tai. Chong Fah was put in prison for three days and questioned about visits to me. The Postmaster and Di Alvis, a senior company clerk, were also interrogated. Twice in one month, Japanese soldiers suddenly arrived in trucks in front of government quarters, poured out and held brief but exciting skirmishing exercises, using blank cartridges, around and even underneath our quarters. The first time, for one brief moment, I thought it was the real thing and help was on its way.

One mid-day, when most of the town was resting, I went across to neighbour Chong Thau's house. Frank Chin was present and it was thus a rather dangerous gathering — wireless operator, suspected insurrectionist and the only European in town. Because of this, Chong Thau was on the alert and when his immediate neighbour went down his steps he went behind his quarters and watched him go down the road to Kempei-tai. At the Seria crossroads, near the House of Terror, the fellow stopped and looked back. Across the padang he could see Chong Thau standing, hands on hips, watching him. He lost courage and came slowly back along the road.

I had a feeling that things were moving towards a change; something was going to happen.

Early one morning Sezuki and an M.P. came to my quarters, in full dress. As usual, Sezuki was friendly and polite. "Tuan Doktor, the Chief M.P. says there are many sick people at Kuching. Do you agree to go there and give them medicine?"

"Certainly, Mr Sezuki." Kuching was the capital of Sarawak.

"Thank you. It is most kind of Doktor."

"When do I go?"

"In half an hour. Arrangements have been made. Two Europeans are coming from Brunei in a car. If you wish you can go with them."

Some four hours later, George Graham and Old Bill arrived. They had been roused from bed at 2 a.m. in the middle of a thunderstorm and given five minutes to pack essential belongings. The electric light had failed, of course. They waited at the District Office for hours before setting out.

My cook turned on quite a good lunch and the four of us drank the bottle of Superior Quality Lychee Wine: after which Graham and Bill and I were bundled into the back of a truck. I waved goodbye to Kuki: the old chap was weeping. By evening, we were in the prison by the river mouth at Miri. It was deja vu with a vengeance.

For three weeks we laboured under guard in the gaol compound, raking, chipping and picking up mango leaves. At night, we had local brandy with our evening meal obtained with help from a profit-seeking Dyak policeman. Once, I reckon we must have had a bit too much, for George started to talk about his wife and declared she was the only girl in the world he could possibly have married. As bachelors, Bill and I were moderately amused, but completely taken aback when we realised he was serious.

"Do you mean to say that if you had been born in Woop-Woop and never met this dietician from Medicine Hat, you wouldn't have got married?"

"That's right."

"What utter nonsense!"

Anyway, she must have been a stunning girl. Later in the evening, Bill became tired; in fact, completely knocked-out.

During the day, as well as Japanese guards, there were two armed Sikh policemen in charge of us. One was as good as gold, one was lousy. The latter was on our backs all the time. "Keredja! Keredja! Work! Work!" Bill was getting on in years and he had to bear the brunt of it. Just before he went to sleep he said, "You mark my words, one of these days Hitler will be regarded as a God." For my part, I said nothing silly enough to rest in memory, but I haven't the slightest doubt I held my own: if I didn't, it was indeed a memorable occasion.

Then, one morning, our luggage was inspected and we were taken on board a Straits Steamship Company coastal ship, *Sabuk* which was lying offshore. On board were a number of North Borneo Europeans. Recently, there had been serious trouble in Sandakan, with Australian P.O.W.s in the thick of it. Wireless sets and contact with the local people seemed to be the basis of the trouble: and Captain Matthews and other Australians, and many civilians, both European and local, were now in the Kempei-tai; amongst them an old friend, Johnny Funk.

Graham, Old Bill and I were directed to the saloon deck, to join two other doctors, their wives and children. A chalk line drawn down the deck separated us from Japanese officers. The ship was crowded. Moored aft was a heavy barge into which additional cargo was being loaded. In the late afternoon I was leaning over the rails when Graham approached and said, "From what I have just heard I am afraid this is going to be a genuine hell-ship." His expression gave no indication as to whether he was serious or joking. Tenth-rate sanitation and Allied attack on the ship by bombs or torpedoes were the only worries I had already conjured up to frighten myself. I hid my uncertainty by asking abruptly, "Why?".

Graham laughed. "It's really bad. Brace yourself! You and I have been selected to do the cooking for this deck."

The ferry crossing at Miri River. The town, which had a peace time population of 10,000 was later occupied by members of the 2/13 Battalion.

Chapter 10

1944-45 KUCHING (SARAWAK)

Our ship was old and handicapped by towing the barge and the few available toilets were choked with maggots. After a short, but seemingly endless journey, we arrived at Kuching, Sarawak, constipated beyond belief and with appropriate expressions of concern upon our faces.

At the wharf we were loaded into two trucks and driven through Kuching to the internment camp at Lintang Barracks, a few kilometres out of town. At the entrance to the camp was a guardhouse with a barbed-wire fence running away from it on either side. The trucks went up a slight incline to some weatherboard buildings. Here, we got out.

A dozen British P.O.W.s were working on the road, dressed only in brief loincloths. They were incredibly thin, as if afflicted with advanced phthisis: no expression on their faces, no sign of any welcome to us. This did nothing for our peace of mind. There was a sentry in the square. On the right hand side of the road were barbed-wire fences dividing the area into a number of separate camps which looked vaguely like cattle yards before a sale; admittedly in an off-season. A squad of Punjabi soldiers marched down from an office further up the hill: at their head was Jemedar Mohammed Hasham, formerly in Seria. He smiled and nodded.

Our belongings were laid out on the road and inspected. I had a bigger pile than most. Then the women went off by truck to the womens' camp down the hill near the guardhouse. The men carried their bags across to the gate of the Male Civilian Camp 30 metres away. We were met by a small group of internees, amongst whom were John Savage and Sam Timberlake. After hasty greetings, the pair took my luggage. I followed them, meeting a few friends and acquaintances. There was a beard on every second face; grey seemed to be the predominant colour.

In front of the second hut from the gate, Savage said, "Sam and I and a planter, Poynton, have just built a sulap (small hut). It will hold four, so join us. We've arranged your bed in this hut. Let's stow your things." I was falling on my feet from the word "go" — the service was excellent!

When I came out of the hut again a lanky figure came up to me. "How are you, Doctor?"

I looked at the man's thin face but recognition escaped me.

"I suppose I have changed since we had some whisky together in Brunei Prison."

It was Anderson — formerly Resident, Limbang. His appearance had altered completely.

The sulap mentioned by Savage was amongst some rubber trees behind the second hut. It was called Clitoris Villa (for that was the name of a vine crawling up one side of it) and was just big enough to hold a small table. In front, the ground had been levelled for home-made chairs.

I hadn't met Poynton before. The planter was a young sixty, serious, rather like a professor in one of the technical faculties.

The first evening in camp was one to remember. At meal time I received so much rice that I gave half of it away. Afterwards, we sat out in chairs exchanging news. Both Timberlake and Savage looked in perfect health. They were very brown and smoked short Manila cigars with their tea. I was staggered by contrasts. In the Civilian Camp, only a handful seemed to be in the same pitiable condition as the soldiers I had seen working on the road. Indeed, many middle-aged men looked much the better for the loss of superfluous weight. Separation from clubs and refrigerators had benefited their physical health greatly. Englishmen were now addressing each other by christian names.

About 8.30 p.m. a Jap guard came into the camp and spent half an hour giving someone in the nearest hut a dressing-down. "That goes on regularly", said Timberlake. As the guard came and went, everyone near at hand stood at attention and bowed like slaves to shouts of "Kyo-tsuki" and "Kirei". It was clear the Japanese had them well trained.

A little later, Savage said, "After that exhibition you will be surprised to learn we have a secret wireless called Mrs Harris or Mrs H. We get the news once a fortnight. It's on next Sunday."

The Male Civilian Camp was a P-shaped area, a hundred metres long by seventy metres at its widest point. There were six weatherboard huts, each accommodating about forty people. In the centre of the camp was a large, open kitchen. On lower ground were open-air bathrooms with showers, benches with taps for washing clothes and latrine cubicles. We were lucky: originally, the camp had been built to accommodate Indian troops. There was over-crowding, but buildings, water supply, sanitation and kitchen amenities gave no serious ground for complaint.

My allotted bed-space consisted of 7 planks on one side of the second hut from the gate. Two Sarawak men gave me a wooden bed of three widely spaced planks and refused the rice I offered as payment. I slept between a pink Eurasian from Malaya and a swarthy English parson. Savage, Timberlake and Poynton had their beds further down the hut. Savage had a Heath Robinson affair: an end of one plank had fallen to the floor and it looked like a ramp for the convenience of mice and cockroaches. If it had been bigger or Savage smaller he could have slid to the floor in the morning.

In the Lintang Camp there were about 3,000 P.O.W.s and internees. Australian, Dutch and British officers were quartered in separate compounds on gentle slopes above the Civilian Camp. Further down were camps for Dutch and British other ranks, Punjabi soldiers and the women. The hospital was opposite the Punjabi Camp and was already full of emaciated patients. On the far side of the central road were two camps for Roman Catholic priests and Indonesian soldiers from the island of Ambon.

All ten camps were surrounded by barbed-wire aprons. There were sentry boxes at points around the camp and every hour a small squad of small guards set out from the guardhouse to relieve the sentries on duty. Between the Civilian and British officers' camp was a strip of land about 30 metres wide with a sentry path running through it. Most of it was planted in sweet potatoes.

Major Suga, the commandant, whom I had met outside a kitchen in Belait, had his offices on top of the hill. The 120-odd Koreans, Formosans, Chinese and Japs forming the guard were known as Sugar Babies. Nearly all had nicknames — Big Pig, Little Pig, Measles, Pimples, Wife-beater, Stammering Stephen, Rubber Lips and so on. Most of the officers and N.C.O.s in charge of this ugly, hysterical rabble were known by their correct names, but a few had been tagged otherwise — Piano Legs, Benjo Bill, Flannel Foot.

Into the Male Civilian Camp the Japanese net had drawn a moderately interesting collection of internees — tobacco and rubber planters, missionaries, barons of commerce, several dozen Dutchmen, three Chinese civil servants, British administrators, some beachcombers, a brace of anthropologists, a small corroboree of Australians and enough medical men to hold an annual dinner. I met (by appointment) Noel Turner, the former Assistant Resident, Kuala Belait, who had left such a fund of goodwill behind him. I was hoping to pass on news of Belait but, alas, by the time the Assistant Resident had finished his opening remarks, it was lunchtime. He had had several of his front teeth damaged by a blow from a rifle butt.

On Saturday night, Savage kindly invited me to a concert in the soldiers' camp next door. The place was out of bounds to us, of course.

'Have you got some tickets?" I asked.

"If they're necessary we'll get them over there. Come on!"

We dressed in khaki and after dark struggled along a pee drain into the soldiers' camp. The Japanese had put barbed-wire across the drain and Savage tore his forehead on it. As we sat in forbidden territory amongst the soldiers, watching the female inpersonators, Savage made valiant efforts to stem the flow of blood. I asked, "As a matter of interest, John, how do you explain these scratches?"

"Up to the present, I haven't had to, thank heavens."

The concert was very good, the Poms being born comedians, but next day, this performance was bettered in the Civilian Camp. A Sarawak officer named Aikman visited each hut in turn and delivered, without notes, a summary of news obtained from Mrs Harris during the past fortnight. It was a masterly performance: by closing one's eyes it was possible to imagine it coming from the B.B.C. Later, I met Graham. "Well, what do you think of it? This is a better method of getting the news than giving Pangiran Mohommet weekly injections in the bottom at the hospital."

"A bit more ethical, anyway!" laughed Graham.

The Civilian Camp was well organised. Everyone was expected to do at least 21 hours communal work a week. There was a wide selection of jobs. Timberlake prompted, "Come out with us and see agricultural officers and planters actually using a hoe!" Any such work seemed a waste of time. I was convinced the war was nearly over. Nevertheless, curiosity aroused, I joined the gardening squad.

My Villa companions had already established themselves on sloping land beside the road near the ration shed. For a time, the four of us worked together. However, Timberlake and Poynton set about mass cultivation of shallots so seriously that Savage and I soon refused to be associated with them except at morning and afternoon tea. The pair maintained that taste was just as important as calories. A Sarawak officer, Dennis White, and the Beaufort planter, Ace Wren, took over a thin strip of soil immediately below the shallot patch. Savage and I were left with a plot about 15 metres square, formed of solid, white clay. A more hopeless task than coaxing anything edible from this area could scarcely be imagined. The rainy season commenced before we got going and the lower half of our garden was soon converted into a quagmire. Nevertheless, over several weeks we succeeded in hoeing and ridging half the plot and planting it with lengths of potato runners. Our garden was well placed for communication with men from other camps. Savage, a natural liaison officer, decided on a screen of tapioca to give protection from Japanese eyes: so we put the rest of the garden under tapioca (manioc), the easiest thing in the world to grow. The garden was completed by erecting a trellis for four-angled beans and planting a few banana palms for shade and some pineapple tops as a joke — these latter take over a year to mature and we knew for certain the rout of the Japanese was imminent: why else would we all be suddenly rounded up and sent to Kuching?

The rubbish heap beside the garden became, in time, a veritable goldmine. When produce considered unfit for consumption was dumped from the ration shed, Savage and I stepped on to the heap and salvaged anything edible: often there was nothing, but sometimes a half papaya, 2 centimetres of banana or a slice of watermelon turned up. On one occasion, from a cartload of rotten turtle eggs, we retrieved about two dozen which could be eaten without distaste. If Savage and I were absent when rubbish was dumped, residents, visiting agents and barons of commerce scrambled on to the heap and helped themselves without any sense of shame.

A few weeks after internment, I was returning from the garden when we passed a group of Australian officers outside the office: they were 8th Division, fresh from Sandakan.

"Kell!"

Hearing my name, I searched amongst the Australians but recognised no one. Jap guards were present and I walked slowly on.

"Kell!"

An officer standing to one side of the main group moved his arm and nodded. I did likewise. I half recognised the face. Back in camp, it suddenly struck me — it was Frank Mills, an old university friend. I had not seen him for years. We had played together for several years as a pair in inter-collegiate tennis. I kicked myself for not giving better evidence of recognition. However, a few days later, he sent a message through the hospital. This was fairly easy because parties went to it on daily sick parade from the various camps.

As Christmas approached, Mills showed initiative. He made a successful application to the Japanese for permission to meet me in the office, claiming relationship. On Christmas morning I donned a pair of white trousers to mark the occasion. Some priests were taken into the office first: when they had finished we were called and were given two chairs at a table. Little Wilfred, the interpreter, sat between us.

When time is limited it is surprising how easily speech can be wasted. I told of my coming to North Borneo: then Frank spoke of his hospital experience, joining-up and going to Malaya with the 8th Division. He described the fighting at Mersing, the retreat on Singapore, the capitulation and his transfer to Sandakan with nearly 3,000 others of the 8th Division. Little Wilfred was called away by Lt Nagata. Immediately, Mills bent forward. "Derwent, can we get out of here?"

He had only just arrived and apparently wasn't settling in. Grinning broadly, I answered, "We'll give it a go. Any time you like."

"Well, you know the country. Get cracking. Two others want to come with me."

"Who?"

"Better not mention names." The Australians knew what a Kempei-tai investigation meant.

Little Wilfred returned. Frank had said what he wanted to say and now filled in with an innocuous account of the harsh conditions in the P.O.W. Camp at Sandakan.

Little Wilfred had difficulty in following what Mills was saying. Presently, he said, "Finish now, Doctors, please" and sent us back to camp.

On Christmas night, Savage threw a party. For months he had traded and smuggled with such success that an underground cellar had been established beside the Villa. It cost me half my clothes. Two of the Dutch, Kummelkampf (Bill) and Van der Brink (Brinko) were invited. When everyone was present, Savage took a hoe and loosened the soil over the cellar. Then he plunged a hand underground and drew out a bottle of Mr Red. Everyone sat on chairs in front of the Villa. At intervals, someone got up and tunnelled about in the soil. When Savage proposed a toast to Queen Wilhelmina we stood and said, ''Queen Wilhelmina!'' and drank to Her Majesty. Brinko responded by proposing a toast to His Majesty, The King. Other toasts were drunk to Mr Churchill, Victory and Speedy Relief.

As a result of my interview with Mills, I had something to think about. Jungle-covered, malaria-ridden Borneo was completely surrounded by Jap-occupied territory. We could go hundreds of kilometres and still be nowhere. The mainland of Asia was far away and not inviting. Our best bet lay in making our way eastwards.

One day, Dr Stookes of Sandakan approached me in the square and said, ''Have you thought about escaping from here?''.

This was sudden. ''Why?''

''I'd like to talk it over with you. I think we might be able to manage it.''

''We might.''

''I know the coast as well as anyone, having flown over it for years. You know the oil-fields, the interior and some of the east coast. You went down the Kinabatagan to Sandakan in 1940, didn't you?''

''You're well briefed!''

Stookes smiled. ''There's no telling what will happen here. If we stay, we're probably for it. If we can get away we might be of some use. Anyway, we can discuss possibilities.''

''No harm in that.''

''You know my new plot near the pigsty? We can talk there any time. Too dangerous inside.''

Thus, within a short time, three people, all doctors, were considering plans to escape. We had dealt with such things as virulent streptococci as well as Nips and had as much confidence in the sporting instincts of the one as in the other. Anyway, planning was a hobby of sorts and it helped to pass away the time.

Stookes was much older than myself but had kept his condition well. In World War I he had been a pilot. He spoke Malay fluently and had the right mentality for an escape of this sort. Satisfied that he was in earnest, I admitted, without personal particulars, the interest Mills was showing. We agreed our only chance lay in travelling towards the Philippines and Tawi-Tawi. Too many people had lost their heads to Dyaks earlier in the war to make the inland safe: also, endemic malaria was a major factor there, and if one native in twenty whom we met was pro-Japanese, we could not get away with it. The sea was the answer. Stookes told me he had established first contact with two people in Kuching through working parties of British soldiers. They lived by the river and had two boats. Stookes was always at the fence, talking and trading with the Tommies. We discussed our minimum requirements. Parangs: if possible one each; water bottles; fishing gear; a saucepan; a compass; Archdeacon Mercer's reading glass. This last article we borrowed one lunch hour and confirmed that it worked as a sunglass. Looking at the paper burning, Stookes said, laughingly, ''Let him keep it for the moment. It couldn't be in better hands!''. The poor Archdeacon was completely dependent on it for reading.

Stookes had a parang. There were water bottles in the soldiers' camp. The fishing line was a problem; the saucepan not difficult. But the compass? I thought this impossible to obtain. For a sea trip it was essential. Stookes said, ''I'll see what I can do''.

Six weeks later he came to me with a broad smile showing through his beard. ''It's coming over the fence tonight at 9.30.''

"What is?"

"The compass."

"Ye Gods! How did you get it?"

"It's a present from the Japanese Society for the Advancement of Amateur Navigation."

At 9.30 p.m. I kept watch whilst Stookes got the compass over the fence. Then we went to the latrines to inspect it. I was so surprised I burst out laughing. "What the hell!"

It was a huge ship's compass: with attachments, it weighed over 7 kilograms. A British soldier had accomplished the remarkable feat of stealing it from a Jap ship at the docks.

"What did you give him for it?"

"A shirt and five katis of tobacco. Look here! I think we'd better get this underground smartly. How would we explain if caught with it?"

The danger of it set Stookes laughing. I said, "Better hurry before it explodes in your hands'."

I went to the gate to watch the Sugar Babies. Fifteen minutes later Stookes waved to me. The deed was done.

Weeks passed, as we waited for the wet season to end. In an attempt to get medicines we found out where A.R.P. (Air Raid Precautions) Depots had been established round Kuching — two of them, in fact. When we questioned Sarawak officers, you would have thought we were either Japanese or Germans, they were so cagey. We also learnt that the patients at the leper colony some kilometres away were being neglected; the Japanese did not visit the place and the Dresser-in-Charge was Chinese and therefore, trustworthy. The leper colony seemed a promising first port of call when we escaped and Stookes set about contacting the Dresser-in-Charge.

Then suddenly, one day, the Japanese Kempei-tai swooped on the camp and took nine civilians away; one of the nine was Stookes and we never saw him again. It seemed that the trouble was over the smuggling into camp of newspapers which the Japanese themselves had printed. There was no telling where Kempei-tai interrogation might lead and I sent word to Mills that I was coming over to see him.

After the Last Post, everyone in the Civilian Camp went to bed except myself and Savage. We stood near the Dispensary and watched the Jap guard go past. I was secretly pleased with the opportunity of giving Savage something to worry about for a change. I went down and slipped between two strands of barbed-wire and lay on the grass in the centre of the apron. Then I went through the other side of the wire and stepped down on the sentry path. Bending low, I crossed it and crept along between potato ridges to the boundary of the British officers' camp; then through the wire and across their garden to a pee drain coming from the Dutch officers' camp. I entered the drain. Near a narrow bridge I heard footsteps approaching. I slipped under the bridge — it was barely 46 centimetres wide — and remained still. Someone came and stood on the bridge, pee'd, spat and walked away. I went on, to reach the edge of the Australian compound. Here, the fence was a mixture of barbed-wire and a leafy, edible shrub called chekur manis. The end of an Australian hut reached almost to the fence. I came close to the fence and gently separated several stems of chekur manis. Five metres away someone was standing perfectly still. I called softly, "Frank! Frank!".

There was no answer. I lay low for nearly a minute, then called a little louder. The figure came towards me. It was Frank. This last fence proved difficult.

We sat on a bench between two rubber trees. In the hut a few metres from us were scores of Australian officers, sleeping in tiers from floor to rafters. I told Frank about my colleague, his plans and the compass buried underground. Stookes alone knew where it was hidden. We discussed escape, balancing possibilities against risks and the trouble it would cause for those remaining. In the end, we decided to stay put; for the present at least. By now, Frank was in poor shape. He had lost 19 kilograms and had a gastric ulcer for which he was taking charcoal several times a day. He had an inventive mind and told me of an artificial heart and kidney which he was planning, with the help of an engineer in his camp. He was still holding forth earnestly on the dialysing ability of membranes when the eleven o'clock guard marched around. I took the chance to say goodnight and slipped through the fence into the Dutch camp. The stars were very bright. After a fashion, it was an amusing business crawling across potato beds and slipping through barbed-wire aprons while everyone slept: very like the hunting excursions of the interior. But here there were no honey bears, tree leopards or king cobras to worry about — only Sugar Babies.

I found Savage sitting outside the Dispensary, where he could see any guard entering the camp. He was news hungry, as ever.

"Oh, Derwent! Take a seat. What's doing? Anything?"

When I had no news other than that Frank Mills was designing an artificial heart and eating charcoal, Savage was indignant. He exclaimed, "I've never known anyone who could find out so little in such a long time as you!". This sounded a little like Churchill, in reverse gear.

In the next few days I walked every centimeter of our camp looking for evidence of a buried compass. There was none. I decided Stookes had buried it in the bottom of the pee drain.

Visits by the Military Police to the camp were unsettling. Over the newspaper-smuggling business their representatives came to Lintang Camp several times. During one visit, Little Wilfred came towards the Male Civilian Camp calling, "Mistah Savage! Mistah Savage! Come to the office, please!".

John quickly dressed in "beating-up" equipment — extra underclothes, shoes and socks and the best khaki shirt and trousers available. Poynton, Timberlake and I stood near the camp entrance and saw him leave in a car for Kempei-tai headquarters; this time, without golf sticks and luggage.

We were worried, but hours later, he returned, much to our relief: we needed him for Christmas. Down in the Kempei-tai an internee who had been beaten mercilessly was forced to kneel beside him. On being questioned, Savage denied ever having smuggled newspapers into camp; then, looking at the battered man beside him he realised some information had been extracted from him and therefore corrected himself — yes, months ago, he had brought in a half-sheet of Japanese newspaper which he had found on the rubbish heap beside his garden. This admission probably saved his life. After further interrogation an M.P. walked across to a diagram on a large black-board fixed to the wall. The kneeling internee's name was in the centre and arrows went from it to other names arranged in a circle about it; amongst these, Savage's name was found and erased. Of all those with their names on the diagram — and there were over twenty — Savage was the only one to survive.

I was not in the camp for many months when Edrich Selous came to me and said, "I hear you know some Japanese."

"I know about 50 words and can say 'Open cherry blossom, open!' That's about all."

Selous smiled. "Would you like me to teach you?"

I made up my mind quickly — filling in time was a major problem. "O.K. If you feel up to it: I'm not much chop at languages."

"I'll teach you to speak it pretty well in two months. Actually, it will help me too."

I knew I could not become fluent without more effort than I was willing to expend. But it interested me to find out how a man with an extraordinary gift for languages went about it. We arranged to meet three days a week after lunch, in the Villa, when everyone else was having a post-prandial snooze. Selous spoke three Chinese dialects and Malay as well as any European can ever speak it. He was at home in French, and a refugee Doctor in the camp praised a short story he had written in German. He had come into camp not knowing a word of Dutch: when I asked Brinko about Selous' proficiency in Dutch, Brinko answered, "Well, you *can* tell he's a foreigner".

After a few days my tutor insisted that all conversation take place in Japanese. His mind was very active and crystal clear. Over several weeks, I learned some 1,500 words. Every evening, just before lights out, we walked up and down the square chattering together in Japanese. Selous never lost an opportunity to speak to the Sugar Babies and urged me to do likewise: but I had had a wider experience of Japs abroad than my tutor and would have none of it. Thus, while I had little difficulty in talking to Selous in the language, I did not progress to the stage of being able to swop everyday chit-chat with a Sugar Baby.

However, the time was not wasted. I got to know Selous well and this in itself was sufficient. He had a heavy head of fair hair, high cheekbones and a short, pointed, well-trimmed beard, which gave him quite an Elizabethan air.

His thoughtful eyes were narrow, almost Asiatic. In speech he was precise and very English. There was a hard, smiling intellectual coolness about him that almost masked a capacity for feeling intensely. Apparently, he played most games with more than average ability and was enthusiastic about real tennis. At one stage, before the war, he had had a clouded leopard as a pet. He was related to a well-known hunter of African game.

One afternoon, Selous asked me: "If we were released this afternoon and had the opportunity of ordering dinner — anything at all — what would you do about it?".

We were hungry and this was interesting. I answered almost immediately, in English — and he did not check me. "Toheroa soup, a dozen Sydney oysters, steak and chops with fried eggs and chipped potatoes: then a man-sized helping of ice-cream." The prospect delighted me, but Selous was enormously amused. "That certainly would be filling," he said. "What drinks would you use to float all this on?"

"A pint of beer — as recommended by Archimedes himself."

I felt Selous had an advantage and I thought I might as well try to be funny about it: the idea of an upthrust on the chops and ice-cream equal to the weight of beer displaced amused me, but Selous, with his classical education, could scarcely be expected to see the humour in this.

I turned to him and said, with a hint of aggression, "Well, what would you have?"

Selous looked out across the garden. He took a long draw at his native cigarette, exhaled, and then started. In a few moments, I was lost. I did not even know what Selous was talking about as he wandered amongst the Alpine peaks of continental eating and drinking. I had never thought it possible for anyone to talk so completely over my head on what was basically a question of satisfying metabolic requirements. Nothing he mentioned had an honest-to-God name.

Selous was fastidious, yet, paradoxically, he was one of the first in camp to tackle the giant African snails. At night, these great slimy creatures slid about on the grass: in the early morning, they crawled up on shrubs and bushes to shady places below the leaves.

Selous asked me, "These things contain protein, don't they?"

"Yes, of course. They must."

"And that's the chief thing we're short of, isn't it?"

"Yes. That and animal fat. And vitamins A to Z."

And so Selous set about collecting, washing, cooking and consuming these ugly snails. One day, I asked him how he found them. "Not too bad", he said. "If you wash them well to get the mucus off. It's best to dissect out the gall-bladder — it's rather bitter."

One day, with unholy glee, he showed me a whole basin full of them — shelled, washed and ready for the pot. It was a revolting sight.

"Are you going to eat those?"

"Yes."

He now appeared to be wandering in a swamp in Mozambique in his culinary activities. I myself was rather partial to cobras and occasionally ate one or two. The blind, double-headed snakes dug up in swampy ground were scarcely worth the effort, but, after a fashion, they made a passable soup. But snails!

In order to have time for study, Selous became a member of the "benjo" squad. Twice a day he appeared at the latrines, with a team-mate lifted two tongs of "doings" on a large pole and set off for pits dug in the garden. Two such trips had to be made twice daily, three if unpolished rice was included in the rations. He was meticulously correct in bowing to sentries. This was necessary and it did not appear to worry him in the least.

He was easily roused by injustice. One morning, in the garden, he talked about several pre-war controversies. One concerned the leg-irons which were automatically put on every wrong-doer in Sarawak sentenced to imprisonment for more than one year. With some heat, he explained to me how the irons were attached to the ankle and waist and locked so that prisoners could not escape. The practice had ceased years ago and seemed little enough to get excited about so late in the day. But Edrich was exasperated by the type of mind that had thought up such a practice and indolently permitted it to continue.

One morning, Selous was one of five gardeners who failed to notice a Jap officer passing along a nearby road. The matter was reported and an N.C.O. named Benjo Bill was sent to deal with the offenders. Benjo Bill was as sturdy as an Himalayan foothill and enough to frighten a year's growth out of anyone. He lined the five garden workers up along the road and hit them.

That evening, as we walked up and down the camp square, Selous told me about the incident in Japanese. He remembered being hit only once. Actually, he was hit several times and was in the ditch by the roadside when he came to .

The spectacle of starvation as seen in the adjacent soldiers' camp made a deeper impression on him than on most civilians. A large part of the daily news passing round the camp consisted of items such as Lt. Inagaki throwing an emaciated British soldier over his shoulder on the gravel road; or a quiet surveyor named Smallfield being stood for hours in the sun with his hands above his head; or such things as happened to the elderly Anglican bishop. Some days the bishop was allowed to visit other camps to hold services and often he took messages, clothes or money to persons there. He never refused any request, always answering, "Certainly, I'll be glad to". However, one Sabbath, he was caught handing money to a British soldier and was taken to the guardhouse. One of the things they did was to make him kneel on the floor holding a basin of water at arm's length. He was beaten when his arms fell.

"Would you believe it!" exclaimed Selous. "A bishop! It's incredible, isn't it? If they ever tried anything like that on me I wouldn't tolerate the indignity of it. Would you?"

"I've already shown that I'll tolerate almost anything."

Selous smiled for a moment and said more quietly, "Well, I wouldn't tolerate it. I'm damned if I would."

The Allied forces did not come surging up from the south to the relief of Kuching as I expected. Eventually, I was driven to extend my gardening activities. I joined a morose handful labouring in a swamp near the pigsty. I selected one of the least boggy areas and heaped up the mud and swamp compost into four curved beds; often, I turned up leeches as thick as a finger and once, a pair of blind ground snakes. Old Bill supplied me with some small, very "hot" chillies called chubi lada to cook with them. I planted bananas, potatoes, egg-plants and corn. Weeks later, the firewood gang cleared a dry area nearby. I acquired another plot, entirely covered with small scrub and stumps: obviously, it would keep me occupied until the end of internment. My plan was to clear a narrow strip, turn the soil over, ridge it and plant potato runners; then on to the next strip.

Ridge by ridge I advanced across my plot. But shortly, I came to a hardwood stump, a metre thick, with roots shooting out under the surface like the legs of an octopus. It blocked all progress.

At this point, I was joined by Dennis White, wearing what appeared to be an old Stetson hat turned up all round: as well as a loincloth, of course. We sat for days looking at the arthropod squatting malignly in the centre of our land and decided to build a hut before tackling it. This took several days. By the time we tackled the monster we already loathed the sight of it. With infinite trouble, we hacked through the ironwood roots where they joined the trunk, then dug out every separate root and finally dealt with the trunk itself. During the operation we each lost 3 kilograms in weight.

Afterwards, the going was easier. It was a great day when we finished. The soil was good and the sweet potatoes flourished. One day at lunch, Timberlake remarked, "I went down to your new garden for tea. The rows of potatoes — they looked fine. What a sight!"

White was pleased to hear about this. "A compliment, what? Come to think of it, his shallots aren't bad, are they?"

"Not bad at all."

"How many beds have Poynton and he got now?"

"Forty-one — and still going strong."

As Jap-supplied rations diminished, the internees were compelled to take gardening seriously. The head gardener was a north-countryman, Danny Lascelles, county footballer and a very fine fellow. Day in, day out, he and his second-in-command, Bob Snellis, led a team of clergymen, doctors, barons of commerce, planters and dull, incorruptible civil servants from the camp. On and on they worked and in time, the whole of the swamp area was converted into a magnificent garden.

More land became available between the Civilian and British officers' camps, towards the perimeter. Between two mounds there was an area of flat land which Savage maintained he could hoe in a day. In my opinion, he couldn't and I said so, and so we bet a theoretical $50 on it. We agreed on at least half the hoe in depth, soil turned over, no gap between sods. Next morning, Savage ran to the stipulated area and started work. Normally, he was rather a lazy gardener, but in sport and betting, he was highly competitive. Dressed in a colonial helmet and a loincloth, he worked strenuously throughout the day, losing litres of sweat and valuable salt with it. He returned for a tapioca lunch, then slogged on throughout the afternoon. He won the bet with ten minutes to spare and returned to camp exhausted. It was a first-rate exhibition: but for the next two months he paid for it. The skin of his hands and feet came off at the slightest knock and often blood blisters appeared spontaneously on parts of his body. A more foolish bet I have never seen, but we did not realise how we were failing. He was never the same man again; either physically or mentally.

One memorable day, I was weeding in my garden when I heard an incredible sound. I tiptoed across to a nearby drain and peered in. What a sight! Several wonderful ducks had wandered in from a Chinese farm outside the perimeter. I retreated to think things over and, after my heart had settled, I called two fellow-gardeners, carefully selected. In a sentry tower fifty metres away was a Sugar Baby. One of my companions, a Hollander named "Swivel Navel" (the closest to his name we could get) disappeared into a branch drain; the second crouched among some kangkong (a green-leafed vegetable). Both were trembling with excitement. I armed myself with a short iron bar and entered the ditch. The ducks backed away nervously towards the ambush. Finally, they stopped, their necks standing together with a clump of coconut palms. I looked towards the sentry and then flung the iron bar like a boomerang. My friends closed in, eyes glinting murderously. Only one duck escaped this planned assault. It ran across the British P.O.W. camp and there, I presume, it met its fate — no one would want to raise it as a pet.

An hour later, two members of the latrine squad came to the drain to wash their buckets and collected the ducks. That evening, the birds were plucked in the Villa. Disposal of the feathers was a major problem. Unhappily, the ducks were young and caused considerable disappointment, even anger, due to their lack of physical development. One was given to the patients in the Lazarette; one to a mildly corrupt element amongst our splendid kitchen staff; the rest were divided amongst a number which, alas, had grown fantastically, due in part to downy feathers floating in the air and attracting shameless "friends" to Clitoris Villa.

Compared with life at Kuala Belait, I found Lintang camp like a convalescent home. Personal prestige was completely unimportant. No one protested when struck by a guard and no one was expected to. Almost daily, someone was "clocked" and the routine was to stand at attention and take it. This soon brought each incident to a close. Sometimes, a protest was lodged at the office, but the only result was to take another month off the liaison officer's life. Proof that slavery was complete was provided at every roll-call. The numbering and shouting of commands and the precision and fervour of the obsequious bows was quite enough to demonstrate this. We could have been marched over a cliff into the sea without protest. Only two Japanese seemed to have any insight into our condition at these times. One was the Taxi-driver, the best of all the Sugar Babies, who, on several occasions, stood well behind his officer and gave a silly bow like a comedian. The other was Benjo Bill, a quiet, tough soldier who did his duty without rancour. As he saluted to our bows, a faint but unmistakable smile frequently played upon his face.

The first year, I escaped scot-free from any trouble. Then my luck changed. Several times, I was caught accidentally in group slappings and other minor incidents. Later, I was involved in two more serious affairs. The first was almost worth it, for it had some resemblance to entertainment.

One evening, an officious Jap cadet approached a table where a game of cards was in progress. The players stood and bowed. The cadet was about to leave when he noticed some coins and tin counters on the table. Gambling! He produced a notebook and took the names of the six players.

Next morning, Little Wilfred, the interpreter, cried, "Mistah Timberlake! Mistah Savage! Mistah Moore! Doctah O'Connor! Doctah Kell! Mistah Stackhall! Come to the office please."

Savage quickly put on his "beating up" clothes. I thought so lightly of the matter that I went across in shirt and shorts and clogs. The officer on duty that morning was a priggish little man called Flannel Foot with the bonhomie of a pavement stone. I felt nervous as I took a position in the line of three District Officers, one rubber baron in the making and two doctors. As we bowed, the Jap looked very severe.

Little Wilfred stood beside Flannel Foot. The latter reprimanded us at length in words charged with emotion. Gambling was prevalent amongst the British, a third-class people without culture. Japanese did not gamble. Hadn't everyone memorised the camp regulations? I, for one, hadn't read a word of them.

Six adult Europeans, all previously holding responsible positions, stood with shaking knees before a gentleman half their size physically and rather less intellectually and were told off with a fanatical and brainless fervour on a matter of the utmost inconsequence. Not the faintest sign of a smile, impatience or irritation was permitted to appear on any face. Flannel Foot had a way with him that forbade the slightest liberty. Running out of caustic criticisms, he counted the coins and metal counters; from time to time he made what must have been an absurd observation on paper. There were 65 cents all told and two dozen pieces of tin.

Finally, there was a lull. It occurred to Stackhall that an explanation would clarify and finalise the matter. Unfortunately, Flannel Foot was eager for provocation. To the interpreter, Stackhall said, "The officer does not understand. These coins do not have their face value; they represent a false value."

Little Wilfred translated this rather woolly statement. One can only imagine how it went into Japanese, a language where everything is back to front to start with: perhaps it went in upside down. Flannel Foot leapt round the table and assaulted Stackhall with a volley of slaps which forced him backwards towards the wall. Stackhall was tall and the Jap had to strike upwards: nevertheless, the slaps sounded like whip cracks in the confined space of the office. The other five gamblers stood like a row of plaster-of-Paris statues. Immobility, we hoped, was not far removed from invisibility.

Presently, Stackhall rejoined us, but almost immediately fell in a faint. I caught him before he hit the floor.

The matter had now advanced beyond a reprimand and the gamblers were sent to the guardhouse. There, we were welcomed by a group of Sugar Babies and ordered to kneel on the gravel in front of the guardhouse, sitting back on our heels with hands resting lightly on our thighs. This position is quite easy to maintain for several minutes. Then, persons unaccustomed to it begin to feel uncomfortable. In ten minutes pain is felt, in half an hour the victim suspects he has reached the limit of endurance. The trial continues on until grunts and groans can no longer be suppressed. I was nearest the guard and for several hours had little opportunity of lifting and throwing my weight to one side.

Finally, we were transferred to a section of closed-in verandah in the guardhouse. For a time, we stood faces to the wall; afterwards, we were ordered to sit in a circle on our heels in front of the cells. Two cells were occupied by British privates who could be seen through the coarsely latticed timber walls.

What a night it proved to be! I attempted to ignore the pain impulses streaming in from my knees and ankles by an improvised form of yoga. To some extent, it worked. Timberlake's face was a heartrending study; Savage was deft at removing his weight from his heels when he felt too uncomfortable; Moore, a good, tough Pom, gave me consolation by grunting and turning his grimacing face to the ceiling. At odd intervals, the guards granted short rests. One internee attempted to converse with a soldier and was beaten for his trouble. About midnight, Flannel Foot appeared and enlivened proceedings. Dr O'Connor was approaching retirement and his joints were such that it was physically impossible for him to get into and maintain the upright position with his weight resting on his heels. He therefore frequently assumed a more convenient quadruped position and occasionally edged forward slowly towards the centre of the circle. One guard lifted his head and forced his buttocks back on his heels, causing his joints to protest audibly. Finally, O'Connor fell full-length on the floor. The guard asked me to examine him. "Is he dead?" I felt my colleague's pulse and said, "Belum. Not yet."

Stackhall very cleverly took Dr O'Connor's head and put it on his lap. I resumed my former position, annoyed at having overlooked this opportunity of doing a little nursing. A rest was granted shortly afterwards and Dr O'Connor recovered.

There was a roughly built fireplace on the verandah beside us. One guard ordered Savage to stand on tiptoe with knees bent and arms extended above his head. He took some red-hot embers from the fire and put them under and behind Savage's heels. Savage, showing remarkable endurance, remained in this position for fifteen minutes before being told to resume his place. It was as remarkable a scene as most men see in a lifetime — five men in a circle, sitting on their heels with evidence of pain on their faces; leaping flames throwing flickering shadows on a Jap soldier bent over the fireplace warming his hands; a powerfully-built man maintaining a fantastically impossible position and the latticed cell front reaching to the ceiling. The P.O.W. in the end cell came forward and stood peering through the gaps in the latticed walls: the light played upon his thin, white knuckles as he grasped the timber and held his wasted face against the grill.

The guards took hourly turns in watching us. The Taxi Driver turned up trumps. He took two watches and gave rests lasting almost throughout the hour. He passed cigarettes around and told us that Flannel Foot said we were to be sent back to the office at 9 a.m. This news set a probable limit to the ordeal. Other guards reacted petulantly to this kindness.

Dawn seemed late in coming. The soldier in the end cell was released to assist his friend. The latter was down with dysentery and the lower part of his bowel had prolapsed and his friend tried to replace it. It was clear he did not have long to live.

There was a wall clock in the corridor of the guardhouse and those who could see it through the door watched the minutes pass. As nine o'clock approached, Timberlake's expression became increasingly anxious. It was difficult to witness such anguish and keep a straight face.

The hour struck and nothing happened. Minutes passed and there was some irritable fidgetting amongst the civilians who expected an immediate yasumi (at ease). In due course, it came. Later, a very light breakfast was served. The gamblers were marched back to the office to face Flannel Foot. One slip meant the guardhouse for another night.

The six of us lined up in front of the humourless little Jap, tense, windy and depressed beyond all joking. Flannel Foot fastened his gimlet eyes on each of us in turn for at least twenty seconds. Under this critical observation I focussed on infinity and did my best to appear thoroughly chastened. It wasn't hard. From my mother, I had inherited a sadness which at odd times was reflected in the countenance. On this particular morning, it was a godsend.

Flannel Foot called upon each individual to state frankly what was in his mind about our third-class conduct and the punishment awarded for it. Down the line came the explanations, commendably brief, penitent in character and increasingly difficult to paraphrase. Flannel Foot would not tolerate expression of agreement with the previous speaker. Somehow, everyone managed to confess error and acknowledge the justice of the punishment given.

Flannel Foot completed his notes and sent us back to camp. By this time, except in the case of the older O'Connor, all pain and even stiffness had worn off. We walked without limping and our bodies were completely unmarked. In a short time people were asking, "What's all the fuss about?"

My second visit to the guardhouse was a much more serious and severe affair.

With another Christmas approaching, Savage set about obtaining the nearest equivalent to champagne and oysters available. Obstacles he had to overcome were Sugar Babies, kilometres of barbed-wire, lack of credit or ready cash and the absence of a supermarket or even a pub. However, one night, when everyone was sleeping, he and I sat in the villa sampling the first of three bottles of Chinese wine to come over the fence. To my disappointment, two were Mr White, but the third one was definitely Mr Red.

As we sipped, Savage entered a reminiscent vein. He spoke of experiences at Cambridge, of golf, of Betsy, Pretty Polly and then, of course, of food. He was fond of dressing for dinner and enjoyed his period as the Governor's Private Secretary. He recalled one dinner party at Government House at which there were twelve guests at table. A Malay "boy" came in with exactly twelve chops on a dish. The distinguished lady on His Excellency's right was served first and took two. His Excellency was served last; rather than go without, he drew her attention to something on the far side of the room and leant across and transferred a chop from her plate to his own.

It was a good story and I chuckled my appreciation.

"Help yourself, Derwent."

"Thanks, John. I don't mind if I do."

The eleven o'clock guard approached. The pair of bon viveurs sat in silence while four sleepy soldiers and a corporal trudged along the path twenty metres away. The wine finished, we decided to go to bed. Unfortunately, in the square Savage thought of another anecdote, about a girl he had met in Spain. Suddenly, to our astonishment, wide-awake Japanese conquistadors with fixed bayonets appeared everywhere about us. Savage said quickly, "Don't admit we've had anything to drink."

We were marched off to the guardhouse. The guards put down their rifles and gave us a slapping and then stood us at attention on either side of the steps. We remained like this for an hour. I heard one of the guards say, "We'll send them back to camp later." When the chance offered, I whispered this information to Savage.

Two hours later, we were still standing. Savage, who was devoid of antipodean apprehensions, decided on taking a sporting chance on forcing the issue. He turned, bowed neatly and, in Cambridge Malay, asked if we could return to camp as we had to turn out for work early in the morning.

The guards came pouring down the steps like molten lava. They set about Savage with fists and rifle butts. He fell to the ground. They took a long wooden post and began to ram his prostrate figure. Looking across, I saw him lying against the bank, his hands clasped over his head while two Japs pounded his back and buttocks with the post. Another was using his boots.

For a time I escaped notice. Then Measles came across, cocked a leg behind me and pushed me over backwards. This was repeated several times. Another fetched a post and as I lay on the ground he raised it above his head and brought it down across my lower abdomen and left thigh. It was a sickening blow. I felt myself fainting and then was almost sick. The guard was kicking me: as soon as possible, I got to my feet again.

The guards concentrated chiefly on Savage. Eventually, one of them rammed the end of the post down into his face and kicked him on the head. Savage cried, "Derwent, they've blinded me!"

I was free of attention at that moment and was able to go across. I said in Japanese, "You've damaged his eyes. He can't see. There'll be trouble. It's best to take him to hospital."

The guards hesitated. I bent down and helped Savage to his feet. Savage held his forearm across his blood-stained face and I repeated what he said in Malay. Possibly the Japs felt they had gone too far. One took Savage's arm and he and I led Savage up the steps into the guardhouse. Savage said, "It's not as bad as I am making out." But I was not sure of this — he had already lost one eye accidentally earlier in life. Savage was left on the closed-in verandah. I was taken outside. Pig Face confronted me and said in Japanese, "Have you been drinking?"

"No."

Pig Face closed his fist and caught me a swinging blow on the left cheek. He repeated his question and I repeated my answer. This time my right cheek took the blow.

And so it went on. I had no option other than to persist in my denial. To smuggle anything into camp from outside was a matter for the Kempei-tai, conceivably ending on the chopping block. By morning, we would be in a much stronger position. No Japanese officer ever had much faith in the word of any member of this rabble of Sugar Babies.

Eventually, Pig Face tired. He ordered me to kneel in the drain in front of the guardhouse. At dawn, I was sent inside to join Savage on the verandah. By this time Savage had recovered the use of his eye.

Shortly after 6 a.m. a car drew up in front of the guardhouse and the Japanese Commandant, Major Suga, came up the steps on a chance inspection. He received a report from the senior guard on duty. I heard the guard say that we had been drinking and were caught attempting to escape. Suga turned towards us. Our clothing was torn and filthy and our faces swollen. He asked our names and where we had worked before the war. He said the guards alleged that we were attempting to escape. This Savage and I denied: it was too hot to sleep in the huts; we had come out for a breath of fresh air. Suga accepted our explanation and told us to return to camp. We went down the steps. Savage stopped to look for one of his crude latex boots. Some guards were openly hostile and I said "Oh, come on, John, for heaven's sake!"

We walked up the road, bowed to the sentry in the square and entered the camp.

On a shelf in the Villa, were two bottles of sugared water with native yeast added to it: already, small bubbles were rising to the top.

"See!" said Timberlake, patting himself on the back, "Any questions and we made it ourselves! How's that for quick thinking?"

Savage laughed. "The yeast is obviously making the bubbles, but who did the thinking?

Needless to say, on the next Christmas Eve and New Year's Eve Mine Host, Savage, entertained his friends as usual. Once again, toasts were drunk to Queen Wilhelmina, His Majesty the King, Mr Churchill, Victory and Speedy Relief.

During my second year in camp, conditions deteriorated. Bulletins from the secret wireless in the British soldiers camp were no longer released; when the electricity supply was cut off, Mrs Harris went off the air completely. It was rumoured that the soldiers had stolen a Japanese bicycle and now used it to rotate an armature which they had constructed from scratch. Be that as it may, we received no more wireless news. A latrine squad attending the Japanese occasionally salvaged scraps of news sheets in the vernacular and sold them to civilians for food. Soothsayers and deliberate fabricators of events sprang up like weeds, for news of any sort had a saleable value. Traders softened prospective clients with rumours. Some compositions were plausible enough to be authentic, e.g. Roosevelt was reported as saying, "We have lit a fuse in the Pacific: now watch it burn."

Rations went down in quantity and quality. Half our garden was taken away. Rice was largely replaced by sago and tapioca. Practically the only animal protein came from a little dried fish and stinking fish preserved in stone jars. Once every ten days, the head of a half-grown pig was carried into camp and the kitchen staff tried to satisfy two hundred and forty people with it. There was little fat or salt in the diet. The effects of general starvation became more apparent. By the middle of 1945, only a handful of internees weighed more than 63 kilograms. Old Bill's enormously valuable paunch, once deposited with such pride on George Graham's lounge table, shrunk to ludicrous proportions. Graham himself developed "the runs" and I thought he was for it. He was no longer fit for outside work and was appointed Assistant to Dr Sternfeldt.

One day, without warning, everyone was ordered to the square while huts were searched. The Bishop had in his hands the camp atlas which had dangerous markings on it, particularly so on the map of Burma. But beside him stood a noble Dutchman, now 70 kilograms below pre-war weight and dressed only in a loincloth. The Dutchman noticed the Bishop's dilemma. He quickly lifted up a flap of skin hanging from his abdomen and tucked the atlas underneath and safely out of sight: then he stood at attention again until the search was over.

The Sarawak internees had had a rougher time at the beginning and had been interned longer; a number gradually lost their sight due to malnutrition. I attended one, Daubenny, every day for nine months. His legs and arms were scaling from knees and elbows down and he wore an eye-shade to protect his failing eyes from the light.

As real hunger developed, many began to eat all sorts of rubbish — snails, banana and pineapple skins, rubber nuts and even earth worms. At night, one ingenious fellow often entered the kitchen quietly and, with a pocket knife, searched along the edges and in the cracks of the table on which dough was rolled. One night, on the way to the latrines, I walked through the open kitchen to find him lying stretched out on the floor. Seeing me, he sprang to his feet. "Oh, Derwent, when you come to England you must come trout fishing with me." I suppose I had interrupted his dreams.

Some hungry men became involved in sizeable financial deals for scraps of food. I said to one reckless buyer, "Don't be a fool, that's a lot of money. The war's nearly finished!".

"And so am I!" he said. I dare say he had his priorities right.

Savage and I were sitting at the edge of the kitchen one night after lights out when a small pariah dog appeared in the square. We watched it intently for a few seconds, then Savage picked up a piece of firewood and, holding it behind his back, left the shadows and entered the moonlight. He made towards the dog saying coaxingly, "Pup — pup — puppy! Come here, puppy!" The little dog sized up his intentions exactly and backed away snarling quietly.

The introduction of chain gang work seemed to be the last straw. For months on end, one hundred internees had to turn out daily on compulsory labour. Hectares of land were cleared of rubber trees and planted with tapioca. The trees were cut up for firewood: later, the stumps were dug out and used similarly. N.C.O.s and Sugar Babies became much tougher and beatings more frequent.

Increasingly, the prisoners looked towards the New World and its General MacArthur to bring an end to this slavery.

On 25 March 1945, two, perhaps three, four-engined planes appeared in cloudy sky overhead. I looked up and in a moment took my eyes off a plane to gaze at two peculiar shimmering objects some distance behind them. "What the devil are those? Flocks of birds?"

A German refugee cried, "Lethal gas!"

Then an American engineer, George Colley, hit the nail on the head. "Pamphlets!" he cried. "Allied planes! Allied planes!"

It was good of him to say "Allied". One of the great planes came low and went towards the aerodrome some kilometres away. Crummph!! At long last something had happened.

"They're on their way, boys!"

"Three weeks to go!"

"We'll be out in a month! It's a cinch!".

But weeks and months passed. Planes continued to come; sometimes one, sometimes half a dozen. On one occasion twenty-odd four-engined bombers pounded the aerodrome furiously. We could see the bombs coming from the bomb bays and drifting over our heads. Later, Australians based on Labuan Island took over from the Americans and Spitfires, Hurricanes and Mosquitoes appeared. As time went on without relief, prisoners actually became exasperated when planes appeared. Often, we had to sit in slit trenches for hours.

The Japs invited everyone to send a card of fifteen words home with a certain proportion containing Japanese composed propaganda sentences such as "Borneo is a land flowing with milk and honey".

Savage was very brief. "Not dead yet," he wrote.

Everyone in the Villa laughed, including Savage, but he was very angry. Timberlake said, "Come, come, maestro! You can't send this home!".

"Why can't I? What the deuce are they doing to get us out of here? That's what I'd like to know! This will let them know just how things are."

The cemetery was within sight of the Civilian camp. It began to enlarge rapidly. Once, twice and then three times daily, everyone stood at attention while a bugler sounded the melancholy notes of the Last Post. Multiple burials replaced single burials. Coffins were used again and again. Deaths occurred in the Male Civilian camp; not many, but just enough to show it was possible to die. One who died was the Eurasian who slept beside me. His skin was pink and he developed a skin cancer on his thumb and he would not let us amputate it. He was a cricket fanatic and a spin bowler. "How will I bowl without a thumb?" he said heatedly. People watched themselves more closely, the older men particularly. The camp doctor was a quiet, courageous Jew who himself suffered a great deal from peptic ulcers. He was given no rest.

For a few weeks I had colic at night. When my right side became tense I consulted Dr Sternfeldt. He had hidden ten ampoules of emetine in a banana palm. He gave me six daily injections, standing on his toes and biting his lower lip as he did so: the only camp needle was extraordinarily large and very blunt. The emetine worked — perhaps too well; presently, I found myself on the head gardener's special squad of half a dozen who went to the garden to bring in produce when the chain gang complement could be filled without us.

In 1944, Poynton used to lead the rush of garden workers to the showers after work. He worked hard amongst his shallots, carrying tongs of urine and ashes to them, digging and transplanting and cutting the tops for the kitchen. He began to feel the strain but worked on just as hard, saying, "I won't let it get the better of me". In the end, it did. He then spent long hours lying on his bed conserving every remnant of strength:; his skin broke down completely and he was transferred to the Lazarette, a special end room for persons in precisely his condition.

Ace Wren did exactly the same. He too felt himself going and he worked on obstinately and would not listen to anyone. "I'm going to pull my weight," he said. But he could not see that even this meant doing less and less each day. Frequently, he broke out into a cold sweat and turned pale and his head was pushed down between his knees until he felt better; then he picked up his hoe and went on working. One day, a Jap guard went beserk and from a line of internees standing rigidly at attention he picked on Wren and knocked him unconscious with his rifle butt. And we stood like heroes while Ace lay on the ground in front of us.

For some reason unknown Edrich Selous was called from camp one afternoon and spent hours in an office with a Mr Kubu. Sounds from the office were frightening. A British soldier saw through the door for a moment. Selous was on the floor and Mr Kubu was jumping on and kicking at his chest.

As the chaingang was returning to camp, Selous passed down the road to the guardhouse under armed guard, looking white and tense. Most of the Sugar Babies respected him and apparently in the guardhouse he was treated with some consideration. However, he took an opportunity and deliberately ended his own life with glass from a broken bottle.

As he had seen it, life only had a certain value and now that value had been exceeded.

He was probably the most gifted man in the Lintang camp and his death shocked in a way no other ever did.

Frank Mills sent word that a friend of his, Harold St John of Brisbane, was in trouble. Could I help? A German refugee dentist had been in Sandakan and described St John as the finest looking man he had ever seen in uniform. Timberlake was now in the kitchen where he was proving a first-class fastidious cook. Somehow, he made half a dozen things that looked like meat pies, but of course, had no meat in them. However, he managed a teaspoonful of fat in each. Savage obtained a small bottle of red palm oil from a Tommy and once again, I went through the wires and across no-mans-land and through the British and Dutch camps to the Australians. St. John sat on the edge of his bunk and apologised for not standing as we shook hands. He was in poor physical condition but mentally was sparking on all cylinders and soon had us all laughing. I complimented them on the magnificent choir that had been got together by a Sydney conductor in their camp. To my surprise St John was a member of this group. In peacetime, there would be less than one chance in a million of such a talent being unearthed.

Most of the officers were asleep in the three-tiered bunks which seemed to be constructed mainly of lichen-covered rubber tree branches, but I met several doctors. I asked one had he examined Harold's chest for occasionally Harold had the taste of blood in his mouth. "What's the use?" he said: and, of course, he was right. In the circumstances, ignorance was a form of bliss. A stethoscope couldn't do anything for him nor in the long run, unfortunately, did a little palm oil and a few well-shaped pieces of tapioca pastry.

The Japs began to watch the strip of land between the British officers' and the internees' camp closely. In addition to the regular change of guard, snoopers began to appear at odd times. N.C.O.s checked on the sentries being awake by knocking on the corner post of the Briitish officers' camp; Sugar Babies on duty nearby responded by knocking on the walls of their sentry boxes. A friend of Savage's named Monty of the British officers' camp, visited the Villa at night on several occasions. One such evening we discussed the increasing danger of such visits and the possibility of signalling by tapping on a water pipe running through both camps. Next mid-day, I applied a stethoscope to the pipe while Monty hammered out dots and dashes a hundred yards away. I could hear nothing, even though I could see him striking the pipe. "We expected that" said Timberlake, laughing outright. I took the professional slur in my stride and returned the stethoscope to the camp doctor.

Very late one night, a sentry raised the alarm: in a few seconds, Jap guards were shouting from one end of the camp to the other. I woke from a deep sleep and sat up in bed. First one and then a second person could be heard running bare-footed behind our hut, an unmistakable element of desperation in their haste. Within the next hour, using torches and flares, the Japs examined nearly two thousand men, all stripped to the waist. They found a British P.O.W. with tell-tale scratches on his shoulders. His companion stepped forward when the Japs threatened to beat him until both offenders were discovered. Subsequently, Jap guards were under orders to shoot immediately if any other P.O.W.s were seen outside their own compounds.

Every night, groups of ten collected in huts, in the kitchen and under the trees and drained each other dry of reminiscences. I was driven to giving a talk on coral reefs and the coraligenous actinozoa, of which I knew very little! Evening after evening, Timberlake left the villa to speak to a group somewhere in the camp. After one such departure Savage asked curiously, "What the devil is he lecturing on?".

I also was puzzled. "I can't imagine. My guess is either shallot cultivation or women."

There wasn't much to talk about. Everyone drew on reserves of memory until they were exhausted. Some unexpectedly good talks were given by the most unlikely characters. One cheerful reprobate — incidentally, a pre-war member of the Beaufort Club — casually remarked that he had made love to women of 37 different nationalities. That evening, all over camp, people could be seen counting on their fingers and even toes. They reminded me of Rungus Dusuns solving a simple mathematical problem.

At one stage, we got so bored in the Villa that we decided to learn Dutch. We asked Bill Kummelkamph to teach us and he was delighted. He had written a thesis for a doctorate just before war broke out. It was typed on one side only and in double spacing. He tore the thesis to pieces and distributed the pages amongst us. We had three lessons and could count to ten and say, "good morning, good evening" and perhaps a little more. Then the

Kempei-tai picked Bill up and that was that. We decided it would be bad joss to get another teacher while Bill was away. We never saw him again.

It was a very curious thing that with the guards striking at the roots of all personal dignity and under circumstances of prolonged overcrowding when everyone could be expected to detest the sight of everyone else, most people developed a healthy respect for the vast majority of their companions. Japanese eagerness, determination and brutality had produced an illuminating quietness in the compulsive strong characters, the born leaders of men, amongst us: these colonial clones led the march into deliberate self-protecting anonymity. We had to carry on best we could with a core of calmly resolute, balanced fellows like Smallfield, Parnell, Timberlake, Barrett, Noakes, McLaren and others who were a great comfort to us. The campmasters, liaison officers and ration masters had the unenviable task of confronting the Japanese almost daily, fortunately with the bulldog example of little Mrs. Adams from the Women's Camp to inspire them. Rutter, reserved and cynical, turned on an immaculate performance as our Liaison Officer. Eric Meredith, of Cable and Wireless, employed as a clerk in the Japanese office, amused both himself and all internees by typing out the underground newsletter ''Adversity'' right under Japanese noses. The two champions in our camp were Danny Lascelles, indefatigable gardener, and Dr Sternfeldt, the camp doctor, German refugee and a credit to his profession. The Anglican bishop wasn't far behind them.

Several people only retained a sense of humour — Tuxford, an Englishman, a common man uncommonly funny at times; Vietch, the camp barber (''I can corrupt anyone,'' he said with glee one day after he had persuaded a senior administrator to eat some illicit potato, albeit with studied absent-mindedness); Bryant, sometime cricketer from Western Australia, who professed concern about the colour of his palms and soles and the size of his supra-orbital ridges nearly every time he met me; and White, the only English public servant in the Far East who knew how to laugh outright. And finally, Lutter, a man who actually invented jokes. Bryant was as quick with his hands as with his tongue. One day he sneezed as he was walking across the square. His false teeth shot out; he caught them in his right hand, tossed them a metre into the air, caught them in his left hand and threw them back into his mouth, all in a flash and continued on walking as if it wasn't a fluke.

The period of internment eventually extended beyond the limits of interesting and profitable experience. Too many people were affected physically and mentally; some irreversibly so. Two dozen odd in the Male Civilian camp developed ruptures due to wasting and forced labour and nearly everyone passed into a mild anxiety state. The Japs went to a great deal of trouble to reinforce the barbed-wire aprons; actually, if they had replaced them with pink ribbons, it would not have made the slightest difference.

Major Suga declared that he regarded the camp as an excellent training ground for bushido, the cult of the warrior, and announced that he had been promoted to Colonel. Lt Takino, the polite, good-natured paymaster, declared that he had had enough of the whole business and wanted to resign and return to Japan. A few other Japanese felt the same way, but they were prisoners just as surely as were the internees and P.O.W.s they guarded. The Japs performed one public service — by the time they had finished with us, there wasn't one self opinionated blowhard in the camp. Colonial snobbery and excessive self esteem were revealed as only skin deep cancers, eminently curable by a few slaps and harsh words.

After June 1945, everyone grew more confident that somehow, sometime, our present experience was coming to an end.

''What I'd like to see is the Household cavalry coming into camp — scarlet and blue tunics, breast-plates, plumed helmets and all the rest of it: and well-groomed, thoroughbred horses; and carriage after carriage, with members of the royal family and celebrated people. Something first class for a change. Wouldn't it be just the stuff?''

''Not bad. Bernard Shaw amongst them. He should get an eyeful of this.''

''Or everyone from a Chelsea Arts Ball coming dancing up the guardhouse road —

cardinals, negresses, arabs, fauns, mimes and friendly senoritas. . . . . but maybe I'm crazy.''

"A fleet of taxis would do me.''

"Five hundred nurses in scarlet capes!''

"Fifty head of prime beef cattle!''

Timberlake managed to infuse an element of the uncanny. He said, "Last night I went to the pee-tong in the square. Everyone was sleeping and the whole of Kuching was silent, just as if it was waiting for something to happen.''

And that was about it: everyone was waiting. They were fed up to the teeth with chaingangs, bashings, starvation, hookworms, itch, bed-bugs and poverty of every kind. Then something took place which worried the fittest amongst us very much. The P.O.W.s were set to work making small wooden boxes with shoulder straps, something like the boungins we used in North Borneo to transport our medical supplies and luggage on jungle tours. Who was to carry them? We soon found out. We were called over to the office in small groups. Then, one by one, a Jap officer asked us to comment briefly on our health while, with a quick eye, he noted and then recorded our physical condition. A reasonable guess was that the Japanese were contemplating a retreat into the hills for a last stand. And following arrival at the unknown destination what would happen to the carriers? They would be expendable, of course.

The edge of sorrow became blunted by repetition. As with other emotions, it does best on a full stomach.

I myself had little contact with the soldiers' camp. But one night, about 11 p.m. I was down at the wash-basins when someone across the wire called "Good evening, Sir''.

I went closer to the fence. Standing in the moonlight was a P.O.W. dressed in shorts. There was a bandage on each leg. One leg seemed much bigger than the other.

"Good evening; how's things?''

"Not too bad, Sir.''

"That's good. Can't you sleep?''

"No. The ulcers are giving me jip.''

"What are you doing for them?''

"Nothing. I am one of the stingah mats. Half dead-uns. Too bloomin' tired after work to do anything. I wash the bandages once a week. There's no more rag.''

There was a pause and I was just thinking of saying "good night'' when the P.O.W. said, "You wouldn't like to come over for a bit? Swatow Bill's on. He's all right''.

I hesitated. The P.O.W. prompted "There's a seat here at the end of the hut. I'd like to meet you and have a talk. I'd like advice.''

The Last Post had been sounded and everyone was in bed. I could think of no good reason for refusing. I slipped through the wire. The young man introduced himself as Bennett, George Bennett.

I gave my own name, Kell, Dr Derwent Kell. It sounded slightly clumsy by comparison, out of rhythm as it were. We went to a seat hard up against the nearest hut. In this position we were fairly well hidden by young tapioca stems about 120 centimetres high.

"Did you say you were a doctor?''

"Yes.''

"There's a lot of patients in this camp.''

"You're having a worse trot than us. Never mind, it can't be long now. They're on their way.''

The tops of Bennett's feet were very swollen. He was sitting with his back bent and the top of his stomach curved outwards as if the muscles were giving way. He was not in the least bit fat. His voice was slightly husky and he came out with each sentence as if it would take an effort to follow it up with another. He said, "It was good of you to come over. I wanted to talk to someone. Funny how you get like that sometimes.''

"Where do you come from?"

"The bush."

I was surprised. "The bush? You're not Australian?"

"No. no! The Bush. Shepherd's Bush, London. what's more, I'm not going back."

"Oh?"

"No. I've 'ad it. Look at this!"

He pushed his legs out in front of him. "I dunno what it is. I'm for the 'igh jump and I seem ter know it."

I did not argue. It was pretty obvious.

"Maybe I'm crazy. I feel so certain that I gave away some blasted ubi (potato) today. I know in a matter of days I'll be dead."

This was certain if he continued to give food away. I tried to think of some way in which to break this run of thought. "Don't let that worry you. We all get that idea sometimes and nothing ever happens. In three or four weeks we might be on our way home. They can move fast once they start."

Bennett put his elbows on his knees and then his cheeks in his cupped hands. With his toe he traced a simple pattern in the soil and stared at it. Finally, he lifted his head and said, "Well, we'll see if I know. My mind is clear and I just seem to know what is going on".

"Look here, George, cut out this kind of talk. It only—."

Bennett interrupted. He was quite worked up. "You listen, Sir, you listen to me. Look, I'll show you I know."

He stood half up and pointed to a papaya tree growing in a drain running round the hut. At its top the fruit tree curved outwards in its search for light, beyond the overhanging roof. About two metres from the ground there was a cluster of fruit.

"You see that papaya?"

"Yes, I see."

"You see that big one just turning yellow at the end?"

"Yes."

"Well, I know someone's coming to pinch it."

"Nonsense."

"You wait."

I was keen on getting to bed. The man seemed cuckoo, but nevertheless, it was intriguing. I had to sit for some time, anyway.

Conversation languished. It wasn't so necessary now. There was something of an object in just sitting quietly. I sat back and looked at the papayas. The moon was falling but there was still plenty of light. Some of the fruit was getting on. Yes, one in particular seemed to be ripening at the end. My mouth began to water. Bennett's guess or "know" was probably not as wild as it seemed. Plenty of people would like that papaya. From inside the hut came muttering and even muffled cries from sleeping Tommies.

It occurred to me that Bennett himself might be the fellow who contemplated the felony. And if anyone saw me going back through the wire, who would get the blame? The thought made me smile. And I decided on sitting it out a little longer.

Bennett spoke again. His mind wasn't as clear as he thought it was and he rambled on and I lost interest in his conversation and was scarcely aware when he stopped. I was dreaming of something else when he touched my knee.

I stiffened. My first feeling was one of apprehension. Someone was coming towards us from the fence. No, it wasn't a guard — too quiet, too big, no rifle. In a moment the figure stepped out into the moonlight and moved with the alert caution of a pariah dog towards the papaya tree. A short distance from the tree the prowler stopped and looked up at the fruit. I felt as if I had found a golden sovereign. It was a close acquaintance of mine, almost a friend. The intent, hungry look on his face was something to be remembered.

Bennett stood and shuffled towards the newcomer. "Good evening, Sir."

I decided to stay put. Bennett's body almost hid the adventurous civilian from me.

"Good evening."

"Can I do anything for you, Sir?"

A pause, then, "No. Not at the moment. Who are you?"

Bennett did not answer. "I think you'd better go back, Sir. The guard's in camp. He might come this way."

"Is he? Oh! Then I'll be on my way. How's things in your camp?"

"Not bad."

"That's good. Well, good night."

"Good night, Sir."

Bennett watched the man go through the wire and limped quietly back to me. He was beside himself with excitement. "What'd I tell you! What'd I tell you! I knew someone would come!"

He grasped his knees and his head shook with barely suppressed laughter.

"How's that for knowing! I told you, didn't I?"

"Yes, you told me. You were right, as it happened. Well, I must be off. If I can do anything for you let me know. Kell's the name, if you can remember it. Dr Derwent Kell."

I doubted whether Bennett was listening, he was so pleased with the fact that he was right. I went back through the wire. As luck would have it, I met my acquaintance near the steps of the hut, coming back from the latrines.

"Ho, there!"

"Oh, Derwent! What are you up to?"

"Nothing. But tell me!"

"What?"

"You don't mind: but were you really going to pinch that papaya?"

We looked at each other for a second, then both grinned broadly. The wandering civilian said rather loudly, "Of course I damn well wasn't!"

He was laughing quietly now and went up the steps into his hut.

Some ten days later a Dutchman who was always at the fence trading with the soldiers, met me in a food queue and said in an exceptionally deep voice, "Doctor, I've got a message for you. One of the P.O.W.s died half an hour ago and left word for you to be told at once."

I smiled. I felt I should not, but I could not help it. "I suppose his name was Bennett, George Bennett?" My heart felt cold.

The Dutchman gave a short laugh. "How did you know that, Doctor?"

I hesitated; "I guess I must be psychic", I said.

This is the secret wireless, christened 'Mrs. H.', which for a while supplied us with news. It was made by WO L.T.A. Beckett of the Radio Instrument and Maintenance Unit, Royal Air Force Far East, whilst he was a prisoner of war in Kuching. Photograph shows WO Beckett demonstrating the wireless to Brigadier T.C. Eastwick, Commander Kuching Force and Lt-Col. A.W. Walsh, C.O., 2/10 Aust Field Regt. after surrender of the Japanese.

Chapter 11

1945 THE WAR ENDS

Slowly but surely the Japanese came to realise that they could not win this particular war. They never seemed to lose an opportunity of announcing that they would fight to the last man, a rather grisly self-defeating exercise, scarcely compatible with ultimate victory.

To a few ill-fed despised Sarawak internees fell the honour of supporting and even reinforcing this pessimistic opinion, and in quite an amusing way.

Over a long period a group of earnest administrators had been meeting in the evenings to produce a blue-print for post-war administration and reconstruction of the zoological garden territory formerly presided over by their White Rajah. No doubt they were planning a model, lily-white democracy, the sort of thing all the goodies were fighting for. In time, they completed a document and with commendable caution (being immensely security conscious) they hid it underground: but even malnutrition cannot suppress brilliant new ideas. One day the papers were dug up for revision and no doubt for a check for spelling and punctuation errors. As luck would have it the Japanese raided the camp and captured the lot. One can imagine their feelings as they browsed through the pages — not a single Japanese name in all the proposed post-war public service!

The exact manner in which liberation would come did occupy our thoughts from time to time, but not unduly. It seemed a waste of effort: there was nothing we could do about it, at least in our section, full as it was of middle-aged and aging brow-beaten civilians. My idea was that there would be an amphibious landing on the coast to attract the local Japanese forces, and then suddenly out of the sky over Lintang would come hundreds of parachutists. For half-an-hour or so there would be hell-to-pay, after which Colonel Suga, his officers, and all the Sugar Babies, and perhaps some of us and some of our saviours would be dead. It seemed as good a guess as any.

But one evening in mid-August 1945, about two years after I had arrived in Kuching, there was quiet excitement amongst internees at Lintang Barracks: a rumour that hostilities had ceased had come in from the British P.O.W. camp next door.

In the very early hours of the next morning, two P.O.W.s were caught in our camp kitchen: were they stealing potatoes? No indeed! They declared they were on their way to rob the Japanese stores. There was no risk now — the war was over.

The story was soon on everyone's lips. At 8 a.m. I stood with others on high ground overlooking the P.O.W. camp. The Tommies were digging up their potatoes, knocking timber from huts and lighting fires for private cooking — actions forbidden both by Japanese and their own camp regulations. A Japanese guard came in and spoke angrily to a soldier removing a plank from his hut. He was told to ''fook off'' — and actually did so! This was very convincing. Something had happened.

Lintang Barracks.

Then on 15 August the R.A.A.F. (Royal Australian Air Force) dropped pamphlets over the internment camp. As they fluttered down there was a general alarm and Sugar Babies rushed into each section of the camp. Nevertheless, we managed to get and conceal one of the messages and so we learnt for certain that Japan had accepted the Potsdam terms.

No admission of an armistice came from the Japanese office, and chaingang work continued as usual. Rations, however, were suddenly increased. Sweet potatoes, tapioca and yams were supplied in quantity and everyone began to put on weight rapidly. Many developed swollen faces and legs. Timberlake's feet suddenly came up like balloons and his thin, strong features were given a comical snootiness by oedema over his cheekbones.

The first newspapers dropped by the R.A.A.F. were hidden before guards could seize them. First a Hollander and then the Resident, Brunei, read the news in each hut in turn. The news of the atomic bomb was staggering. There was was a burst of laughter when a paragraph about the Australian censor banning *Brave New World* was read. An English padre remarked that reading it was part of his theological training.

At 5 p.m. on 23 August, working parties were recalled to camp and ordered to a general parade in front of Colonel Suga's office. For all concerned it was a momentous gathering. Colonel Suga was in the unhappy position of having to admit that in the matter of surrendering in battle the only difference between the Allies and the Japanese was that the latter surrendered totally and in unprecedented numbers.

Suga admitted to "good tidings". He spoke very solemnly in his slightly broken English. His gestures were ample and his hesitations rather emphasized the deep emotion under which he was speaking. Amongst other things, he said that the Japanese could understand soldier fighting soldier, and sailor fighting sailor — that sort of thing is easy to

Surrender.

understand. But, speaking of the atomic bomb, he said that he could not understand. It was war on civilians. Swinging his arms in an expressive circle he said, "This is war upside down."

He admitted that the Emperor had agreed to accept the Potsdam terms, but said that the undefeated Japanese Army overseas was restless. Many soldiers wished to fight on in the hills. We could quite believe it. They were resolute and determined men: moreover, there was the ruthless, monstrous Kempei-tai to make sure they did as they were told. There was movement in the audience and a quiet murmur when Colonel Suga said that he intended to follow the Emperor's orders. Lifting his head he cried, "Be calm! Be patient! Don't excitement!"

Release was at hand. I was particulary struck as Suga, grasping the edge of the table, leant forward and said in a much lower voice, "I will give you more food." Producing asthenia via malnutrition had been official policy. In the crowd were scores of men and women as thin as matchsticks. Hundreds more were too weak to walk up the hill to hear the address. Over 600 P.O.W.s, or about half the British other-ranks camp, had died of starvation that year.

To even matters a little, Suga had had his home and family in Hiroshima when the bomb fell. In spite of everything, few must have felt anything but compassion for him.

With improved nutrition, tempers sharpened. Several fights occurred in our camp, none of them very classy exhibitions. They were stopped after the minute or two legitimately allowed by curiosity to see how the contestants shaped. Even in Clitoris Villa signs of strain appeared. One morning, some eggs obtained by barter from the Weasel had to be cooked. Timberlake obtained some glowing embers from the kitchen, put a few damp twigs on them and blew himself purple in the face trying to make a fire. He got into a rage and strode from the Villa. However, he soon settled down and returned: and later, when he contemplated his egg perched on top of a little heap of fried rice, he exclaimed, "Whenever I see a sight like that it makes me certain there is a guiding hand behind this Universe of ours. A greater brain than a fowl's is at work here. Don't you agree?"

"Of course, Sam."

In the evening, groups of ten still collected to hear speakers discourse on their various experiences. An expert on elephants gave a talk on doings in a place in Siam called Chiangmai. One tale concerned a visit by Somerset Maugham. The European community gave a dinner for the distinguished author. When Maugham appeared, a local character started the ball rolling by removing the flowers from a vase, pouring in gin liberally and putting it down the hatch in a single draught. "That's how we drink in Chiangmai," he said. Maugham replied, "Oh, is it?" and then did the same, winning the first round. The local character was a bad loser, but at least he proved that everyone in the Far East didn't quite take Maugham lying down. After dinner, and quite tipsy, he seized the drumsticks from the roast and used Maugham's head as a kettle-drum until the compleat scandal-monger promised not to write any derogatory stories about Chiangmai.

The deliberations of one group of ten interested me. They took a vote on whom they considered least affected by Japanese ill-treatment, and I was the one selected. This at a time when I felt something was going wrong up topside! I had difficulty in concentrating my thoughts on any subject for long, and to initiate and maintain a conversation called for deliberate, almost painful effort. Thinking it might be cerebral beri-beri setting in I began to chew a few green leaves! It was probably simple disuse atrophy.

Another question the group considered was, "If you had to be captured by any race in Asia, which would you choose?" Opinion was unanimous — the Japanese. I was inclined to agree. I think the reason was that the Japanese took all prisoners seriously — in fact, with deadly earnestness — and seldom laughed at them. This, in a way, raised morale: traditionally, prisoners have always been regarded with a mixture of mirth and contempt.

Before long, Savage's friend Monty in the British officers' camp heard about the newspapers in the civilian camp, and requested a summary — urgently, of course. Papers were borrowed, summaries prepared, and plans made to carry them through the aprons at night. No-one was anxious to get into trouble at this late stage, but as I was the one who could fit between the barbed-wire strands most easily, that was that. The movements of the Japanese guards were studied carefully. In the midst of all this planning, the Rajah's elephant expert came to the Villa. He wanted us to join him in a raid on the Japanese pigsty that night. "I think we could get away with it alright," he said, quite seriously, as if he had considered the proposal carefully from all angles.

We began to laugh. Our own impending adventure of slipping stealthily through the wires suddenly seemed absurdly trifling. An extremely hazardous operation was being proposed to us in all seriousness. The Japs had their pigsty close to their quarters and not far from a sentry box. At the first disturbance two hundred pigs would create porcine uproar. And how could one cross the square with a pig (preferably dead) during the inevitable alert? After all, three thousand hungry people had been living peacefully beside these fat old pigs for up to four years. Hunger wasn't responsible for this Elizabethan proposal, for its sponsor was still distended like a drum from the evening meal!

Our news summary was coiled inside an old piece of bamboo which could be discarded at a moment's notice, and, shortly after 11 p.m. I slipped through the barbed-wire apron and made my way across the sentry path and potato patch into the British officers' camp. Monty met me and I handed him the summary, asking that it be passed on to the Australians. I was introduced very formally to a number of the officers and spoke briefly to Hodges who had apparently spent most of the last few months on his bed. He was very thin. Then I was taken to the perimeter of the Australian camp to see Mills. Mills was very pleased with himself — he had made the distance. We spoke briefly and I then returned to our camp. Savage and Timberlake were sitting in the Villa, waiting like two old hens for grains of gossip.

Every day, R.A.A.F. planes came from Labuan several hundred kilometres away. They performed miraculously, roaring over and around the camp just above the tree tops. Big Brother was keeping an eye on us! Good for him! It was exhilarating to watch their carefree antics. On occasions, it wasn't clear whether they were bent on liberation or destruction, so close did they come. Faith in our race was completely restored.

On 30 August, a big Douglas appeared overhead and several dozen Red Cross parcels were dropped from it. For breakfast next morning there was bread and butter. How delicious it was! But in the Women's Camp some of the youngest children had never seen bread before and they tried to peel it before eating it. Some were very upset. "Where's our rice?" they cried. Unfortunately, a young member of our camp was killed instantly by a falling parcel. Another heavy parcel crashed through the hospital roof but, by a miracle, no-one there was killed.

A fortnight after the Armistice doctors were given Red Cross armbands and were allowed to move between camps for "consultations". George Graham and I were shown the hospital by Colonel Shepherd, a wonderful man, and later, around the British soldiers' camp by Colonel King. At the hospital we walked round almost in silence. It was difficult to say anything, conditions were so appalling. After we had completed the wards and verandahs, I fell a few metres behind the others and happened to look into a small, very dark room underneath the verandah. On the floor was a single naked emaciated corpse lying at an untidy angle to one of the walls. Why I do not know, but my chest tightened and a brief feeling of horror seized me. The soldier may have fired a shot in self-defence in Malaya or Singapore — who knows? Here, he had merely wasted away. If this was war then as far as I was concerned they could stuff it. One could only hope that in some beautiful church or cathedral in the British Isles the soldier's death would ultimately be recorded in a manner imparting simplicity and dignity and even honour. The Poms have a genius for such things.

Of 750 left in the British soldiers' camp, only a hundred were now classed as "effectives". Five hundred odd were in sick bay. Some were very low, a few hours or only minutes remaining to them. Moving amongst them were Roman Catholic Sisters and other women, cleaning and dressing them, saying all sorts of comforting things.

As we walked back to our own camp, George said, "The Australians had better hurry."

With restrictions on movement lessening, concerts were arranged. One was held in an open shed. An Australian sextet sang; Tod Morgan recited Dennis's poem of the Sentimental Bloke at Hamlet; Dr Wand's wife was recalled twice for several songs; finally there was a recitation of "This Royal Throne of Kings" by an Australian, followed by "Land of Hope and Glory" and then "God Save the King". Many women broke down.

On 8 September, two Australian medical practitioners, now officers in the Ninth Division, were permitted to visit the camp from Labuan. One was Lt. Colonel "Cobber" Morgan, a Queenslander; the other, Major Hutson, from Victoria. Morgan was an old university friend of Frank Mills and myself. Mills ran down the hill to call me. "Come up and see him, it's Cobber Morgan," he shouted. "He looks magnificent!" We had played together against him in inter-collegiate tennis. We hurried back to the Australian camp. There, in an open space between two huts, was something no-one had seen for years — two free Europeans in normal health. It was a most striking sight. Colonel Suga stood beside them, occasionally licking his dry lips, not exactly at ease. There was no evident jubilation amongst the Australian officers, no laughter, nothing but quiet, matter-of-fact conversation, and little of that. Two and a half thousand of their companions (some British, mostly Australians) whom they left behind in Sandakan had died — of exhaustion, malnutrition, disease, bullets and bayonets, and even crucifixion — mainly during a series of death marches between Sandakan on the East Coast and Ranau in the Interior. Six had escaped to Tawi Tawi. Another half-dozen had slipped away during or after the death marches. One of the latter had fled in fear until he was exhausted then had sat down to rest on a log. Presently he was on the run again. To his horror, the log moved — it happened to be a giant python, sleeping deeply after swallowing a jungle pig.

The following day, I attended a lunch given by the Punjabis. Three civilians who had been associated with them in some way were invited. Everyone ate to full satisfaction. The fried terong (eggplant) particularly were delicious. It was a very dignified occasion. Several people made speeches, including the old Indian doctor Kalyan Singh Gupta, who had had a particularly bad time. It seemed to be the beginning of civilised life again. The Regiment had lost 217 men killed in action or dead of disease and malnutrition as P.O.W.s Twenty-seven men had died in Seria alone of beri-beri and dysentery. Of Subedar Makhmad Anwar, it is recorded in the Batallion Newsletter (April to September 1947), "He was starved, beaten and tortured over a prolonged period and given no medical care. He died hanging from his heels with his wound maggot-infested and in a semi-conscious condition. The result of such a superb example of courage and loyalty was that no single man under his command then or later gave way to the Japanese methods of persuasion, facing death rather than do so."

Four other V.C.O's were taken to Kuala Belait from Seria, forced to dig their own graves and were beheaded. Five Sikhs taking refuge in Balwant Singh's house were bayoneted and killed. As for Balwant Singh himself, "he first had his hands cut off, then his eyes gouged out, and was finally beheaded". My friend and benefactor, Chong Fah, died with him, in the same manner.

On 11 September, the internees played a game of mini-cricket against the Australian officers. The game was still in progress when a white car shot up the hill. An order for a general parade was issued, and everyone dressed and gathered in front of a platform near the rice store. I found myself on the edge of the women and children. As Brigadier Eastick walked onto the platform, one of the children said, "Mummy, here's a man going to sing to us." The Brigadier did not sing, but he smiled all the time he was speaking. The points he made were simply stated. Everyone was now free. We would be given food, medicine, and doctors to attend the sick, and arrangements were being made to send us home as soon as possible. When he had finished, he was given a great cheer. He was followed by an American Naval Captain who said that the experience of being present at the relief of Kuching had made all the hardships of war worthwhile. Mrs Agnes Keith ("Land Below the wind", "Three came Home") declared it was the only perfect speech she had ever heard.

General Wootten, commanding the Ninth Australian Division, arrived to see us in a very small sedan car. He was a huge man, probably over 130 kilograms, and as he stepped from the car an involuntary exclamation of wonder came from the crowd. Half-starved Colonel Walsh from the Australian officers' camp stood on the platform beside him, looking quite infinitesimal. The General made a solid, workmanlike speech. Fighters and light bombers flew low overhead as he was speaking. The gathering closed with an expression of thanks to General Wootten. Colonel Walsh stepped forward and thrust out his hand towards the General and the big man took it amidst general acclamation.

This was really the end of internment. Australian soldiers appeared about the place, big men, fit as fiddles and atebrin-stained, not a trace of the heeby-jeebies afflicting us evident in their faces. What they thought of us I cannot imagine. One went to the cemetery and was so angry at what he saw that he threatened to put a bullet into the Jap sentry on duty nearby. He was restrained because it happened to be Swatow Bill from North China, a family man with six children, one of the best of the Sugar Babies. Presently, Japanese sentries went off duty, and prisoners of war and internees began to leave for Labuan by destroyer and plane. Poynton was taken as a stretcher case to

Scene at the Prisoner of War and Internee Camp where, after the surrender ceremony at Kuching, Brigadier T.C. Eastwick, Commander Kuching Force, 9th Aust. Division, tells the assembled POW's of their liberation.

Kuching, Sarawak. 12th September 1945.
8th Aust. Division officers, ex-POW's of the Japanese get a rousing cheer as they leave the Kuching POW and Internment Camp for the journey into town. The author is one of the cheer squad.

Johnny Funk.

Kuching hospital and died shortly after. Savage and Timberlake, both of whom had developed oedema, left before me. Johnny Funk and several others from North Borneo were released from prison in Kuching. They came to our camp and sat quietly on the ground in front of our hut looking stunned and exhausted. As punishment for helping Allied P.O.W.s in Sandakan they had spent almost the last two years on road construction, felling and cutting timber for military use, burying dead soldiers and prisoners at any time of day or night and unloading cargo from ships at the wharf. When Allied planes strafed and bombed, they were forced to continue work while the Japanese directed operations from air raid shelters nearby. From mid-June 1945, Johnny was a member of one of ten teams transporting general supplies from Kuching to the Indonesian town of Sambas about a 160 kilometres away, where the Japs intended to make a stand. They used buffalo carts, one man between the shafts, another six men pushing behind. They worked from 5.30 a.m. to 7 p.m. and made several such trips. They were informed by a friendly Jap soldier that on the last trip they would be joined by more "buffaloes" from Lintang Barracks: after arrival with the last load, that was it for all the human buffaloes — kaput.

Johnny and his companions told us of a man who assuredly will live in Australian military history — Captain Mathews of South Australia. He was executed in Kuching for his part in planning revolt against the Japanese in Sandakan. Johnny had been present when Mathews and Dr Stookes had met one evening in the jungle at Mile 8, Sandakan. Stookes was dressed as a kuli and Johnny said he was regarded as the key man in the local resistance. Often, he had flown Japanese officers in his small plane to various places on the East Coast. Stookes and a handful of Europeans (Mavor, Laband, Taylor and brave Mrs Cohen) still free and working in Sandakan, and numerous other local people (notably shopkeeper Khoo Siak Chiew, a corporal in the volunteers) had smuggled food, medicines, wireless sets and even arms to the Australian soldiers. Unfortunately, the

Japanese became aware of what was going on and disaster followed. Stookes was killed in Keningau shortly before the war ended.

Slowly the stories of what had happened elsewhere filtered into our camp. The medical department had not fared too well. Dresser Peter Lai of Sandakan had received a fifteen-year sentence and ended the war as Dresser at the gaol in Kuching. Senior Dresser Thomas of Kudat was dead. Nurse Alice Watson survived but her brother Richard was executed with Kong Su En, the chief clerk to the Principal Medical Officer, Dr Taylor. Dr Taylor himself was in a gaol in Singapore when hostilities ceased. An attendant at an outstation dispensary had been killed by the Japanese and eaten. In 1944 all adult males (Ubians or seagypsies) living on the small islands of Sulug and Denawan off Jesselton had been slaughtered. The human race can be the end.

One morning, with two friends, I went to Kuching. We borrowed some bicycles and rode through the streets and along the river for several kilometres. It was interesting to see a town in which we had lived for two years. We dismounted opposite the Rajah's Palace. It was rumoured that the White Rajah would never return to Sarawak: an institution which had seemed to suit the territory of mixed population in many ways had ended. Our vague feelings of regret were dated. The old British Empire was on the way out. No tears need be shed at its passing. From a doctor's point of view, in large part it was a vast slum, filled with poverty-stricken, illiterate, disease-ridden people. It was time for a spring-cleaning. One blessing at least had been bestowed upon the subject peoples. They could wander anywhere they wished in their own territories in perfect safety. And, in the colonial Territories, there was religious freedom and a high degree of financial integrity within Government.

The following morning I went down with a sharp attack of malaria. For some hours I was in delirium, and finally woke drenched in perspiration. Frank Mills was standing by my bed and said arrangements had been made for me to go to hospital. To hospital with *malaria*? This was something new, but at the time I was too dazed to resist. I walked unsteadily to the showers. In hospital, I was put in a private ward and slept most of the afternoon; by evening I had recovered. I was then transferred to the labour ward, not because of any revision of diagnosis, but because Colonel Morgan had come in and tapped my excellent bed and said I must have something better.

Colonel Suga died in a tent surrounded by barbed wire on Labuan Island. I understand that he attempted suicide by slashing his wrists and throat with a table knife. Finally his orderly, using an empty bottle filled with sand, hammered the utensil into his heart. Later, several of the officers who had served under him were hanged. One was Takino, who seemed to me to be a good sort of bloke, unfortunate enough to be trapped and enslaved by his country's military killing machine.

On 21 September, Mills and I and a number of other doctors left for Labuan. We went down the river in a launch. At Pending, there were two Catalinas on the water and we made towards one of them and clambered aboard. The pilot was Bimbo White, an old university friend and international footballer, 100 kilograms and more of muscle and happy-go-luckiness.

Twenty minutes later the flying boat raced along the river and took to the air. We circled over Kuching and obtained a last glimpse of the internment camp at Lintang Barracks. It was a strange sensation looking down on the small huts with their attap roofs; the thin lines of barbed wire aprons; the gardens; and the short grey roads. Nothing could have looked more benign. As we climbed and flew away, the camp area grew smaller and smaller, and then, quite suddenly, was lost in the immense stretch between widening horizons.

Thanks to the Armed Forces, freedom was ours.

Cocos-Keeling Islands
December 1976

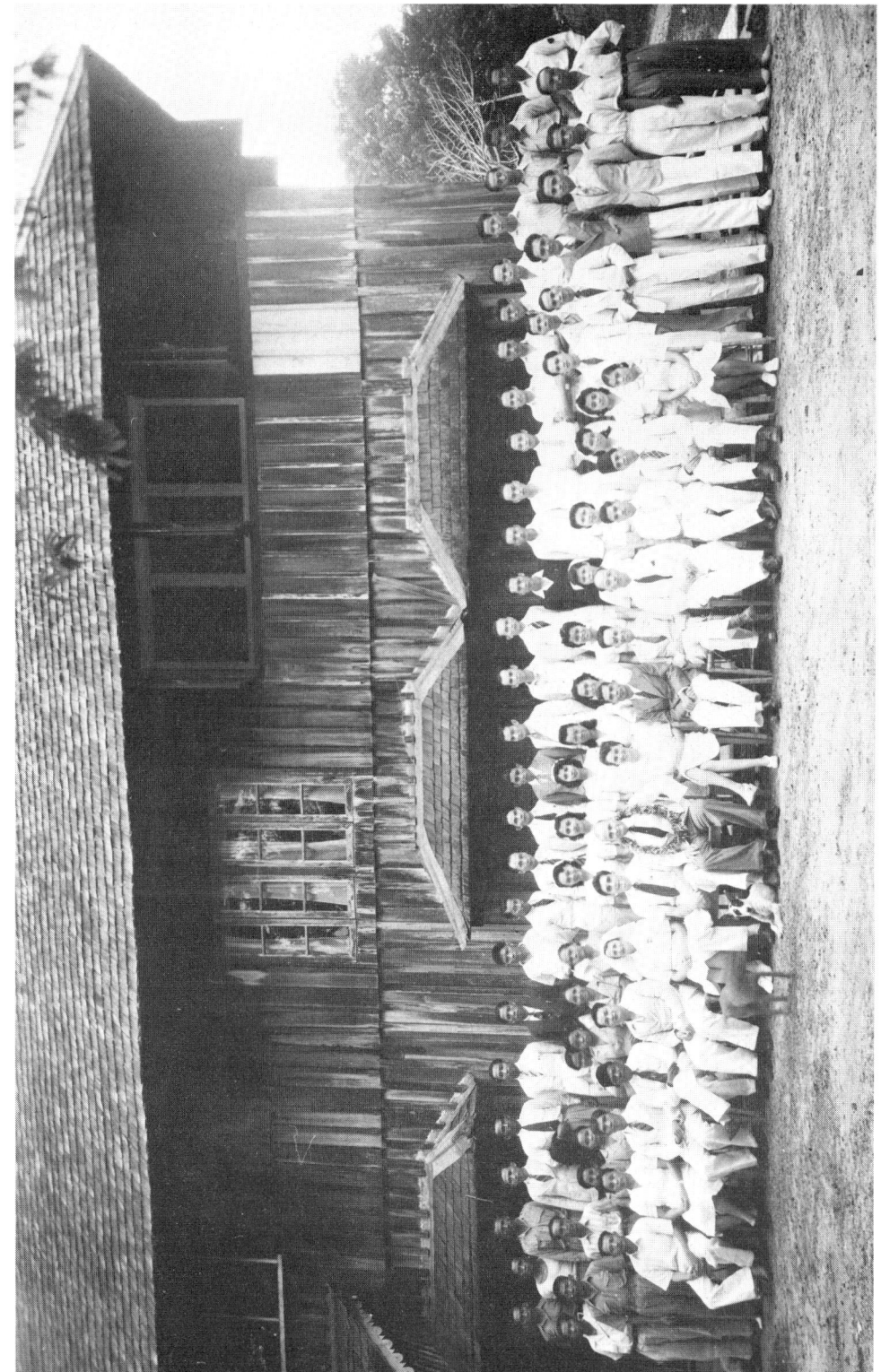

Jesselton Medical Staff — August 1947.

A section of the Allied cemetery in the Lintang Prisoner of War Barracks.